T0326305

# WHOSE ARMY?

# WHOSE ARMY?

## Afghanistan's Future and the Blueprint for Civil War

MUSA KHAN JALALZAI

Algora Publishing
New York

Library of Congress Cataloging-in-Publication Data —

Jalalza'i, Musa Khan.
    Whose army: Afghanistan's Future and the Blueprint for Civil War / Musa Khan
Jalalzai.
        pages cm
    Includes bibliographical references and index.
        ISBN 978-1-62894-054-1 (soft cover: alk. paper) — ISBN 978-1-62894-055-8
(hard cover: alk. paper) — ISBN 978-1-62894-056-5 (ebook) 1. Afghanistan. Afghan
National Army. 2. National security—Afghanistan. 3. Internal security—Afghanistan.
4. Insurgency—Afghanistan. 5. Nation-building—Afghanistan. 6. Afghan War, 2001- 7.
Afghanistan—History—2001- I. Title.
    UA853.A3J354 2014
    355'.0330581—dc23
                            2013050024

Printed in the United States

ACKNOWLEDGEMENTS


This book could not have been completed without the strong encouragement and support of former Director General, Inter Service Intelligence (ISI), General Asad Durrani and my Afghan friends in both the Interior and Defense Ministries of Afghanistan. I would like to thank former Chief of ISI, General Hamid Gul, who rang up me from Islamabad, Pakistan, and provided information regarding the importance of time and space in modern military conflicts. My friends Saqalain Imam of BBC Urdu Service London and Wadood Mushtaq of ARY TV Channel updated my knowledge of the war on terrorism in Pakistan and Afghanistan.

Musa Khan Jalalzai

# ABBREVIATIONS

| | |
|---|---|
| ABP | Afghan Border Police |
| ANCOP | Afghan Civil National Order Police |
| AUP | Afghan Uniformed Police |
| ANAAC | Afghanistan National Army Air Corps |
| ANBP | Afghanistan New Beginning Program |
| ANCO | Afghan National Civil Order Police |
| ANDS | Afghanistan's National Development Strategy |
| ANA | Afghan National Army |
| ANCO | Afghan National Civil Order Police |
| ACPF | Anti Crime Police Force |
| ANP | Afghan National Police |
| ANAP | Afghan National Auxiliary Police |
| ANBP | Afghanistan's National Border Police |
| ANSF | Afghan National Security Forces |
| ACP | Anti Crime Police |
| AQ | Al-Qaeda |
| ARSIC | Afghan Regional Security Integrated Command |
| ASG | Area Support Group |
| ASV | Armored Security Vehicles |
| AUP | Afghan Uniformed Police |
| CIA | Central Intelligence Agency |
| BSA | Border Security Agency |
| CID | Criminal Investigation Department |
| CSTC-A | Combined Security Transition Command-Afghanistan |
| Europol | EU Police Mission in Afghanistan |
| FATA | Federally Administered Tribal Areas |

| | |
|---|---|
| GBA | Green on Blue Attacks |
| GDPSU | General Directorate of Police Unites |
| HN | Haqqani Network |
| HQ | Holy Quran |
| HRW | Human Rights Watch |
| IC | International Community |
| ICG | International Crisis Group |
| ISAF | International Security Assistance Force |
| ISI | Inter Services Intelligence |
| K | Kandahar Security Group |
| KHAD | Khidmat-e-Atlaat Daulat |
| KPRT | Kandahar Provincial Reconstruction Team |
| LDI | Local Defense Initiatives |
| MI | Military Intelligence |
| NDS | National Directorate of Security |
| NGO | Non-Governmental Organization |
| NATO | North Atlantic Treaty Organization |
| OEF | Operation Enduring Freedom |
| PA | Pakistan Army |
| PCCM | Private Contractor's Criminal Militias. |
| PDPA | People Democratic Party of Afghanistan |
| PMC | Private Military Contractor |
| QS | Quetta Shura |
| RAMA | Riasat-e-Amniate-e-Milli |
| RAW | Research and Analysis Wing |
| RCSANP | Regional Command Structure of the Afghan National Police |
| SIGAR | Special Inspector General for Afghanistan Reconstruction |
| TQA | Taliban Qatar Office |
| UA | US Army |
| UDD | US Department of Defense |
| UK | The United Kingdom |
| UNDO | United Nations Development Program |
| UNDP | United Nation Developed Program |
| US | The United States |
| USJSOC | US Joint Special Operations Command |
| VSP | Village Stability Program |
| WZ | War Zone |

# TABLE OF CONTENTS

Acknowledgements                                                                    vii

Abbreviations                                                           ·           ix

Preface                                                                             1

Foreword                                                                            5

Chapter 1. The Afghan Army from Alexander the Great to Hamid Karzai    11

Chapter 2. The Afghan National Army and Green on Blue Attacks          21
    The Challenge of Green on Blue Attacks                   29

Chapter 3.  International Military Efforts and the Uncertain Future of
    the ANA                                                  35
    The Taliban Office in Qatar                              41
    The Transition of Security, ANA and the Taliban          43
    The Security Transition                                  45
      *Phase One*                                  45
      *Phase Two*                                  46
      *Phase Three*                                46
      *Phase Four and Five*                        46

Chapter 4. Brigade-888, ANA, and War Criminals                         47

Chapter 5. Blackwater, Private Contractors and Criminal Militias       57

The Business of Private Militias in Afghanistan     66

Chapter 6. The US Joint Special Operations Command, Blackwater and
the Drone War     69

    Drone Attacks in Pakistan from 2005 to 2013     77

Chapter. 7. State-Owned Criminal Militias     79

    Regional Command Structure of the Afghan National Police     83
    The Oath of Afghan National Police     84

Chapter 8. Marketing Terrorism and the Import/Export of Suicide
Bombers     85

    Marketing Terrorism and the Business of Fear     92

Chapter 9. An Incoherent Approach to the War     95

Chapter 10. War on Terror in a Failed Afghan State     103

Chapter 11. Afghan Intelligence, the Intelligence War and
Intelligence Failure     111

    The Intelligence War Among 50 Nations in Afghanistan     116
    Afghan Intelligence: Foreign Influence and Allegations of Torture     119

Chapter 12. Social Media, Cyber Terrorism and the Taliban's Tactical
Intelligence     123

    Cyber Terrorism     126
    Licenses issued to Internet Services Provider Companies in
    Afghanistan     130

Chapter 13. The US–Afghan Strategic Partnership and the Pentagon's
China-Phobia Policy     133

    The Pentagon, the CIA and The Defense Clandestine Service     137

Chapter 14. The Pakistan Army War on Pashtuns     141

Chapter 15. Afghanistan's Future and the Blueprint for Civil War     147

Postscript     155

Appendix 1. Durand Line Agreement, November 12, 1893     161

    Agreement between Amir Abdur Rahman Khan, G. C. S. I., and
    Sir Henry Mortimer Durand, K. C. I. E., C. S. I.     161

Appendix 2. Decree of the President of the Islamic Transitional
   State of Afghanistan    165

Appendix 3. Afghan Security Forces Command and Control Structure    169
   Afghan National Army    169
   Afghan National Army Air Corps Command and Control System    169
   Defense Ministers of Afghanistan    170
   Generals of ANA Military Command    170

Appendix 4. Size of the Afghan Security Forces 1978–2012    173
   Afghan National Army plus Police    173

Appendix 5. Foreign Forces Deployed in Afghanistan 2001–2012    175
   Troops Committed to NATO's International Security Assistance
     Force (ISAF) by Country    177
   NATO Training Mission in Afghanistan    178
     *Mission*    178
     *Area* of *Responsibility*    178
     *Contributing Nations*    178

Appendix 6. Resolution against Drone Attacks    179

Bibliography    183

Index    189

# Preface

Many mis-steps have been made in the war in Afghanistan, some by Pakistani generals and some by US and Russian generals. When American generals plunged their military forces into Iraq, they were underestimating the importance of Afghanistan. They also gave a free hand to Pakistani generals to set the future direction of that war. Military operational errors, high rates of collateral damage, illegal night raids, unnecessary killings, humiliation of innocent civilians and desecration of the Holy Koran at the hands of American soldiers all combined to create what might euphemistically be called a "relationship gap" between US and NATO allied forces and the people of Afghanistan. The criminal acts of US Special Forces and unaccountable Blackwater militias created permanent hostility towards foreign forces.

The former Mujahedeen Commander and Minister for Water and Power, Ismail Khan, criticized US and ISAF generals for their incoherent approach to the war in Afghanistan. On 23 September, 2013, in an interview with German magazine Der Spiegel, Ismail Khan said that international coalition "has taken away" his country artillery and tanks and turned them into scrap metal.

> The arrogant Americans drove the most important Taliban out of Kabul, bombed the rest from the air and then ended the war.... Mr. Ismail Khan categorically said that he and his Mujahedeen have 20 years combat experience, and they defeated Soviet Union in 1980s. The Afghan army trained by the West has lost 63,000 men, or one in the three soldiers, to desertion in the last three years.

There are numerous predictions that the country will plunge into brutal civil war. The Afghan Security Forces and Taliban are still in the battlefield and ready to continue the fight till the end. The continued instability and political rivalries in the country leave the door open for the re-emergence of a variety of impatient and intolerant war criminals. A working paper for the Center for Strategic and International Studies (CSIS) has predicted a weak and divided state, a state that devolves into regions controlled either by power brokers or war criminals.

In April 2010, former Afghan parliamentarian Malalai Joya criticized the US strategy and its efforts at peace making in Afghanistan. "The US invaded my country under the banner of the war on terror, women's rights, human rights and democracy. But even with the presence of tens of thousands of troops, not only women, men also suffer from war, terrorism, injustice, the rule of drug mafia and warlordism, insecurity, joblessness, poverty, unprecedented corruption, and many other problems.".

The inability of the ANSF to fight the Taliban and their increasing dependence on foreign forces complicated the war within the country even further. The wider effect of war has promoted the trafficking business; thousands of children are being trafficked within the country for cheap labor. Internal migrants are homeless, jobless, sick and starved. Poverty and starvation have forced hundreds of Afghan families to sell their children. The New York Times has reported on the warlords' business conducted via private militias around the country.

These militias are spying on the Afghan population in breach of privacy laws. Some MPs have established criminal businesses. Afghan parliamentarians are deeply involved in kidnapping for ransom, and drug and human trafficking. They have established close contacts with insurgents and help them in many ways. Northern Afghanistan has turned into an open pedophilia bazaar. War criminals run the business of male prostitution and child sex slaves.

There are also strong links among the Tajik and Uzbek Islamist insurgent groups and the Afghan weapons and drug smugglers. Afghanistan shares porous borders with Tajikistan and Uzbekistan which are used by criminal elements to smuggle weapons, drugs and other illegal items. Once smuggled out of Tajikistan and other countries, the weapons quickly find their way to the Northern and South-Eastern provinces. Afghan drug production is financing terrorism across the country. Opium is often used as a currency in rural areas. The value of the international trade in Afghan opiates is approximately $40 billion, while Afghan farmers receive $600 million. Terrorists and traffickers receive an estimated $2 billion. The Taliban have imposed taxes of 10% on farmers who grow poppy.

In all 34 provinces of the country, thousands of men, women and children are begging on behalf of underground mafia groups. Organized and professional criminal gangs collect millions in Afghan currency from across the country and in big cities share it with their friends in government departments. Pakistani journalist Najjam Sethi says that Afghanistan poses key foreign policy challenges. He also warned that the Afghan national army will not be able to hold the fort for long. And a drift into civil war, Mr. Najjam Sethi says, would lead to a significant backlash for Pakistan as well.

By the end of 2014, once NATO and the US forces leave the country, Afghanistan's neighbors will have to play a larger role. Pakistan will either sincerely try to placate the Taliban or demand its share. Iran already influences the political and military affairs of the country overall. India has played a significant role in rebuilding the country. India has signed a Strategic Partnership Agreement with Afghanistan and continues to train Afghan forces.

The war in Afghanistan has failed. The war, like previous invasions by Russia and the United Kingdom, has been a spectacular failure. Taliban have inflicted serious financial, military and human costs on the US and NATO allies states. The US war strategy has failed to bring peace and stability to Afghanistan. Its military presence in the country causes instability. American and NATO forces have killed thousands of innocent women and children in different provinces during the last twelve years.

Journalist Seumas Milne reported the killings of innocent civilians in Kandahar, noting that the slaughter of innocents in Panjwai, nine of them children, followed an eruption of killings and protests after US troops burned copies of the Koran. Even US General Stanley McChrystal, former commander of NATO troops in Afghanistan, said: "We have shot an amazing number of people, but to my knowledge, none has ever proven to be a threat. . . Many civilians are killed in night raids or air attacks, such as the one that killed eight shepherd boys aged six to 18 in Northern Afghanistan."

More than 350,000 ANA soldiers, 100,000 members of criminal militias, private contractors and over 110,000 foreign forces, are unable to defeat the Taliban and 100 al-Qaeda fighters. The only solution in NATO's and America's mind is to withdraw their forces by the end of 2014, and leave Afghanistan to the terrorists and criminal mafia groups. This means they have been defeated. Now they are trying to save face by handing over the security of the country to a profoundly corrupt and weak Afghan army, an army that cannot defend Afghanistan.

On 18 June 2013, the process of transition and the handover of security to the Afghan National Army was nominally completed. The ANA will have to take the lead in providing security in 34 provinces of Afghanistan. In 2010, the strategy adopted by NATO allies in the Lisbon Summit between Afghanistan and NATO's military command fixed the date of the ISAF Combat Mission's withdrawal from the country. By the end of 2014, the ISAF Combat Mission is set to end and Afghan Security Forces will take full control of security related operations in Afghanistan after a decade-long engagement.

Without continued US assistance, the fragile and war torn country will likely to re-descend into anarchy. At the Chicago Summit, it was agreed that after 2015 the Afghan Security Forces would be reduced from 352,000 to 230,000 personnel, because the "international community" has been unable to reach the goal of 352,000 by January 2013. In fact, the Afghan National Army is shrinking, not growing. As acknowledged even in the report of the Special Inspector General for Afghanistan, the rate of desertion in the ANA is very high.

The decision to downsize received harsh criticism from all sections of Afghan society. Afghans complain that the US and NATO are not sincere with their plan to rebuild a strong force for their country. Coalition forces feel more threatened by the Afghan National Army than the Taliban, as the ANA has established close contacts with Taliban networks for more attacks, in order to force them into immediate withdrawal. Realizing a constant threat from the corrupt officials, and from nationalist and factionalist elements within the Afghan National Army and the police, the ISAF with NATO and the US have turned to the private militias of warlords for the protection of their military installations.

A coherent approach was needed for the reorganization and the reorientation of Afghan's state institutions. The military and political interests of NATO and US, on the one hand, and of India and Pakistan on the other, are in conflict. The collapsed, polarized, fragmented and deeply wounded Afghan state has devolved into a vortex of instability, corruption, regionalism and illegal militarization of society.

In bringing to the public my analysis of this data along with the vital observations of professionals operating in the field, and the remarks of many reporters and commentators, I am highly indebted to Algora Publishing and their staff members who showed deep interest in my book.

Musa Khan Jalalzai
London, UK, January, 2014

# FOREWORD

I am grateful to Mr. Musa Khan Jalalzai for asking me to write this fore-word. The book covers a wide spectrum: the state of the Afghan National Army (ANA); the present situation in Afghanistan; challenges the country is likely to face during the run up to the withdrawal (or the drawdown) of the foreign forces; and much else. I however sought the author's permission to focus primarily on the ANA's ability to carry out the task it has been assigned: "ensuring security in Afghanistan".

My reasons are simple. Firstly: enough has been written and debated on the other themes and the author too has extensively quoted a number of experts; another "two cents" was thus hardly what the reader needs. Secondly, as someone who has served many years in the armed forces, I find myself more qualified to talk about military affairs. Most importantly, if the peace and stability that has eluded Afghanistan for over three decades was now to depend upon an institution like the ANA, its potential to do so needs to be assessed in a dispassionate discourse.

In principle, security is not a 'military only' affair. The armed forces play their role, however important, in an overarching political framework. This umbrella is all the more critical when they are employed within the country. Even when fighting an insurgency, for example — usually as a weapon of last resort — the military's role is specified and limited by the political objective: pacification, reintegration, or elimination of the insurgents; all depending on the environment. The use of force can only create favorable conditions and win time for a process that addresses the genuine or perceived grievances of the people themselves. That is best done by the political leadership and the civil society. These fundamental norms from which all legal norms are derived (Grundnorms in Hans Kelsen's Pure Theory of Law) are also applicable to Afghanistan — especially in view of the country's configuration.

Some of us must have often wondered, what happened to the region once described by the historian Toynbee as the "eastern crossroads" of history, thus dubbed primarily because of its geo-political location but perhaps also because the armies and the people who crisscrossed it did so almost at will! When in 1747 Ahmad Shah Durrani united the major tribes and factions of the area that constitutes today's Afghanistan, whatever motives he might have had, one effect was that the highway he create for the invading armies became a quagmire for them. If Toynbee were not an historian, he might have named it the "eastern Bermuda Triangle"; only this one sucked in whole empires, with similar consequences. For this outcome alone, the founder of the country deserves to be remembered as Ahmad Shah 'Baba'.

Anyone halfway familiar with Afghanistan would understand the algorithm of this transformation. The country is divided along all possible fault lines — geographic, demographic, tribal, even sectarian and cultural. It became a political entity through a grand bargain amongst its components. It is best held together with the broadest possible consensus. And most relevantly, it cannot be subjugated unless all its major centers of resistance are overpowered. That may well explain the logic of consulting an all-inclusive assembly, the Jirga, before decisions of national import are taken. And that may also have led to the syndrome we are now so familiar with: foreign invaders face no resistance from the conventional armies of Afghanistan, but they cannot pacify its people who wage unconventional warfare on their home turf.

The outcome of the Soviet invasion and the predicament of the still unfinished American misadventure continue to resonate. I however find the fate of the first British expedition in 1842 more illustrative. When the expedition reached Kabul, the Khan of Kalat famously quipped: "And how will it get out of there?" That one didn't get out, but it was not because an "army" reduced it to one man. It died a slow death inflicted upon it by the Afghan tribesmen, or, depending upon one's perspective, by bounty hunters. Of course, the sole superpower of that time had to save face. To avenge the disaster, it made another incursion: it bribed its way to Kabul and back.

One may well argue that whereas the foreign invaders fail because of the Afghan natives' propensity to defend their freedom, a "national" force due to its local credentials need not suffer the same fate. But then one only has to recall the post-Soviet plight of the PDPA Army; it was much better equipped, trained and led than the ANA's hired guns. It is true that the Mujahedeen could not dislodge the regulars from entrenched positions, a lesson they learnt at considerable cost at Jalalabad; or, that they had to pay their way to "conquer" Khost, as the elder Haqqani did. But then it is also true that the

PDPA was confined to a few big cities while the resistance controlled the countryside.

As any military strategist knows, the side that enjoys freedom of maneuver ultimately wins the war. Incidentally, contrary to common belief, Najeeb's army did not disintegrate because the Soviets ceased their support but because his regime collapsed when allies like Dostum deserted him after his fateful statement that he would abdicate in favor of a Mujahedeen-led government. Indeed, it is the unity of command, all the way to the very top, that makes an army functional.

A dysfunctional government in Kabul may be just one (albeit the most grievous) of the handicaps the ANA would face. The ethnic divide that has been aggravated a great deal during the last two decades may be equally disabling. Maintaining a healthy ethnic mix is a requisite for a national army. Given a mutually acceptable arrangement, it could work. But in the present environment — to put it mildly, a "trust deficit" — it is a recipe for disaster. Employed against the Taliban, many of its Pashtun soldiers would desert, some of them after using their weapons and skills against their non-Pashtun officers.

And just in case a posse was sent up North, one would be naïve to believe that the Afghans would have forgotten the brutalities perpetrated by the Taliban in Mazar-e-Sharif, or the systematic extermination carried out by the former Northern Alliance operating under the cover of B52s. I have no idea how deeply the Taliban have penetrated the ANA's ranks, but one can reasonably assume that after all the multicolored assaults — green on blue and red on whatever — no Pashtun soldier is above suspicion.

The ANA as an institution may also remain suspect; at least for a time. The Mujahedeen used to call the PDPA Army a "communist tool." The ANA would also be regarded as an imperial instrument, especially when operating under the US/NATO umbrella. Someone once rightly asked me why the Pakistan Army, being a legacy of the Raj, was not similarly labeled? I am not sure if I have the correct or the whole answer, but I believe it must be due to historical and cultural differences. In the Subcontinent the force of arms was feared, even respected, and in "martial areas" envied and eulogized. I do not know of many other countries where the soldiers proudly wear emblems touting that their unit, while in service of a foreign power, massacred its own people. I believe the Afghans, while pragmatic when dealing with power, are too proud to worship it.

One may legitimately ask if the above makes any sense, why would the US sink enormous sums of money into a project that stood no chance to deliver. The honest answer again must be: I do not know; but I can come up with a few hypotheses. A few years back I met a retired US general at the Kabul Airport. He said he was heading one of the companies training the Afghan Army. Other than the defense industry introducing a new weapons system, it had not been common knowledge that private companies were imparting basic skills to armies preparing for combat. Even when employing retired soldiers, these outfits are more interested in getting their contracts extended than anything else. Inadequate training is one way to achieve that end. Training, equipping and building barracks for the Afghan armed forces is a multi-billion dollar business.

Exhausting all options — as Churchill said was the American wont to do before they got it right — may be another possible reason. Having experimented with democracy, nation building and degrading the Taliban — none of them succeeding — handing over Afghanistan to a national army might help Obama to proclaim "mission accomplished".

Then there is another likelihood that is not so benign. Former US Vice-President Dick Cheney once reportedly remarked that turmoil in certain regions is good for America. Indeed, it is. It helps the sole surviving super-power to retain leverage with one or the other side — at times with both; and it keeps its mighty military-industrial complex well oiled. Turmoil in Central Asia has numerous costs and benefits. But at the very least a strong presence in the region would presumably help the US achieve a few objectives: to exploit the region's minerals; restrain "rogue" nuclear — or wannabe nuclear — powers in the neighborhood; block Beijing's strategic goals in Pakistan; and one day even realize its (unpopular in the region) "New Silk Road" project. An ANA unable to keep the peace and promote stability in Afghanistan provides the right pretext for maintaining the desired foothold.

Or maybe there is yet another reason! For a long time, I remained under the impression that the US had understood the limitations of an Afghan army's ability to ensure security and was building up the ANA on some other pretext, or even as a ruse. But since an American friend of mine who is a keen observer of the Afghan scene is convinced that the ANA could carry out its role with some help from its mentors, it is quite possible that Washington, too, actually has faith in its role.

Another friend of mine from across the Atlantic suspects that the Pakistanis, especially from the military, are fearful of an effective Afghan army, believing that it would be an unfriendly force and could spoil Islamabad's designs to influence policies in Kabul. I must admit that I had never given much thought to the type of threat a strong Afghan army could pose to Pakistan's real or perceived goals in the region. But I do recall what the Afghan Security Forces did during our two wars against India. The message from Kabul both in 1965 and 1971 was that we could remove all our forces from the Afghan borders. We did precisely that, and the Afghans ensured that for the duration of the crises all was quiet on the western front. The two countries have their neighborly troubles, but then, their stakes in each other's security and stability are so high that neither would do anything deliberately to hurt the other's core interests.

Every country has the right to keep an army; if for no other reason than as a symbol of its sovereignty. Afghanistan too will have one to suit its own needs. But to expect the ANA in its present shape (or even when it has become an effective fighting force) to ensure security in the absence of a broadly accepted dispensation in Kabul runs counter to a fundamental principle as well as to the genesis of the country. My American friend, the keen observer of the Afghan scene, once told me that before 1977, except for the Panjshir uprising of 1975, it was the local authority that kept peace in the country.

Lt Gen (r) Asad Durrani
Former Director General
Inter Services Intelligence (ISI)
Pakistan
July 2013

# Chapter 1. The Afghan Army from Alexander the Great to Hamid Karzai

Afghanistan has been a strategically important country throughout history. The country has never been occupied by foreign invaders. For more than 2,500 years, Afghanistan has been serving as a vital crossroads for armies and witnessed fighting between various civilizations: Greek, Tatar, Mongol, Arab, British, Russian and American. Historians have called Afghanistan the Central Asian roundabout. From Alexander the Great to US General Allen, they all tasted Afghan food but suffered severe indigestion. A very brief rundown of the relatively recent past will prepare the reader for a more detailed look at what is happening now.

Alexander the Great invaded Afghanistan but faced relentless resistance and was forced to leave the country as soon as possible. After his defeat at the hands of the Afghans, Alexander the Great said to his friends: "Afghanistan is easy to march into but hard to march out of." He remained frustrated, and never forgot Afghanistan all his life.[1]

In 1220, Genghis Khan came to Afghanistan with brutal war tactics but was defeated. Great Britain invaded Afghanistan in 1838 but experienced the same resistance. While its forces were withdrawing over the mountain pass outside Kabul, 4,500 soldiers and 12,500 civilians were killed.[2]

In 1897, as a young British cavalry officer, General Winston Churchill wrote about the war in Afghanistan: "Financially it is ruinous, morally it is wicked, militarily it is an open question and politically it is a blunder." The

---

1 Jason Thomas. 5 July 2013, *Small Wars Journal.* "Post 2014 Afghanistan: Another King upon an Ant Hill".
2 Baxter C, 2011. *The First Anglo Afghan War.*

current Afghan army originated in 1709 when the Hotaki Dynasty was estab-lished in Kandahar. In April 1709, Mirwais Khan Hotak revolted against Gurgin (a Georgian who represented the ruling Persians) and challenged the Safavids in Kandahar. Gurgin was killed. Four days later, Georgian troops arrived to occupy the town, but Mirwais Khan sternly resisted. From 1710 to 1713, the Afghan tribal army defeated several powerful armies of Persians dispatched from Isfahan. Mirwais Khan died in 1715.[1]

In 1747, when Ahmad Shah Durrani created an Afghan empire, his tribal army fought a number of wars in Hindustan in the 18th and 19th centuries. In 1761, Ahmad Shah Durrani was requested by Shah Waliullah Dehlavi, to help the Muslims against the Maratha (a confederacy of Hindu tribes known for guerrilla tactics) atrocities. Ahmad Shah attacked Panipat and decisively defeated the Hindu Maratha Empire. His tribal army was later on challenged by Ranjit Singh's army in Punjab. In the battle of Jamrud, the important Sikh commander Hari Singh Nalwa was killed by Prince Akbar Khan. In 1838, British India invaded Afghanistan.[2]

In 1838, the British Government feared an increased Russian influence in the country, and the Governor General of India tried to bring Afghan foreign policy under Britain's control. Lord Auckland organized an army of 58,000 soldiers and attacked Afghanistan in March 1839.[3]

Afghanistan signed various treaties with Great Britain after the first, second and third Anglo-Afghan wars. In 1809, the treaty of Peshawar was signed between Great Britain and Afghanistan as Shah Shuja sought British support in his battle for the throne. In 1855, a treaty of friendship between Great Britain and Afghanistan was signed after the first Anglo-Afghan War. In confirmation of the 1855 treaty, Britain signed another agreement with Afghanistan in 1857 during the Anglo-Iranian war (1856 to 1857). Under this agreement, Dost Muhammad Khan supported Britain against Iran. The Gan-damak Treaty of 1879 was signed in Gandamak, turning Afghanistan into a state dependent on Great Britain by barring Afghanistan from maintaining an independent foreign policy. In November 1893, finally, Abdur Rehman divided the Pashtuns by signing the Durand Agreement with Great Britain in Kabul.

Moreover, confirming all the treaties between Abdur Rehman and Great Britain, Habibullah Khan signed the Kabul agreement on March 21, 1905. In 1919, Afghanistan signed the Rawalpindi agreement with Great Britain and confirmed the Durand Line. In 1921, Britain recognized Afghanistan as an independent state by signing a friendship agreement with the country.[4]

---

1 Bruce George, 1878, *History of Afghanistan. London.*
2 William Dalrymple. 2010. *"The Ghosts of Gandamak."* New York Times.
3 Macroy Patrick, 2002. *Retreat from Kabul: The Catastrophic British Defeat in Afghanistan.* The Lyons Press. USA.
4 Stephen Tanner. 2009. *Afghanistan: A Military History from Alexander the Great to the War against the Taliban.*

In the 19th century, Afghan rulers needed a strong army to defend their territory. Afghanistan was a poor, weak and scattered nation while Abdur Rahman Khan further divided it into pieces. Amir Abdur Rahman Khan, who ruled Afghanistan from 1880 to 1901, killed and tortured hundreds of men and women of Hazara Muslim communities, and those who opposed him. He propelled 10,000 Hazara Afghans towards Pakistan and introduced the military conscription program in 1895, called "Hasht Nafari" (one man out of eight). He asked various tribes to provide manpower for the army, but the majority of the Pashtun tribes refused to help the Amir in building national security forces, because he had already divided the Pashtuns under the Durand Agreement in 1893. He received no encouragement or support from the Pashtun tribes.[1]

His grandson Amanullah Khan decided to follow his father's military strategy and introduced a conscription program after he defeated the British Army in 1919. He wanted to professionalize the army by removing all vestiges of tribal authority, creating an organized force trained by Turkish advisors, but his confrontation with tribal leaders and religious clerics led to the collapse of his government.[2]

Afghan military expert Ali Ahmad Jalali views the era of Nadir Shah as the era of modernization. In his understanding, from 1929 to 1933 Nadir Khan shored up the Afghan army because he was aware that future development in the region would entail military action. Therefore, he tried to establish an army of 70,000 soldiers and reopened Kabul's military academy to train his tribal soldiers. After his assassination, the process of conscription stopped. His young son, Zahir Shah, became the king of a weak and vulnerable Afghanistan. He entered the political game and raised the issue of so called Pashtunistan, instead of providing jobs and food to the poor people of his country.[3]

In fact, the establishment of regular Afghan armed forces does date back to the 1920s and 1930s, when Nadir Khan attempted to organize his army as a modern force. By 1938, the size of the Afghan army reached 90,000 soldiers. From 1939 to 1953, he tried to train an organized military force but failed, because Pashtuns from Paktika and parts of Paktia provinces rejected the conscription program and refused to serve in the army. Meanwhile, corruption spread through the rank and file of his army and half of the military budget was lost to corruption.[4]

In the 1950s and 1960s, the Afghan army was not in good shape — and Pakistan and Afghanistan came close to war over Pashtunistan. At least in

1  Muhammad Daud. 2010. *Encyclopedia of Britannica.*
2  Mark Sedra. 19 April 2012. *The Army in Afghanistan: from Abdur Rehman to Karzai. Middle East Institute.*
3  Ali Muhammad Zahir Shah. 2010. *Encyclopaedia of Britannica.*
4  Muhammad Zahir Shah. 2010. *Encyclopaedia of Britannica.*

the 1950s, the Afghan army was capable of defeating a tribal revolt. Modern aircraft were purchased from the former Soviet Union. In 1959, a revolt in the Mengal area was put down with the use of tanks. In the 1960s and 1970s, the Afghan army made some progress. In 1973, when Muhammad Daud came to power, the Musahibeen monarchy was defeated. Muhammad Daud decided to re-establish the relationship between the state and society, tipping the balance of power away from the tribes in favor of the state.

He started modernizing his country's military forces and opened military training centers and boarding schools intended to create a well-trained army free from tribal influence. Daud was a committed ruler who worked day and night to create a well-trained military force, but unfortunately his government was toppled in 1978 by the People's Democratic Party of Afghanistan. In the 1970s, the army tried to pick up the pieces again and decided to take men directly from districts — not from the tribes; this strategy also failed.

Finally, in 1979, Soviet forces invaded Afghanistan.[1] In 1980 and 1981 the army was adjusted to the presence of a Soviet garrison. During the late 1980s, the Afghan army even took part in a number of major offensives. More successes occurred in 1984 and 1985, when Babrak Karmal built a strong security apparatus. However, by 1985, the Afghan army was completely politicized and from 1986 to 1992 the desertion rate was very high.

The Khalq and Parcham governments brought new changes to the rank and file of the national army. Appointments and promotions were based on political loyalties, affiliations and ideology. From 1980 to 1992, Afghan and Soviet forces were unable to fight effectively or secure the territory. More Afghan army soldiers joined mujahedeen forces every year — the desertion rate was 20,000 to 30,000. The army faced serious difficulties in training new soldiers. In 1992, after the collapse of Dr. Najibullah's government, the army disintegrated.[2]

From 1992 to 2001, there was no regular army in Afghanistan. After the fall of the Taliban regime in 2001, the international community hurriedly reached out to contact the major Afghan groups to form a broad-based government in Afghanistan. On 5 December 2001, members of various political parties signed an agreement (the Bonn Agreement) in Germany, which was endorsed by UN Security Council Resolution No. 1385. In June, 2002, an Emergency Loya Jirga (Grand Assembly) of 1550 participants from all major political parties across the country, and a 35-member Constitutional Commission was formed.[3]

---

1 Hayes and Mark Sedra, *Afghanistan Transition under Threat*, Oct, 2008.
2 Stephanie Cronin. *"Afghanistan's Armies Past and Present"*. Research paper, Institute of Contemporary British History. Kings college London.
3 Nilanthi Samaranayake. "Conscription in the Afghan Army: Compulsory Service Versus an All Volunteer Force." Academia. Edu. 2012.

In 2002, with the establishment of the Afghan National Army (ANA), the process of conscription resumed. Between 2002 and 2004, more than 4,000 soldiers were trained. The Commission later on drafted Afghanistan's Constitution. From December 2003 to January 2004, the Constitutional Jirga approved a new Afghan constitution with some changes. Thus, in December 2004, Hamid Karzai became the President of Afghanistan and, on 19 December 2005, Grand Assembly was inaugurated. Notwithstanding, all these efforts of international community for stabilizing the war torn Afghanistan, there was a constant need for a strong Security Forces to keep the country united.[1]

The 2001 Bonn Agreement clearly stipulates that ensuring security in Afghanistan rests with the Afghans, but unfortunately, after investing over 12 years in training the Afghan National Security Forces, they still remain incapable to protect the territorial integrity of the country.[2]

In December 2002, with the decree of the President of Afghanistan, the Afghan National Army was re-established. The military objectives of the Afghan National army are, of course, nationwide: ensuring independence, fighting insurgencies, safeguarding territorial integrity and maintaining stability. The Afghan National Army managed to grow, increasing in size and operational capabilities. The ANA is growing gradually, month by month and year by year, but desertion continues day by day.[3]

Kenneth Katzman, in his CRS Report for US Congress, discussed the mission of the US military in Afghanistan: "To combat the insurgency, the United States is in partnership with 49 other countries and the Afghan government and security forces. There were 100,000 US troops in mid-2011, which fell to 90,000 by the end of 2011 and to 68,000 (the "surge recovery") by September 20, 2012. The vast majority operates under NATO/ISAF command, but about 9,000 remain part of the post-September 11 anti-terrorism mission Operation Enduring Freedom (OEF)".[4]

Member states of the NATO-led ISAF met in Chicago in May 2012 and renewed their commitment to a stable and democratic Afghanistan. In March 2013, NATO's Secretary General visited Afghanistan and reaffirmed that the organization will continue its mission of training Afghan security forces, but Afghanistan's presidential spokesman termed their military operation "aimless and unwise." In fact, Aimal Faizi was reacting to Anders Fogh

1  Kenneth Katzman. Congressional Research Service, 23 May 2013. *Afghanistan: Politics, Election and Government Performance.*
2  BBC News, "Afghans agree on New Constitution," 04 January 2004.
3  Imam Hasan. *The News International,* 06 February, 2013. "Afghan President lakes faith in his own National Security Forces In 2001, Bonn Agreement clearly stipulates that the ultimate responsibility for ensuring security throughout Afghanistan rests with the Afghans themselves."
4  Beata Gorka Winter, March 28-30, 2012. *Challenges for the Security Sector in Afghanistan: How to Save Reform.* Chicago, USA.

Rasmussen's rejection of Afghan President Hamid Karzai's allegations of US collusion with the Taliban insurgents.[1]

On March 20 2013, *Dawn* reported the deep anger of the Afghan government about the secret cooperation between the Taliban and US forces. "The people of Afghanistan ask NATO to define the purpose and aim of the so called war on terror... (They) consider this war as aimless and unwise to continue."[2]

These statements by the Afghan government deeply disappointed the international coalition. They started thinking about withdrawing their forces from Afghanistan. A London-based independent think tank, Chatham House, in its August 2012 analysis, criticized the withdrawal of NATO and US forces from Afghanistan:

> NATO's announcement that it will pull out its 130,000 troops from Afghanistan by the end of 2014 and hand over control to Afghan Security Forces has been open to criticism. On the one hand it was seen as giving hope to the Taliban, allowing them to believe that all they need do is to sit patiently and wait as Western forces withdraw. On the other, it was seen as jeopardizing attempts to strengthen the Afghan state, by creating disincentives for Afghan officials to invest time and money in the country's future.[3]

Kenneth Katzman in his CRS Report on Afghanistan described the actual size of the Afghan Security Forces: "In January 21, 2010, the UN–Afghan Joint Coordination and Monitoring Board (JCMB) agreed that, by October 2011, the ANA would expand to 171,600 and the ANP to about 134,000, (total ANSF of 305,600). Both forces reached that level in September 2011. In August 2011, larger target size of 352,000 (195,000 ANA and 157,000 ANP) was set, to be reached by November 2012".[4]

In 2010, President Hamid Karzai gave a speech in which he stressed the need for national unity and said: "Conscription could serve as a vehicle for national unity." Now Afghans don't know what to do and where to go. There is no hope, no dream and support, all dreams vanished. The present artificial state and its corrupt institutions including armed forces are unable to protect the unity of the nation.

Afghan civil society asks whether the process of peace building has reached a state where NATO and the US can handover the responsibility to ANA for a stable Afghanistan. In spite of several attempts to reinvent the state, the state mostly remained weak and corrupt, having multiple and conflicting legal and political systems. The state has not been in position to sup-

---

1  *NATO Press Release, 2009. "The Afghan National army is divided into five combat corps. Sentinels of Afghan Democracy: Afghan National army", Military Review, January February 2009.*

2  Kenneth Katzman, 25 June 2013. "Afghanistan: Post Taliban Governance, Security and US Policy". *Congressional Research Report.*

3  *Ibid*

4  March 20 2013, *Daily Dawn.* "The deep anger of Afghan government about the secret cooperation between the Taliban and US forces".

port the army. Afghans have been disconnected and alienated from the state and government since 2002. Afghan civil society and neighboring states are anxious about the possibility of a future civil war, after the withdrawal of foreign forces in 2014. Thus, all neighbors are demanding the extension of the stay of US and NATO forces in Afghanistan. However, in November 2011, President Karzai convened Afghan Jirga and extended the stay of US and NATO forces until at least 2024.[1]

In 2012, President Obama, in his visit to Afghanistan reassured the government of Afghanistan, and its neighbors, that the end of 2014 will not produce a complete US withdrawal. In May 2012, The Chicago Conference also expressed the same resolve.[2]

Paul D. Miller, in his article in *Survival*, March 2013, reveals his doubts about the US withdrawal strategy and says the United States is not scheduled to withdraw from Afghanistan in 2014. President Obama is changing his statement about Afghanistan which created controversies in his own country. His inconsistent policy regarding his country's military mission in Afghanistan has badly affected the morale of US forces.[3]

Massive corruption and ethnic divides have badly interfered with the development of professional skills in all these forces. They are unable to undertake a single military operation without the support of US and NATO forces. In April 2013, a British general warned that cutting British forces in Afghanistan too quickly could endanger the peace efforts. The main fear among the Afghans is that their country could plunge into another civil war after the withdrawal of US and NATO in the end of 2014.[4]

As the date of withdrawal of US, NATO and ISAF force from Afghanistan approaches, every mature Afghan asks whether the Afghan National army and the police will be in position to defend the ethnically divided country.[5] The ethnic imbalance within the ANA, police and other state institutions has further exacerbated in their anxiety. Afghan National Army and the police are unable to recruit more than a disproportionally low number of Pashtuns from the Southern and Eastern parts of the country.[6]

The challenge of factionalization within the ANA, police forces and intelligence infrastructure (KHAD, NDS, RAMA, CID, and Military Intel-

---

1   Gareth Price, "NATO's announcement that it will pull out its 130,000 troops from Afghanistan by the end of 2014 and hand over control to Afghan Security Forces has been open to criticism". Chatham House. *The World Today, Volume 68 Number-7*.

2   Kenneth Katzman, 25 June 2013. "Afghanistan: Post Taliban Governance, Security and US Policy". *Congressional Research Report*.

3   Press Release (2012) 062, issued on 20 May 2012. "Chicago Summit Declaration, issued by the Heads of State and Governments participating in the meeting of North Atlantic Council in Chicago on" 20 May 2012.

4   *Ibid*

5   Paul D. Miller, *Survival*, March 2013.

6   *The Independent* "Top British general warn of dangerous troop cuts in Afghanistan," 01 April 2013.

ligence), however, is the main cause of despondency among Afghans.[1] An expert on Afghan issues, author Vanda Felbab Brown, in her well-written book, analyzed the post withdrawal scenario. She mainly focused on the danger of future ethnic violence and individual loyalties within the ANA and police forces:

> Deep ethnic fissure and patronage networks run through the Afghan military, with segments of the force loyal to particular top-level commanders rather than to the institution overall or — more important — the government in Kabul. Until mid 2010, the two chief power brokers within the Afghan Ministry of Defense were Minister Abdul Rahim Wardak (a Pashtun) and Chief of Staff of the Army Bismullah Khan Mohammadi (a Tajik and a former lieutenant of the famous northern commander Ahmad Shah Massoud. . . . Not surprisingly, power and loyalty in Afghanistan continue to be attached to individuals rather than institutions. . . . In the post 2014 civil war, the fighting can be expected to be highly localized and complex.[2]

Most Pakistani experts understand that Afghan civil war will be fought among various ethnic and sectarian groups and the military interference of regional states cannot be ruled out. Author Vanda Felbab Brown has also analyzed the destabilization and ethnic politics in Afghanistan:

> The destabilizing political process in the country — from ethnic mobilization to the increasingly narrow and exclusionary nature of the patronage networks—and overwhelmingly poor governance are even more disconcerting. Afghans are deeply alienated from a government and power structure they see as abusive and unaccountable. Many speak of living under mafia rule".[3]

In view of the above-mentioned despondency of the people of Afghanistan, the international community forced the country to talk to the Taliban insurgents. Kabul has already been in contact with the Taliban since 2005, when the reconciliation efforts started for the first time, but all their mutual contacts ended with no result. In 2010, the Afghan Peace Council was formed to initiate talks with the Taliban. In September 2011, former Afghan President Burhanuddin Rabbani, head of the Peace Council, was killed. In 2012, Afghanistan continued to negotiate with the Taliban in and outside the country.[4]

On February 2013, in London, a trilateral summit (Britain, Afghanistan and Pakistan) ended with the commitment that all necessary measures will be taken to achieve the goal of peace. But the result of talks between the

---

1  Vanda Felbab Brown. 2013. *Aspiration and Ambivalence.*
2  *Ibid.*
3  Thomas Rutting. May 2011. "The battle for Afghanistan Negotiations with the Taliban: History and Prospect for the Future". Policy Paper of National Security Studies Program.
4  *Ibid*

Taliban and Kabul remained uncertain, as Qatar refused to close the Taliban office.[1]

In June 2012, the negotiation process resumed. Pakistan continued its support for insurgent groups against Afghanistan. Taliban groups, like Quetta Shura, the Haqqani group, minor insurgents groups of North and South Waziristan, all receive their share from Islamabad. Pakistan tried to persuade its own Taliban that the real jihad is in Afghanistan not in Pakistan. In 2004, the country's talks with its own Taliban resulted in an agreement (the Shakai Agreement) between the two sides. In 2005, the Sararogha Peace Agreement was signed between Baitullah Mehsud and the Army. In May 2008, the Swat agreement was also signed between Sufi Muhammad's Taliban leaders and the ANP government.[2]

In 2009, President Obama proposed direct talks between the United States and Taliban representatives, and in 2010, direct contact between the Taliban and US government was proposed in Munich. In February 2011, the Taliban and the Obama administration discussed the peace process in Doha. In 2011, they discussed the reconciliation process in Germany. In January 2012, the Taliban met with US officials in Qatar and established their office in Doha.[3]

In all these talks (2004–2012), disagreements among the Taliban, Pakistan, Afghanistan and the United States on the issue of peace and reconciliation have been irksome. All sides were determined to stick to their own agendas.[4]

1  Associated Press 04 February 2013. "Afghanistan, Pakistan and the UK called on the Taliban to come to the table for talks. They decided to open a Taliban office in Qatar to facilitate such talks".

2  Shanthie Mariet D'Souza. 10 January 2013.*Transition in Afghanistan: A War of Perceptions.*

3  "Taliban Peace Talks", *the Guardian*, 19 June 2013.

4  *New York Times*, 27 November 2012.

## Chapter 2. The Afghan National Army and Green on Blue Attacks

In April 2003, Afghan warlords and war criminals agreed to support President Karzai's Government in rebuilding the Afghan Security Forces. All the war criminals agreed to support the Afghan Defense Ministry in expanding the writ of the government to every part of the country. Unfortunately, these commitments remained on paper while the warlords entered into a series of agreements with foreign-led entities such as the ISAF, NATO and US forces to protect their military convoys and installations across the country. They are receiving millions of dollars from these international forces.[1]

As regards Afghan military strategy, the principal internal and external threats to the nation's security are: the Taliban insurgency, non-state actors and extremist groups. Illegal armed groups and warlords' criminal militias also threaten the country's stability.

Long term, the stability of Afghanistan depends on the performance of the Afghan National Army. But due to the existence of more than one hundred thousand armed men working for criminal militias across the country, the ANA's non-professional way of operations weak approach to the prevailing insurgency across the country has raised serious questions. It is not clear why the international coalition maintain a parallel army instead of strengthening the ANA.

Some Afghans ask why the present command and control system of the Afghan army was established in Germany, not in Afghanistan? The former Director General of Pakistan's Inter Services Intelligence (ISI), Gen. Asad Durrani, suggests why Afghans must have missed feelings about the ANA:

---

1 *The Long March: Building an Afghan National army.* National Defense Research Institute, 2009.

"The Afghan National army that arose under foreign tutelage, and in the foreseeable future will remain dependent upon its support, will be seen by most Afghans as a legacy of the occupation and not really [a] 'national' [institution]."

In Bonn, President Hamid Karzai in December 2002 told journalists: "Hoping that our endeavor will be endowed with success by the Almighty God, we are embarking on the renewal and reconstruction of the ANA as an essential step for the realization of the idea of the Afghan Mujahedeen who were martyred during the Afghan jihad, of all the people of the Afghan nation, and for the securing of national unity, peace and stability in our country. Success is from God".[1]

The Afghan National army is undergoing numerous crises simultaneously. Desertion, ethnic imbalances, sectarianism, regionalism and lack of resources are causing deep trouble. The United States, UK and NATO allies supported the ANA with training and equipment but corruption, nepotism and ethnic politics undermine its morale. During the last twelve years, Afghans have poured thousands of young people into an army that cannot defend the country. In spite of all its illegal practices, the international community has tried continued providing funds and equipment.

In May 2012, at the Chicago conference, leaders of NATO states reaffirmed the Lisbon resolve for security transition, endorsed a NATO strategic plan and vowed to support the Afghan National Security Forces (ANSF) after their withdrawal in the end of 2014. Alongside the Bonn process and Operation Enduring Freedom, G8 donors demanded security sector reforms according to five segments: The United Kingdom would reform counter-narcotics policies, the US would reform the Afghan Security Infrastructure, Italy would introduce Judicial Reforms, and Germany would introduce reforms in the Police Department, while Japan would facilitate the Disarmament and Demobilization Program.[2]

These were just verbal commitments; in practice no encouraging steps have been taken to improve the operational capability of the ANA so far. No specific reforms were introduced within the police, the judicial system, education, health or the ANA infrastructure. The ANA still needs to be balanced ethnically. The disarmament program failed badly while warlords started rearming their criminal militias and the smuggling of narcotics is only accelerating. After failing to put down the Taliban insurgency in the last 12 years, the US, NATO and ISAF announced the withdrawal of their forces by the end of 2014. The US and its allies won nothing, the insurgency is very much in place, the threat of the return of al-Qaeda and extremist forces are there and the threat of civil war is also there, nothing has changed. The Taliban re-

---

1  Patrick Hennessey. *Kandak: Fighting with Afghans*. Allen Lane. 2012.
2  Press Release, 2012, 062. 20 May, 2012, *Chicago Summit Declaration*.

emerged to challenge the national power and established an office in Qatar in June 2013.

The announcement of the 2014 withdrawal has raised the fear that the country might once again become an epicenter of terrorism in the region. As Afghanistan will not be able to maintain its security infrastructure, the process of state building will be put on ice; and further, the return of al-Qaeda and the Taliban will jeopardize the stability of other Central and South Asian states.[1]

On 12 January 2013, in its print edition, *The Economist* painted a hopeless picture:

> Despite an improving combat performance, it is highly uncertain whether the ANSF will cope. Hastily recruited and trained, the ANSF is still a work in progress. It was deliberately denied heavy weapons or much of an air force on the assumption that America would provide key "enablers" for years to come. It now takes the lead security role in about 85% of the country by population, and overall levels of violence are slightly down on previous years. But according to the Pentagon's latest report on the progress of Afghan forces, only one out of 23 brigades is capable of operating without any outside help. It now looks as if the ANSF will be on its own in Southern Afghanistan where the Taliban is strongest, as well as in the wild east of the country which borders the lair in the North Waziristan of the Haqqani network.[2]

The Obama administration has assured Afghanistan and its neighbors that a large contingent of US and ISAF forces will remain in the country after the "withdrawal." Though the United States has not stipulated number of forces to remain in Afghanistan, some experts have floated numbers as high as 20,000.3

There is a deep concern among the Afghans that the US and its allies have no intention of strengthening the national army. Britain and the United States first announced their withdrawal at the end of 2011, then 2013, and now by the end of 2014. In November 2011, nearly 2,000 Afghan elders granted permission to US forces to stay beyond 2014.

On the consecutive signing of strategic partnership agreements between Afghanistan, US and NATO member countries, Afghan intellectuals and politicians scrupulously warned that on the pretext of these agreements they want to keep their forces in the country beyond 2014, while there is deep suspicion that these so called strategic partnership agreements cannot save the state from collapse. The US and NATO member states have already predicted that the Afghan state and its army will collapse after 2014.

---

1  Kenneth Katzman, *Afghanistan: Post Taliban Governance, Security and US Policy*. Congressional Research. 2012.

2  CJ Randin. "How many US Troops will remain in Afghanistan after 2014". 10 January 2013, *Long War Journal*. And also see, *The Economist*, 12 January 2013. "In fact Afghans are suffering from frustration when they hear about the internal turmoil in Afghan Armed Forces command and control system."

The attitude of most Afghans towards foreign forces has changed considerably. Commenting on this, Kenneth Katzman in his CRS report for Congress (2012) has warned that:

> The attitude of the Afghan public might be a factor for those international forces that remain in Afghanistan after 2014. Insurgent forces have always used the presence of foreign forces as a rallying and recruiting point, but the vast bulk of Afghans have, in surveys, generally supported having foreign forces to secure Afghanistan. Yet, there are growing signs that the public welcome of foreign forces might be eroding. On April 1, 2011, crowds of Afghans in the Northern city of Mazar-e-Sharif demonstrated against the March 2011 burning of the Holy Quran by a Florida pastor. The demonstration turned violent, with protesters storming the UN compound in the city and killing 12, including 7 UN staff. Demonstrations in other Afghan cities followed, including anti US slogans and posters echoing the Taliban's anti-US, anti-Western rhetoric.[1]

Afghans are disappointed and don't wish to support further deployment of NATO forces on their soil. The atrocities committed by US Special Forces in Wardak and other provinces further enraged the civilian population. On February 24, 2013, the Afghan President ordered US Special Forces to immediately withdraw from Maidan Wardak Province. The President accused American forces of involvement in the torture, disappearance and even killing of civilians.

Taliban infiltration is another threat. Debates on Taliban infiltration and their secret networks within the Afghan army, police and intelligence infrastructures show that the killing of Afghan soldiers by their own partners show that this threat has grabbed the attention to the changing attitude of the Afghan government.[2] In February 2012, a senior Afghan military official disclosed that his country wanted to act quickly to clear the military barracks of Taliban sympathizers.

Another incident in which the Holy Quran was burned, this time by six American soldiers, caused further mistrust between the Afghans and their foreign friends in 2012. Abhorrence for the US forces spread across Afghanistan. In reprisal, an Afghan intelligence man killed a US lieutenant, a colonel and a major in their office inside the Interior Ministry.[3]

On 1 March, 2012, an Afghan soldier and a teacher killed two NATO soldiers in Kandahar. The ISAF press release stated that two individuals turned their weapons indiscriminately against their comrades, killing two soldiers. Having realized the sensitivity of the situation, the Pentagon and the Obama administration apologized for the act of desecration but at the same time

1  Kenneth Katzman, *Afghanistan: Post Taliban Governance, Security and US Policy*. Congressional Research. 2012.
2  Bill Radolino, "President Karzai was nervous on the issue of killing in Wardak province". *Long War Journal*. 24 February 2013.
3  *Daily Times*, "*The Taliban infiltration is another threat by NATO and ISAF members' states across the country*." 15 March 2012.

complained that the Afghan army had failed into protect American soldiers. President Obama was in trouble over the act of desecration; French President Sarkozy simply announced the withdrawal of his country's forces from Afghanistan by the end of 2013.[1]

The story became more involved when an Afghan military commander said that the large size of the Afghan army had led to Taliban infiltration. Military experts viewed this statement as a new policy shift on the part of the Afghan government against ethnic Pashtun officers within the Army. Moreover, the Afghan Defense Ministry warned all Pashtun officers within the army and police forces that if they did not shift their families back from Pakistan to Afghanistan, they might lose their jobs. This announcement was based on KHAD's secret report that ISI is using these people for intelligence gathering in Afghanistan.[2]

The report claimed that Afghans living in Pakistan were being brainwashed by the ISI. Afghan intelligence then proposed a plan of tapping and recording the telephone calls of the Afghan military officers and started monitoring their movements and personal relations in order to expose ISI links within the army. Links with the CIA, RAW, the Iranian Ansarul Muslimeen Secret Service, and Central Asian states are not mentioned in the report. Meanwhile, European and other Western intelligence agencies criticized KHAD, WAD and NDS for their brutal and nonprofessional ways of "intelligence gathering".[3]

Corruption and embezzlement within the ANA is matter of great concern. Afghan soldiers and officers, while participating in military training, sell their promotions and positions. According to the Review Draft assessment:

> [The] breakdown of the ANA makes a deeper problem. Promotions within the ANA also are often based upon patronage, money, or personal loyalty rather than upon ability. Entrenched and powerful patronage networks dominate the promotion system in the ANA and have created a large bloc of officers whose loyalty to the central government is dubious at best."[4]

Article 1 of the Military Law of Afghanistan regulates the affairs (appointment, transfer, promotion, holidays and retirement) of the soldiers and officers of the Afghan Armed Forces, but unfortunately, transfers and appointments are still founded on ethnic, sectarian and patronage ties.

Article 12 of the Military Law clarifies the appointment of officers on the following grounds:

> The personnel of the armed forces shall be promoted based on available positions, political merits, practical personnel qualifications, and capabil-

---

1  *The Nation, 2011.*

2  *Daily Times, "President Obama complained that the Afghan army has failed to protect American soldiers in Afghanistan". 15 March 2012.*

3  *Daily Times,* 03 November 2011.

4  Anthony H. Cordesman, Adam Mausner. Lemieux. *Afghan Security Forces: What it will take to implement the ISAF.* CSIS 2010.

ity in combat and work performance." However, Article 19 elucidates the promotion of high ranking officers: "The issue of promoting an officer to the rank Colonel or General shall be discussed and evaluated in a meeting held by consultancy delegations of relevant ministries and the Department of the State Intelligence Services, and the final decision of the consultancy delegation shall then be signed as a protocol by all members.[1]

Different affiliations and allegiances, trends of regionalism, ethnic loyalties, corruption, sectarian inclinations and associations within the Afghan security forces and intelligence infrastructure have created many suspicions about their loyalties to the state, the government, and their colleagues. Reports have revealed a horrifying degree of sympathy with Taliban militant groups among Afghan soldiers and officers.[2]

As the mistrust between NATO allies and Afghan security forces deepens, jeopardizing the "war on terror," Afghans have started viewing NATO and US forces as occupying forces. In their understanding, the way NATO is tackling the insurgency in Afghanistan is ultimately wrong because they kill innocent civilian instead of terrorist Taliban militias.

On August 5, 2012, the Afghan President accepted the decision of parliament to dismiss Defense Minister Abdul Rahim Wardak and Interior Minister Bismillah Khan Muhammadi for their weak response to the internal security threats and the issue of cross-border infiltration, amid ongoing rocket attacks from Pakistan and political assassinations across the country.[3]

Their removal was a blow to ISAF, as the NATO military command had planned to hand over security to the Afghan forces in 2013, but their removal was necessary as they were involved in corruption and power abuse. They had appointed illiterate members of rogue militias within the Defense and Interior Ministries and removed their political opponents from high posts. Western officials had already argued that President Karzai must end the game of politics within the armed forces. Analysts suggested that the shake up in the defense and interior ministries might diminish the political influence of the Northern Alliance in the police and armed forces in near future.

In view of the ethnic and political rivalries within the ANA and ANP, in 2012 British Prime Minister David Cameron warned that the Afghanistan pullout could allow al-Qaeda to return. Military commanders agreed that Afghanistan's future could be jeopardized if foreign troops are withdrawn too quickly. The issue of desertion, too, from the rolls of the police and the ANA soldiers makes the NATO military command doubt whether stability can be maintained after the US and NATO withdrawal.[4]

---

1 "Political loyalties are another problem which dominates the promotion system in ANA". *Review Draft of the Centre for Strategic Studies*, Washington. 2012.
2 *Daily Times*. 15 March 2012.
3 Telegraph, *"The US and NATO doesn't trust the ANA as they have deep sympathy with the Taliban militant groups."* 7 August 2012.
4 *Ibid*, 4 August 2012.

Senior ANA military commanders confirm that Afghan army soldiers are deserting by the thousands. In 2011, more than 15,000 ANA soldiers went AWOL and as many as 25,000 had in effect been written off as permanent absentees or deserters. These defections are further evidence that the Afghan police and ANA lack loyalty and professionalism; they join the Taliban and private militias to kill and kidnap innocent civilians at night. In response to an article of mine published in Daily Outlook Afghanistan, General Zahir Azimi, the spokesperson for the Afghan Defense Ministry, denied reports that 47 percent of soldiers had fled military service, but he was willing to acknowledge a desertion rate of 18 percent.[1]

Article Six of the Military law specifies that: "While on duty in social and political life or private behavior, officers and soldiers of the armed forces shall be exemplary and exhibit discipline, character and high moral[s]. They shall improve their professional and political knowledge, acquire the revolutionary scientific theory and continue developing their military, technical and professional knowledge."[2]

Afghan soldiers receive training and weapons from NATO forces but turn their weapons on them. One Afghan soldier who killed four French soldiers received money from a rogue recruiter to forge his enlistment papers. This is not a solitary incident we mention here; there are many examples of Taliban fighters infiltrating the rank and file of the ANA. On August 3, 2012, a commander of the Afghan police killed 11 civilians in Uruzgan province.

On top of the motives already mentioned, ANA soldiers are suffering frustration and do not want to fight the Taliban. They suffer anxiety due to their uncertain future.

The army is in crisis as thousands of its trained soldiers are quitting and joining Taliban groups and private criminal militias. A NATO warning to this effect was reported in print and electronic media across the United States, UK and Europe in 2013. The rate of evasion increases fear over their ability to protect the geography of their poor and ruined country. The policy of recruitment and retention target is particularly troubling for NATO's International Security Assistance Force (ISAF) as the Afghan army and the police force are seen as vital to preventing the return of the Taliban. Daily Independent in its report quoted British government officials and FCO warned that the rate of recruits leaving is far worse than targets set by coalition leaders, amounting to 63,000 every year.[3]

The Special Inspector General for Afghan Reconstruction reported the number of personnel had shrunk by about 4,000 troops and policemen

---

1  *Daily Times*, 9 August 2012.

2  *Daily Outlook Afghanistan*.10 August 2012- "chapter three of the Afghan Military Law, Promotion of the ranks of colonel and generals shall take place based on an officer's political, military and combat skills and personal merits". *See: www.asianlii.org/af/legis/laws/ml132.*

3  *Independent*, 31 March 2013.

between March 2012 and February 2013; he noted that the crisis is grave indeed. In June 2013, the Special Inspector General for reconstruction in Afghanistan warned that millions of dollars spent for the purchase of aircraft for the Afghan Air Force is going to be wasted. The report deplored US Defense Department expenditures to the tune of $771.8 million on aircraft that the Afghan Air Force cannot operate or even maintain. They simply haven't got the capacity—in terms of man power or expertise—to operate and maintain the existing and planned aircraft the Pentagon buys for them.[1]

The UK Ministry of Defense warned that ANA attrition rates "continue to represent a risk to the sustainability of the future force". The UK Foreign Office, too, warned about the desertion of ANA soldiers. However, within the minds of the Afghan population the concept has developed that it is the US and its coalitions that have failed to build a professional army for Afghanistan.

In Bamyan province, on August 6, 2011, two New Zealand soldiers were killed in a Taliban attack while another six soldiers and 11 ANA soldiers sustained injuries. In 2011, the Afghan Interior Ministry spokesperson confirmed the death of 635 police within three months. In 2012, there were 100 assaults on Afghan soldiers and the police every month. Under these circumstances, the only option foreign forces had was to turn to the private criminal militias.

The record of the criminal militias is not good. They killed thousands civilians in towns and villages during the civil war in 1990s. Civilians have been paying a heavy price, caught between the indiscriminate attacks of criminal militias and terrorist Taliban members since the collapse of the Taliban government. In 2011, Human Rights Watch reported that a 12-year-old girl was raped in her home in a Taluqan village (Qulbars) by men wearing Afghan army uniforms. Reports suggest that private criminal militias kill innocent people, rape young women, detain men and women illegally, kidnap young girls, grab land and raid houses at night in Kunduz, Herat, Baghlan, Uruzgan and Mazar provinces.

In 2012, a local elder in Kunduz province told Human Rights Watch: "The most powerful ones will sometimes select a girl and tell the family that they want to marry her. For families there are only two choices: give the girl, or leave the area and go to Pakistan or Iran."[2]

In the past 11 years, the Afghan army and police have never behaved like a professional force. They have failed to meet security needs. In Northern Afghanistan, especially, militias are proliferating. Male and female prostitution, and sexual assaults and rape, are on the rise. Afghan intelligence agencies, which represent four different political ideologies, many sects and eth-

---

1  *Khaama Press*, 01 April 2013, also; *Herald.* 6 August 2012.

2  *Human Rights Watch*, 12 September 2011.

nicities, provide dangerous weapons to warlords and criminal militias in all parts of the country.[1]

In April 2011, in Baghlan province, HRW reported criminal militiamen entered a house, abducted a 13-year-old boy and took him to the house of their commander where he was gang raped. In Kunduz, in June 2012, Lal Bibi, 18, was gang raped by members of private militias. "I am already a dead person," she said dejectedly in an interview.[2]

The atrocities of warlords and their private militias in towns and cities have been the central issue of public debates. Many Afghans see their country's future as bleak. Public support for the government has declined as the Taliban intensified their attacks on government installations. The prospect of civil war is very much present and the dismemberment of the country along ethnic lines cannot be ruled out. The establishment of the Taliban office in Qatar in June 2013 is the first step towards the partition of Afghanistan along ethnic lines.

## THE CHALLENGE OF GREEN ON BLUE ATTACKS

The story of the US war on terrorism in Afghanistan has become more complex as local recruits have started killing their foreign "guests." This is now a war between guards and guardians. The issue of insider attacks, "green" uniforms on "blue," have generated further distrust and made cooperation virtually impossible.

This is something the US and NATO allies apparently never anticipated. They are stymied as to how to counter this invisible enemy within their ranks. On 9 June 2013, Long War Journal reported that an Afghan soldier opened fire on US troops in Afghanistan, killing two American soldiers and a civilian. On June 12, 2013, *Daily Outlook* reported that a police commander and a police officer had joined the Taliban in Farah province.[3]

The ISAF spokesperson had warned in 2012 that the threat of green on blue attack was constant, and the growing frequency of such attacks is alarming. There are many reasons why Afghan soldiers target foreign partners, but foreign soldiers' urinating on dead bodies of Taliban militants, raiding houses in night and killing innocent women and children are salient.

A US war veteran and a lawmaker who served in Iraq and Afghanistan as a marine demanded the armed services committee to make a closer look at the growing number of this attacks.[4]

Duncan Hunter, a member of the US Armed Services Committee, also demanded that the Pentagon brief lawmakers on this issue. These attacks

---

1  *Daily Outlook Afghanista on 03 May 2012, "Afghan soldier opened fire on US troops in Afghanistan, killing two American soldiers and a civilian".*

2  In 9 June 2013, *Long War Journal.*

3  *Daily Times* 15 April 2012.

4  *The US Today*, 12 March 2012.

have reached an epidemic proportion. Western analysts understand that something is wrong with the battlefield relationship between ANA and foreign forces. President Obama said in a White House meeting: "Obviously we've been watching these attacks with deep concern." Senior police officers like General Muhammad Zaman say the attacks are simply a product of a violent society because no one is safe and everyone is in danger of getting killed.

There is every reason to worry about these attacks and to worry about the security transition as well. In 2012, US military deaths had reached 2,091, according to the US Department of Defense. The Long War Journal reported that attacks by Afghan forces had surged and according to US military sources, the coalition casualties are now 13 percent while in 2011 it was only 6% percent.[1]

Coalition forces in Afghanistan feel more threatened by the Afghan National Army than the Taliban, as it has established close contacts with Taliban networks to create more attacks in order to force them into immediate withdrawal. Commanders of the ANA provide arms and military information including counter-insurgency strategies to the Taliban, in addition to killing their coalition partners on the field of battle.

ISAF Commander General Allen knew the causes of these attacks. Most high ranking officers within ANA understand that the Taliban are fighting for freedom against foreign occupation; therefore, it is incumbent on them to help them in many ways. In a media briefing, ISAF Commander Gen. Allen provided a new perspective about the insider killings. NATO and ISAF understand that elements in Pakistan army are behind these attacks and want to crush the "bad guys" networks across the border. Pakistani defense analyst Zahid Hamid warned, "The US is now well and truly aggressive to provoke more war within Pakistan and to force the Pak army into a head-on collision with the tribe in North Waziristan and against Afghan resistance."[2]

Most Afghan generals understand that NATO and the US do not rely on the ANA but fail to train it properly, and grant more importance and funds to private armies of warlords. The Afghan Army does not approve of the way NATO and the US are tackling the insurgency.[3]

Afghan army officers and police smuggle in weapons at night from across the border and the rearming of warlord militias has become matter of deep concern for the ISAF high command. Weapons are being smuggled from Tajikistan into Northern Afghanistan by warlord militias to prepare for a future civil war. According to an Afghan weapons smuggler, this is going on

---

1  "Afghan National Army," *Daily Times* 2011.
2  Brass Takes, *Threat analysis and situation report.* 26 August, 2012. *In his website, former Pakistan's army officer, Zahid Hamid warned that war is about to shifted from Afghanistan into Pakistan.*
3  *Daily Times*, March 12, 2012, "the US Today reported Afghan officials denying the air force planes involvement in drug and weapon smuggling".

with the consent of local ANA commanders. Smuggling routes are rough, and so smugglers use horses. Light weapons can be smuggled in during daylight hours while heavy ones are brought in at night. The Deputy Director of Afghan intelligence in Baghlan city acknowledged the involvement of war criminals and ethnic leaders in this business. Talking to journalists, the NDS local Chief said that they are powerful people and "nobody can stop them."[1]

The smuggling routes and weapons depots are secured by criminal militias. As these smugglers have business relations with commanders of the border police, they can use police vehicles to convey weapons across the country. This joint network of ANA, police and criminal militias (that seems to have emerged abruptly) undermined the trust between the Afghan National Army and International Coalition forces in Afghanistan.

Until 2012, NATO and Afghan commanders were trying to settle their differences, but after the Panjwai killings, ANA turned its weapons on their foreign partners. The mistrust further intensified when on March 27, 2012, the Afghan Defense Ministry went into a near-total lockdown after the discovery of 10 suicide vests. More than a dozen Afghan soldiers were arrested, suspected of plotting to attack the Ministry and blow up commuter buses for government employees. The security breach took place in one of the most heavily fortified parts of Kabul, less than a mile from the Presidential Palace and the headquarters of the American-led coalition. The killings of 16 civilians in Panjwai by the US army soldiers caused the Afghan Army Chief a major headache.

General Shir Muhammad Karimi was in a state of dismay in a meeting at the Defense Ministry to outline a new military strategy to tackle the Taliban insurgency according to the traditional jirga principles of Afghanistan. General Shir Muhammad's blood pressure went up when he looked at the pictures of killed innocent children. He regretted and said the killing of 16 Afghan civilians including nine children in Kandahar was premeditated murder plan. He was shedding tears with harsh condemnation of the mass murder during the meeting and demanded that the command of military operations be transferred to the Afghan Security Forces.[2]

One of his colleagues asked him whether he and his fellow generals wanted to continue cooperating with the coalition forces in the war against terrorism. He kept silence on that, but confirmed that NATO didn't trust his Mujahedeen- and Taliban-dominated army. In fact, General Shir Muhammad wanted to bring some changes in their military strategy. He was also despondent over the low quality training and intractable behavior of his forces towards foreign forces. In an article published in the Huffington Post Blog on March 21, 2012, John Wight painted the same picture:

---

1  *The Guardian*, 13 March 2012.
2  *Huffington Post Blog* 3, 21 2012.

The [behavior of] soldiers serving in Afghanistan, U.S. and British is the product of the ignorance and racism imbibed not just from military indoctrination but also social conditioning when it comes to the prevailing nationalism and exceptionalism that describes Western cultural values. There can be no doubt that the strain, fear, pressure and stresses suffered by soldiers serving in places where they are not welcome and subject to the constant threat of being killed or maimed takes a massive toll. But the common thread when it comes to the atrocities that result is that the victims are only accorded a minor role in the ensuing fall out, as if their lives and deaths are of less importance than the priority of defending the reputation of the troops and military forces involved.[1]

On the issue Panjwai massacre, *The Guardian* newspaper (13 March, 2012) criticized the way of killing:

The death of innocent civilians is nothing new in Afghanistan, but these 16 victims, nine of whom were children, were allegedly murdered by a rogue soldier, rather than the usual killers — drone attacks, air strikes and stray bullets. This incident has elicited rage among Afghans and westerners alike. But why are westerners not equally outraged when drone attacks kill entire families? Drone attacks that kill civilians usually fall into our category of "collateral damage," because the dead civilians weren't specifically targeted, and we treat this category as an unfortunate consequence of war, not murder.[2]

Now, in light of the above mentioned apprehensions and mistrust between NATO and ANA, it appears that elements of the security forces may also be enraged Afghans against international forces. Since 2007, an estimated 80 NATO service members were killed by Afghan security forces, according to Associated Press. More than 75 percent of the attacks occurred since 2009. [3]

On September 2012, in response to these insider attacks, the International Security Assistance Force (ISAF) said that it would curtail the security partnership with ANA. These incidents badly affected counterinsurgency efforts in Afghanistan. Many Afghans fear that after the drawdown forces from the country by the end of 2014, there would be renewed outbreak of civil war. In April 2012, the outgoing UK Ambassador expressed his outrage at the culture of corruption within the Afghan army and police departments. He warned that if the Afghan government failed to tackle corruption, Britain would withdraw funding for the country.[4]

Sir William told reporters that nobody thinks that Afghanistan will be self-sustaining before 2024 or 2025. Sir William's calculations were quite understandable. He is a well-informed diplomat and understands that the

---

1 "16 Civilian Massacred. Too Bad. They're only Afghans". *Socialist Unity*, 17 March 2012. http://socialistunity.com/ 16-civilians-massacred-too-bad-theyre-only-afghans/
2 *Guardian*, March 13, 2012, Ross Caputi.
3 April 2012, *The New York Times*, 7 March 2012.
4 *Dawn*, 02 April 2013.

future of Afghanistan depends on the level of corruption. Similarly, an Afghan general from the Defense Ministry told this author that the confidence of the forces is crumbling with each passing day and now they have started looking at the Taliban as friends.

Then the brutal killing of six young British soldiers by Taliban insurgents further widened the gap of mistrust that was hampering NATO talks with Taliban representatives that had already been going on for a year, inside and outside Afghanistan. These killings enraged the entire population in the UK. In a statement about that event, the UK Ministry of Defense said the six soldiers were on a security patrol in an armored fighting vehicle when it was caught in an explosion in Kandahar province. Defense Secretary Philip Hammond said the timetable for withdrawal remained on track despite this brutal attack. Yet a September 2010 Review Draft by the Center for Strategic Studies in Washington revealed that failure to try to develop a strong Afghan army was causing more trouble when the Afghan soldiers started attacking their foreign partners in the battlefield.[1]

Afghan soldiers and officers, while completing military training, sell their promotions and positions. According to the Review Draft assessment, Article 21 and Article 2 of the military law state: Promotion of the ranks of colonel and general shall take place based on an officer's political, military and combat skills and personal merits, [given] that there are open posts. The period of service for periodic promotion of officers and personnel serving as crews of helicopters and planes shall be one year less than the periods referred to in article 20 of this law.

---

1  *Long War Journal.* 9 June 2013.

# CHAPTER 3. INTERNATIONAL MILITARY EFFORTS AND THE UNCERTAIN FUTURE OF THE ANA

The Great Game has entered a crucial stage. The involvement of regional competitors in Afghanistan has caused a long running civil war. Pakistan's military intervention through non state actors further intensified ethnic and sectarian violence. Unlike a strong Yugoslavian state in Europe, encompassing various ethnic groups, the Afghan state is a weak polity which has been torn apart by its hostile neighbors. The failure of the Bonn agreement (Ali Jalali, 2011) to design a viable peace plan for Afghanistan further deepened the population's problems.[1]

Building a modern army in Afghanistan has, however, proved to be a difficult task. The US and its allies are now tired of assisting the ANA in their counter terrorism operations. Afghan army is miserably under resourced. This is now a major morale factor for its soldiers and officers. The armed forces are worn down by the three decades long civil war and anarchy.

Pakistan's tacit support for the Haqqani network and its own Taliban proved that the country has adopted two policies for Afghanistan. Research scholar Jayant Singh (2013), in his recent paper, warned that the Pakistani establishment's engagement in Afghanistan is dominated by the overriding fear of India's expanding influence in the country and concern over independent Pashtunistan. In any event, Islamabad does not really support a stable and prosperous Afghanistan.

Stephanie Cronin in her lecture (2010) in the Faculty of Oriental Studies in Oxford University has directed the attention of Afghan government and

---

1 *Joint Report of European Union Institute for Security studies and Carnegie Endowment for International Peace.* June 2011.

international community towards the challenges of building a professional Afghan army:

> Western-sponsored efforts to establish an Afghan National army, as part of a wider program of institution building, are by no means the first such attempt to re construct the Afghan army following its collapse due to the impact of foreign invasion and civil war. Yet an analysis of previous experience offers few grounds for optimism. Since 2001, the Afghan military and its western mentors have encountered a range of problems familiar from the past, including problem of recruitment and troop retention, of force loyalty, cohesion and discipline, and of training and education. So intractable have these problems proved to be that the Afghan government and its Western advisers have seemed increasingly inclined to resort to a solution also familiar from the past an ever greater reliance on local non-state elements, tribal groups, militias and warlords, a reliance which is inevitably at the expense of the state building project itself, although this is rarely acknowledged.[1]

The agony of Afghanistan did not end with the arrival of the US and NATO in 2001. In the absence of a strong army in Afghanistan, a new phase of civil war will be no less destructive than the mujahedeen and Taliban rule in 1990s. In his recent analysis, prominent scholar Dr Rasul Bakhsh Rais sums it up: "The war has accumulated all the elements of a deadly mix — ethnicity, sectarianism, religious extremism and external intervention."[2]

The US and NATO allies are spending vast amounts of money to build a strong Afghan army, but the result remained very disappointed. International Crisis Group, in its Asia Report, analyzed the failure of US attempts in building ANA:

> Although the US has provided more than $10 billion to develop the ANA between 2002 and 2008, and 46 NATO and non NATO nations donated $822 million in equipment to the ANSF, this considerable investment has failed to achieve the desired result because of chronic shortfalls in training personnel, faulty equipment, slow infrastructural development, poor logistics, and the crippling army attrition rates".[3]

In 2013, Afghan President Hamid Karzai and President Obama planned to ensure the handover of combat operations to the Afghan National Army, but the question is whether ANA has gained fighting capabilities or not. Americans say the Afghan army cannot counter the insurgency. In 2012, the Pentagon in its report warned that Afghan National Army brigades haven't achieved the capacity to counter the Taliban insurgency across the country. They are poorly trained and suffer from low morale, a high rate of desertion

---

1 Stephanie Cronin, (2010) lecturer in the Faculty of Oriental Studies in Oxford University, *Afghanistan's Armies Past and Present*, Policy Paper By: Stephanie Cronin, 2010.
2 Dr. Rasul Bakhsh Rais, 1999. *Conflict in Afghanistan: Ethnicity, Religion and Neighbors.*
3 *A Force in Fragments: Reconstituting the Afghan National army.* International Crisis group's Asia Report, 2010.

and drug addiction. Notwithstanding all these challenging problems, in June 2013, the third phase of security transition to ANA was completed.

Many observers suggested that the main objectives of the Afghan National Army must be to safeguard the territorial integrity of the country, but the way it is operating is unprofessional. Bribery, corruption and regionalism have further contradicted their patriotism and professionalism. The force is not yet ethnically balanced; recruitment in Pashtun areas is a difficult task, as most of the commanders of ANA belongs to non Pashtun factions.

Afghan Security Forces (that represents four ethnic and sectarian ideologies) still needs to decide whether they defend an Afghan state or the interests of warlords, Mujahedeen leaders and Taliban. The ethnically divided armed forces of the country now became a bigger challenge for US, NATO and their allies, fighting the Taliban insurgency in the country. The lack of effective coordination and lack of capability is another challenging problem.

Within the NATO and US military command, there is reluctance to directly confront with the problems of corruption, powerbrokers, criminal militia commanders, foreign elements and Taliban influence in the command structure of ANA. In 2011, there were countrywide calls from different quarters, to speed up the reform process in the ANA, but NATO and US allies were struggling to establish their own private militias instead of strengthening Afghan Security Forces.[1]

During the last 12 years, they established several private militias; some are fighting inside Afghanistan and some are fighting outside the country. Having realized the isolation of the Afghan National Army and the police, President Hamid Karzai ordered to abolish private contractors that guard NATO's military convoys. A Review Draft of the Center for Strategic Studies in Washington revealed that, failure to try to develop a strong Afghan army caused more troubles when Afghan army soldiers started attacking their foreign partners in various provinces. According to the Review Draft assessment:

> Ethnic breakdown of the ANA makes a deeper problem. Promotions within the ANA also are often based upon patronage, ethnicity, money, or personal loyalty rather than upon ability. Entrenched and powerful patronage networks dominate the promotion system in the ANA and have created large blocks of officers whose loyalty to the Central Government is dubious at best.[2]

Sectarian and religious affiliation has badly affected the operational skills of ANA. In Review Draft, the fact cannot be denied that most of these ethnic networks are revolving around warlords, military commanders and religious leaders:

---

1  *Daily Times*, 29 April 2011.
2  Washington 2012, *also see*; *Small Wars Journal*, 23 August 2011.

As a chief of staff, moreover, General Bismillah Khan was able to appoint loyal deputies to commanders he did not trust, or to win some degree of support among professional officers who had to lobby General Bismillah Khan in order to get a promotion.[1]

In 2011, ANA graduated its first military intelligence company composed of people belonging to specific ethnicity, but their affiliation and loyalties also raised many questions. Afghan Military Intelligence often prepares fake reports about the activities of Pashtun officers and commanders, makes their position contradictory and trying to convince both the President and Defense Minister, to replace them by non-Pashtuns officers. This is, no doubt a dirty game that badly affected civil military relations in Afghanistan.[2]

Britain's internal papers recently revealed about the corruption culture, desertion and drug abuse among the police recruits and ANA members. As soldiers and officers of police and army receive low pay, they do not show real interest in their duties. In his Small Wars Journal article, A. Lawrence Checkering concludes:

> Widespread apathy among the tribal people of Afghanistan may be the most important impediment to any reasonable outcome there. It is certainly a major impediment to any exit strategy for us, and reducing it is also crucial for our fighting men and women, encouraging them to understand we are not fighting a hopeless and undeserving cause.[3]

The infiltration of non-state actors into the army ranks further exacerbated in the disparity of international community, that if the situation remains the same, what will happen after the NATO withdrawal from the country in the end of 2014. Former US Commander, General McChrystal had a plan to build Afghan police to a force of 160,000, by 2013, but his dream remained incomplete. General McChrystal admitted that his country had a very weak coherent approach to the war in Afghanistan.

The general had realized that US commanders are not sincere in their resolve to build a strong Afghan Army. He was very upset with this unrealistic approach of the US and NATO allies to the war in Afghanistan. Former British Ambassador to Afghanistan, Mr. Sherard Cowper-Coles also expressed the same concern about the ISAF efforts in Afghanistan.[4] Afghan Defense Minister Abdul Rahim Wardak regretted and said this would be a bigger problem as the Afghan Army is taking control of security in various provinces.[5]

The secret distribution of weapons among various ethnic and sectarian groups at night in Northern parts of the country is an irksome devel-

---

1 *Ibid.*
2 *Weekly the Nation* (Urdu), 19 April 2012.
3 *Small Wars Journal*, A. Lawrence Checkering article, 23 August 2011.
4 *The Guardian*, 27 March 2012.
5 In 2011, *Washington Post* reported the desertion of ANA soldiers. Also see *Daily Outlook Afghanistan*, 29 June 2012.

opment.[1] Sectarian and ethnic groups are trying to rearm their private militias across the country. The recent news reports on the drug and weapon trafficking business of Afghan Air Force brought shame to the country. On 12 March 2012, *USA Today* reported Afghan officials denying the air force planes involvement in drug and weapon smuggling, but *Wall Street Journal* confirmed an investigation of the NATO-led forces into the case.[2]

Moreover, in Baghlan province, an Afghan on-line newspaper, Khaama Press, reported police seized at least 40kg hashish and 16 pistols. Security officials confirmed some 40 cases of weapon and drug smuggling in the province. Military experts say, all these weapons are being distributed in Northern Provinces in the pretext that after the withdrawal of foreign forces at the end of 2014, the Taliban might target them.[3]

A recent US military report bemoaned the corruption of ANA soldiers and officers. Military units of ANA sell vehicles, weapons and other military equipment, and indulge in outright theft of fuel provided by the US Army. In 2010, when Kuchi nomads attacked the villages of Hazara Muslims in Behsud districts, military commanders in the Defense Ministry responded on ethnic and sectarian bases. Former Afghan spy

National Directorate of Security (NDS) Chief Amrullah Saleh in his recent article published in the *Daily Outlook* Afghanistan depicted an irksome story about the politicization of Afghan security forces.[4]

The police, he claimed, were far from international attention until 2007, when most of aid was going to the army. Mr. Amrullah Seleh warned that police and military barrack were politicized during the last ten years. He also revealed that intelligence agencies have also been politicized by the Karzai administration.[5]

The disease of drug addiction has also penetrated into the ranks of US army in Afghanistan. As the US fatalities hit a new record, however there are reports of suicide attempt and drug addiction within the US army.[6] Afghan military experts warned that if the US army gets infected by the virus of drugs, all Afghans will soon face the consequences. On World Socialist Website, in his article, Bill Van Auken pointed some facts and figures about the drug addiction and suicide attempts of US soldiers in Afghanistan.[7]

Drug addiction and the trends of suicide in US military barracks forced General Petraeus to put 10,000 unemployed Afghans on the CIA's payroll preparing them, to fight against the Taliban. He gave them arms and dollars to make them effective counterinsurgency force on Pakistani style Qumi

---

1 *Daily Times*, 05 January 2012.
2 *Long War Journal*, 23 August 2011.
3 *Daily Times*, 13 October 2011.
4 *Daily Outlook Afghanistan* 3 January 2011
5 *CNN News*, 21 April 2012.
6 *Foreign Policy Magazine*, 18 October. 2011.
7 Bill Van Auken. On World Socialist Website, *Daily Outlook Afghanistan*, 05 July 2012.

Lashkar (Tribal Force).[1] This was a good step, but Afghans complain that NATO is fighting the Taliban but doing nothing to address ethnic divide, and corruption, therefore, the long-term US presence in Afghanistan is causing more problems.[2]

This newly formed force later on, proved ineffective in fighting insurgent forces. They could not maintain security of the country. The assassination of Burhanuddin Rabbani, former Taliban Minister, Arsala Rehmani and President's brother Wali Karzai in a high security area of Kabul and Kandahar, raised many questions about the ineffectiveness of security efforts of US and Afghan government in protecting civilian life.[3]

Like its American masters, members of this strong private militia and the Afghan army barracks also became the centers of drug users. Afghan authorities admitted many drug cases discovered within military barracks. Opium and hashish are their favorite "food". Some Afghan military officers and soldiers were removed from their service, due to their involvement in drugs offences. Some officers were running their own private businesses and some were promoting drug trafficking across the country to support their families. Every month, one fifth of the soldiers of the Afghan Army go on leave without informing their commanders.[4]

Another issue that made ANA more controversial is the inclusion of war criminals in the command and control units, which created many controversies. Military experts in Kabul have expressed deep concern on the involvement of these people in human rights abuses. The US and UK private security firms, who train Afghan police, are doing their own dirty business. They have been involved in illegal practices. Intelligence website, Wiki Leaks in its Afghan cable revealed about the DynCorp involvement in play boy and sex business.[5]

DynCorp is a private company training Afghan police force. More than ninety five percent budget of the militia comes from the US and a part of that is being spent on child abuse parties and sex trafficking in Northern Afghanistan.[6]

After Wiki Leaks reported on the DynCorp involvement in the sex trade in Northern Afghanistan, Afghan Interior Ministry carried out a thorough investigation into the company activities and arrested two Afghan police and nine civilians for "purchasing sexual service from a child." The US State Department began its own investigation to find out whether DynCorp had ignored signs of drug abuse among employees in Afghanistan or not, but

---

1  2011 CNN *reported the death of eight American soldiers due to overdoses involving heroin and morphine in Afghanistan.* Daily Times 13 October 2011.
2  *Daily Times*, 20 October 2011.
3  http://www.dyn-intl.com /news-events/di-in-the-news.aspx.
4  *Washington Post*, 18 April, 2099.
5  *Daily Times*, 20 October, 2011.
6  *DAWN*, 03 March 2012.

Inspector General of the State Department in its report concluded that dancing boy practice is not an illegal activity in Afghanistan.

This shameless practice also prompted US Defense Department to hire a social scientist, Anna Maria to investigate the problem, as several US soldiers on patrol often passed older men walking hand-in-hand with pretty young boys. There are thousands young boys undergone illegal sexual ordeals, but the actual numbers of these vulnerable boys are not known.[1]

Washington's weak approach of power dynamics in Afghanistan created many challenging problems for its international and Afghan partners. The United States trained 352,000 soldiers, but now 185,000 remained in the army. It means, 165,000 soldiers joined either private militias or Taliban. International community lost between 13 and 27 men per month, while Afghan National Police in 2013 lost 100 men per month. Focused on the looming civil war, international media is now drawing a formidable picture of the future of Afghan National Army and the state.

The main strategy of regional states is clear; they are trying to assert their influence. The six neighboring states of Afghanistan are working on the strategies, based on their own national interests and, all have reasons to worry about the future civil war in the country, which at best could mean the return of refugees or turmoil at home. Iran is opposing the Taliban on one hand and provides arms to the student militia on the other. Pakistan hosts over two million refugees and wants it own share in Kabul. China is much disturbed by the ongoing civil war in the country. The country is concerned about the links between its own extremist Muslim groups with the Afghan extremist groups and Taliban elements.

In 31 December 2013, Chinese President ordered his country forces to prepare for war. The recent terror attacks in Chinese Muslim majority province and suicide attacks in Russia, forced the President to increase his visits to PLA military zones. The threats posed by Japan and the increased US military presence in South Asia, caused major changes in China's military strategy. Tajikistan has strong ties with the Northern Alliance. Uzbekistan also shares ethnic ties with war criminal General Dostum, as does Turkmenistan. All these neighboring states want peace and stability in Afghanistan, but they don't want to see the Taliban back in power.

THE TALIBAN OFFICE IN QATAR

In this chapter, as I have discussed the issue of drug and arms trafficking and prospect of civil war in Afghanistan after the withdrawal of US and NATO forces in the end of 2014, I also want to examine diverse challenges faced by the Afghan National Army. Afghanistan considers the establishment of a Taliban office in Qatar as a challenge to the Afghan security forces.

---

1  *Daily Outlook Afghanistan* 12 October, 2012.

After a long time of a stalled peace process, the Taliban agreed to discuss the future political set up with Afghanistan. The Taliban office was officially named as the Islamic Emirate of Afghanistan with their flag (not Afghan flag) hoisted on it. Afghan politicians termed the Taliban office in Qatar is a dangerous development. Now Taliban demands the control of more than 7 provinces bordering Pakistan and Iran. They want their own government and also want to reorganize their military forces. The Taliban don't accept the Karzai government but want to establish a parallel state of the Islamic Emirate of Afghanistan. They announced that they will improve relations with other states.[1]

The Taliban have the capacity to conquer Afghanistan in a very short time. On 20 June 2013, Fox News reported Mullah Omar, saying that his group will take Kabul within a week, once US troops pulls out from Afghanistan. Taliban also issued a statement on their website about their future intentions and military strategies in Afghanistan:

> Everyone is aware that the Islamic Emirate of Afghanistan has been waging jihad and working tirelessly to bring an end to the invasion of Afghanistan and establish in it an independent Islamic government and has always utilized every legitimate method to achieve this goal. The Islamic Emirate of Afghanistan has both military as well as political objectives which are confined to Afghanistan. Islamic Emirate does not wish to harm other countries from its soil and neither will it allow use Afghan soil to pose a threat to the security of other nations. The Islamic Emirate of Afghanistan wants to have cordial relations on mutual respect with all the countries of the world including it neighbors and desires security for its nation as well as security and justice on international level.
>
> Given these objectives, the Islamic Emirate considered it necessary to open a political office in the Islamic country of Qatar for the following reasons:
>
> 1. To talk and improve relations with the international community through mutual understanding
>
> 2. To back such a political and peaceful solution which ends the occupation of Afghanistan establish an independent Islamic government and bring true security which is the demand and genuine aspiration of the entire nation.
>
> 3. To have meeting with Afghans in due appropriate time
>
> 4. To establish contact with the United Nations, international and regional organizations and non-governmental institutions
>
> 5. To give political statement to the media on the ongoing political situation
>
> 6. We also think the government in Qatar and its Emir, Sheikh Hamad bin Khalifa al Thani to have agreed with inaugurating the political office of Islamic Emirate and to have made everything easy in this regard.[2]

---

1  *Daily Times*, 21-6-2013.
2  *Statement issued regarding the inauguration of political office of the Islamic Emirate in Qatar.* Shahamat-english.com.http://shahamat-english.com/index.php/paighaamoona/32948-

Taliban in Afghanistan represent different groups and councils. The Afghan Taliban leadership council is often referred to as Quetta Shura (Quetta Council) as it is based in the Pakistan city of Quetta. This council directs four regional shuras (councils) and ten committees. The council is led by Mullah Omar, the leader of both the Afghan and Pakistani Taliban. Afghan Taliban established military councils in Quetta, Peshawar, Miran-shah and Gardi Jangle of Baluchistan province. The Taliban have also established ten committees which address specific issues. These committees are: Military Committee, Ulema Council, Finance Committee, Political Affairs Committee, Culture and Information Committee, Interior Affairs committee, Prisoners and Refugees Committee, Education Committee, Recruitment Committee and Repatriation Committee.[1]

### THE TRANSITION OF SECURITY, ANA AND THE TALIBAN

On June 2013, former Chief of Inter Services Intelligence (ISI), General Asad Durrani wrote about the future of the Afghan National Army in an e-mail to this author. General Durrani was not satisfied with the present command of the Afghan army and said,

> The army (ANA) rose under the foreign tutelage, and in the foreseeable future dependent upon its support, would be seen by most Afghans as a legacy of the occupation and not really, 'national'. In the Afghan context, General Durrani said that where the mightiest of the armies fail, how would a half-backed force succeed? General Asad Durrani said that challenges for ANA are more complex. The ANA too suffer from an ethnic imbalance.[2]

Criticizing the US partners and mentors is not the issue; the issue is drug addiction and corruption within the Afghan army quarters. Anyone who has worked closely with ANA has smelled hashish smoke wafting from a guard shack or seen a glassy-eyed, obviously intoxicated soldier on duty. They smoke hashish every day and opium is also provided to them by outsiders.[3]

The army is weak, undisciplined and poorly trained, cannot defeat the Taliban. On 12 April, 2013, *Long War Journal* reported 200 Taliban fighters overran a military outpost, manned by what the New York Times called one of the Afghan army's "highly regarded" combat units. The Taliban attack took place at a small outpost in the Narai district of Kunar province. Reports indicated that more than 13 Afghan soldiers were killed.[4]

Moreover, Special Inspector General of Afghan Reconstruction warned that the strength of ANA is a challenging problem. The Combined Security Transition Command-Afghanistan noted that, in the case of the Afghan

---

statement-regarding-inauguration-of-political-office-of-islamic-emirate-in-qatar,
1  *Long War Journal*, 2010.
2  *Long War Journal*, September,15 2007.
3  *Report of the Department of Defence Inspector General*, Number DODIG-2013-058-March 22 2013.
4  *Long War Journal*, 12 April, 2013.

National army, there is "no viable method of validating their personal number". Thousands of recruited soldiers are quitting the police and ANA every month, raising fear over the capability of the shrinking Afghan army. Daily independent reported Brittan's Ministry of Defense comments on the desertion of Afghan soldiers.[1] The UK Ministry of Defense warned that the ANA attrition rates "continue to represent a risk to the sustainability of the future force. The UK Foreign and Commonwealth Office also admitted that the number of Afghan National Army soldiers exiting the force, the Border Police and National Civil Order Police has caused "a drain on skills".[2]

According to the International Crisis group report:

> Despite billions of dollars of international investment, army combat readiness has been undermined by weak recruitment and retention policies, inadequate logistics, insufficient training and equipment and inconsistent leadership. These shortcomings, combined with the international community's haphazard approach to de-mobilization and reintegration (DR) has undermined the army's professionalism and capacity to counter the insurgency. Kabul powerbrokers are distributing the spoils of increased NATO spending on army development among their constituencies in the officer corps, fuelling ethnic and political factionalism within army ranks.[3]

In May 2012, the NATO Chicago Summit endorsed a plan to end international combat mission in Afghanistan. The United States supported the plan and agreed to exit strategy based on step by step withdrawal forces through 2014. The declaration of the summit stated:

> We, the nations contributing to ISAF, and the Government of the Islamic Republic of Afghanistan, met today in Chicago to renew out firm commitment to a sovereign, secure and democratic Afghanistan. In line with the strategy which we agreed at the Lisbon Summit, ISAF's mission will be concluded by the end of 2014. But thereafter Afghanistan will not stand alone: we reaffirm that our close partnership will continue beyond the end of the transition period.[4]

In July 2012, the post withdrawal scenario was discussed by donor nations in Tokyo to support Afghanistan. Donor nations pledged $16 billion up to 2015 for socio-economic development in the country. In the end of June 2013, NATO military commanders demanded to be allowed to provide extensive logistic support to Afghanistan, until 2014 as they understand Afghan forces will be unprepared to counter insurgency after the NATO withdrawal in the end of 2014.

On 03 July 2013, Daily outlook Afghanistan reported the Tokyo Mutual Accountability Conference, held in Afghan capital Kabul with participation

---

1 ISAF and NATO Chicago summit in May 2012. *The Daily Independent* 31 March 2013.
2 *Reconstituting the Afghan National Army. International Crisis group*, 22 March 2010.
3 "Afghan President announced of the first phase of security transition." 22 March 2011. www. nato.net.
4 "President Karzai announced phase two". *Tolo News*, Kabul. 27 November 2011,

of representatives from 57 states, including Afghanistan. The conference evaluated commitments of the international community towards Afghanistan and also Afghan government performance in meeting the condition set at Tokyo Conference in 2012, for receiving $16 billion dollars assistance after 2014. The United Nations Secretary General's special representative for Afghanistan said:

> Today we jointly confirm both our confidence that Afghanistan and its people supported by the international community will successfully sail through the troubled water of intertwined security, political and economic transition into the stabilizing 'transformation decade' and our mutual commitment to work together supporting each other for Afghanistan's peaceful, stable and prosperous future.[1]

The establishment of a Taliban office in Qatar sparked hot debates in print and electronic media when they announced to establish formal relations with international community. On 4 July, 2013, Taliban announced that they want to appointed representatives in various states, including Afghanistan, to mobilize their supporters. Pakistani leadership announced that it has no formal contacts with Taliban leaders and has no knowledge of militant's leadership whereabouts.

The Qatar office means a government in exile, because it created the sense of legitimacy for them. The office, in fact, challenged the legitimacy of the Karzai government. On 01 July 2013, some Afghan parliamentarian criticized neighboring state and international community for their efforts to divide Afghanistan on ethnic lines. A day earlier, President Karzai claimed that several foreign states, including Pakistan, want to destabilize Afghanistan.

Now the Taliban has established their office in Qatar, the mission of the International Security Assistance Force (ISAF) is expected to end on 31 December 2014. This was agreed by ISAF in NATO Chicago summit in May 2012. It was also agreed that responsibility for security in Afghanistan will gradually be transferred to ANA. This process began in 2011 and will progress through five phased, finishing in 2014.

THE SECURITY TRANSITION

Phase One

On 22 March 2011, Afghan President announced the first phase of the security transition. In this phased, seven provinces were listed: Bamyan Province, Kabul Province, Panjshir Province, Heart Province, Lashkar Gah district of Helmand province, Mazare-e-Sharif and Mehtar Lam.[35]

---

1 "President Karzai announcement about phase three of the security transition", UPI.Com. 13 May 2012.

## Phase Two

On 27 November 2011, President Karzai announced phase two with the list of provinces and districts:

1. Balkh province, Daykundi, Takhar, Samangan, Nimroz and parts of Kabul province.

2. Jalalabad, Chagh Charan, Sheberghan, Faizabad, Ghazni, Maidan Shehr and Qila Now district of Badghis province, Yaftal Safli district, Arghandi district, Tashkan, Kesham and Argu of Badakhshan province, Abkamari, Nawah and Nad Ali.

3. All districts of Heart province except Shindand, Obi and Chisht. Qarghai of Laghman province, Behsud, Koz Kunar and Sorkhrud districts of Jalalabad province.

4. All districts of Parwan province except for Shiwari and Siahghered districts. All district of Sar. e. Pul, except for Sayyed. District of Behsud, Jelriz of Wardak Province

## Phase Three

On 13 May 2012, President Karzai announced phase three of the security transition. Foreign Minister of the United Kingdom, William Hague confirmed that phase three includes Nahr-e-Saraj which is the UK area of operation.

## Phase Four and Five

There is no fixed date for phases four and five.

# CHAPTER 4. BRIGADE-888, ANA, AND WAR CRIMINALS

Throughout the eighteenth and nineteenth centuries, Afghanistan has never been a strong nation state. The country has never had a strong central government, organized professional army and police, to secure the nation. Ethnic identity and religious sectarianism have been politicized to the point that it is difficult to conceive of a national identity. During the Great Game in Central Asia, Afghanistan became a modern state, but the three-decades-long war erased the position of the Afghan state by eliminating, or severely damaging most of its institutions. Afghanistan spent much of the twentieth century as one of the poorest, most divided, weakest and least significant nations in the world. In 1980s and in 1990s, thousands of innocent people were killed in civil wars. In the 1990s, the conflict broke down largely along ethnic and sectarian lines. Mujahedeen commanders killed and raped women, looted houses and destroyed government buildings in various part of the country.

In 1992, for instance, a young woman jumped to her death from the second floor of her house in order to avoid being raped. In another incident, a woman was raped and her husband was killed in the outskirts of Kabul. Today, each ethnic group has its own chief power broker. Warlords and war criminals distribute government posts. They have good representation in Afghan intelligence agencies, army and the police.

After the fall of the Taliban regime and US invasion in 2001, the international community should have dealt with the warlordism and criminal militias in Afghanistan. Instead, they funded them and used their military power to protect their own military installations across the country. In August 2012, the nomination of war criminals and corrupt officials for the key posts enraged the whole population. Every sector of civil society, government officials, politicians and parliamentarians expressed deep concern over the decision of President Hamid Karzai, but there was no reaction from the US and NATO commander. The story became more irksome when President Karzai nominated warlord Mullah Bismillah Khan Muhammadi as the Defense Minister. President Karzai was in trouble; he didn't know what to do and how to manage the affairs of the state. He was under immense pressure from both parliamentarians and the NATO High Command to bring changes into the command structure of the Defense Ministry.[1]

He brought changes, but by appointing his own friends to high posts, saying that in this way he was making a recommended change. In any case, the strategy of changing faces was ineffective as Afghans had already pointed out the weak approach of the Karzai regime and international community to the Taliban insurgency during the last 12 years.[2]

On 29 August 2012, President Karzai removed his Intelligence Chief, Rahmatullah Nabil, and said he wanted to limit the term of an intelligence chief for two years. However, the case is different here; Mr. Nabil with his non-professional conduct and political inclinations had failed to counter the Taliban insurgency, and especially their infiltration into the ranks and file of the police and the Army. There were reports that President Karzai was unhappy with his weak approach to the traditional intelligence mechanism.[3]

President Karzai accused him of power abuse. Like his predecessor, Mr. Nabil's tactics of investigation against Afghan detainees included electric shocks, threats of rape, beatings, extrajudicial killings, torture, humiliation, prolonged pre-trial detention, discrimination against ethnic opponents and sexual abuse of children. He was responsible for the killing of a Pashtun cleric during his brutal investigation tactics in the province of Khost.[4]

Former Intelligence Chief Rahmatullah Nabil was born in 1968 in Wardak province. He received his education in Peshawar as an Afghan refugee and worked with various NGOs. As an engineer by profession, Mr. Nabil had no proper knowledge of intelligence collection and processing. He was newly recruited and less educated in the world of modern technological intelligence work. Then again, he never tried to acquire know-how about modern intelligence gathering and surveillance. President Karzai replaced him with a notorious war criminal, Assadullah Khalid, known for the torture and killings of innocent Afghan men and women in southern Afghanistan. Assadullah Khalid owned a criminal militia, known as Brigade 888, and secret prisons.[5]

---

1   *The New York Times.* 09 March 2012.
2   *Daily Times.* 2 February 2011.
3   *Tribune,* 12 March 2013.
4   *The New York Times.* July 2011.
5   Mark. C. 12 February 2011. *The Great Game: The Reality of Britain War in Afghanistan.*

Khalid and his rogue private Brigade-888 stand accused of human rights abuses, including rape and torture, during his governorship. The Canadian army supported Brigade 888 and considered it as a trusted ally, protecting Canadian outposts in Kandahar. The military and financial support of the Canadian government encouraged criminal activities of the Brigade-888 to torture, rape and murder civilians in Kandahar. Canadians army generals, who knew about the torture business of Brigade-888, said they witnessed no abuse by the Brigade. Nevertheless, common Afghans ask why the Canadian army was abetting the crimes of the Brigade 888. A Canadian newspaper, *The Mail and Globe*, reported: "The Canadian soldiers lived beside [Brigade 888]" personnel in the governor's palace in Kandahar, and "helped train Afghans, who routinely committed torture.[1]

On 29 November 3013, IWPR investigator Abdul Hamid Ezzat reported that leaders of militia force from Ghazni province regularly torture civilians in Ander district. More than 50 villagers complained about the torture and money extortion business of Mokoor-based militias. In their interview with IWPR, militia commanders admitted that they abused and tortured civilians. The militia is backed by Afghan intelligence agencies. In April 2012, residents of Kadimkhel village in Ander district established militia force to fight the Taliban insurgent. War criminal and former governor of Ghazni province, Asadullah Khaled, who headed National Directorate of Security (NDS) in 2012, claimed that these militias were part of his Brigade-888. Commander of the Mokoor militia admitted that he received regular payment from the Brigade-888.

In 2008, Khalid was removed from the governorship of Kandahar and appointed as Minister of Frontier and Tribal Areas. During Khalid's brutal tenure in Kandahar, from 2005 to 2008, the palace became a microcosm of Canada's moral dilemma. Another heartrending story of the Canadian army is related to the use of Brigade 888 against the civilian population. War criminal, Assadullah Khalid is a known human rights violator. He ran a private detention facility for torturing detainees, but Canada never repudiated him or reported his crimes to the ISAF Military Command.

On one occasion, a prisoner handed over to Brigade 888, by the Canadian forces, was severely tortured, abused and humiliated. Interestingly, Canadian Major-General David Fraser spoke in favor of the governor. Canadians who served in Kandahar were not willing to say a single word about their involvement with Brigade 888. Mr. Assadullah Khalid was born in Ghazni province in 1969. He purchased a Bachelors degree from Kabul University in 2001. According to Kabul press reports, Khalid has been involved in widespread misuse and abuse of government funds.

---

1  *The Mail and Globe* reported that the Canadian soldiers "lived beside" Brigade 888 personnel in the governor's palace in Kandahar. *Times*, March 2011.

The nomination of fourth profoundly corrupt and illiterate Mullah, Din Muhammad Jabar Khel, as Minister of Frontiers Affairs, received country-wide condemnation. After the US intervention in Afghanistan, warlord Din Muhammad was appointed as the governor of Jalalabad and in 2009, then became the governor of Kabul. President Karzai brought him back to Kabul. Haji Din Muhammad was born in Jalalabad. His father, Amanullah Khan Jabbar Khel, worked in various posts in the Afghan government.

Corruption in Afghan intelligence, ANA headquarters, and President's office is on the increase. Army officers use army vehicles and helicopters for smuggling and other commercial purposes. Arms are even being sold to the Taliban. Factionalism and ethnic friction among high level players in the Defense and Interior Ministries have put in danger the growth of the Afghan National Army.

The killing of British and NATO soldiers by security forces raised some questions that either the Taliban infiltrated the ranks and file of ANA or probably, security forces receive instructions for the killing of their coalition partners. Afghans ask if the creation of an Afghan National Army was on the agenda of NATO in Germany in 2002, and NATO had agreed that the Afghan army should be ethnically balanced, why that not happened.[1]

The *Globe and Mail* reported that the country's ethnic tensions and recriminations now threaten to undermine the cohesion of the fledgling, multiethnic Afghan army. These concerns, the president's disillusionment, and apprehensions of an impending war within the Afghan army needed to be considered in depth. The President appointed war criminals on high posts in the Defense Ministry, instead of introducing new military reforms.[2]

Amnesty International in its annual Report for 2012 revealed that:

> The National Directorate of Security (NDS), Afghanistan's intelligence service, continued to arbitrarily arrest and detains suspects, denying them access to a lawyer, their families, the courts or other external bodies. The NDS faced credible allegations of torturing detainees and operating secret detention facilities. NATO ceased transferring detainees to Afghan forces after a UN report, issued in October, documented the systematic use of torture by NDS officers. According to the report, prisoners had been tortured in 47 NDS and police detention facilities across 22 provinces. In August, family members of an Afghan man who had been detained by the NDS in Kabul for allegedly selling counterfeit currency told Amnesty International that he had been arrested by the NDS in April and tortured into making a confession. The detainee, who cannot be identified for security reasons, was reportedly punched and kicked until he vomited blood and lost consciousness.[3]

---

1 *Ibid.*
2 *Daily Times*, 03 March 2011.
3 *Amnesty International Annual Report for 2012.* Daily Outlook Afghanistan. 07 March 2012.

From 2001 to 2009, a war of words between the former Defense Minister, Abdul Rahim Wardak, and the Chief of Army Staff, Mullah Bismillah Khan Muhammadi caused deadlocks over the control of staff, resources and operations. The International Crisis Group in its report for 2010 warned that ethnic and political rivalry among high-ranking officers of the Afghan military establishment and general staff has put the popularity and credibility of the forces at stake. Army Chief Mullah Bismillah Khan never allowed General Wardak even to enter the building of the Defense Ministry. Army Chief, Bismillah Khan also expelled a Pashtun woman army general from the Defense Ministry.[1]

In its Annual Report for 2012 on the state of the world's human rights, Amnesty International warned that:

> The Taliban and other armed groups targeting civilians through assassinations and abductions, and harmed civilians indiscriminately in bombings, violating the laws of war and committing a raft of human rights abuses. According to UNAMA, the Taliban and other armed groups accounted for 77 percent of civilian deaths. They increasingly resorted to using improvised explosive devices in mosques, markets and other civilian areas, contributing to a substantial rise in the number of civilian casualties.[2]

Journalist and research scholar Tim Foxley (2012) reported the Taliban allegations against war criminal General Dostum:

> The Taliban have devoted a specific announcement on their website to the subject of ethnic Uzbek former/current warlord Abdul Rashid Dostum, describing him as a war criminal and calling for him to be punished as such. The statement specifically cites the shelling of Kabul as one of Dostum's crimes, the killing of many Taliban prisoners at Dostum's Qala Jangi prison near Mazar-e Sharif and the alleged execution of other Taliban prisoners locked in lorry containers through dehydration and shooting around the same time.[3]

Human Rights Watch reported the killing of more than 3,000 captured Taliban soldiers in Mazar-e-Sharif by the Dostum's criminal militia. The killings followed Malik Palawan's withdrawal from a brief alliance with the Taliban and the capture of the Taliban forces trapped in the city. There were some strategy failures of the US force that could not protect Taliban officials. The Global Security Organization, in its situation report, stated that the US war on terror in Afghanistan created many problems including ethnicity factionalism.[4]

---

1  *Human Rights Watch Report*, 12 September 2011.
2  *Amnesty International Annual Report for* 2012.
3  Tim Foxley July 21 2012, *daily times*, 02 February 2012.
4  *Daily Nation.19 March 2012.* "In 1997 Human Rights Watch reported the killing of more than 3,000 captured Taliban soldiers in Mazar-e-Sharif by the Dostum's criminal militia."

There are still widespread doubts about the ability of ANA to take control of security. Some of the deficiencies are due to ethnic and sectarian divides, regionalism and factionalism. As a Pashtun, the Defense Minister Abdul Rahim Wardak was in control of only two brigades in 2008. Shia or Hazara groups were in control of one brigade and five battalion commanders, while four battalion commanders were loyal to General Dostum.[1]

The Bonn Agreement defines NATO's main role to help the Afghan government in extending its writ to the whole territory of the country, but unfortunately, NATO never tried to extend the writ of the Afghan government to all parts of the country. In addition to this, ISAF has been entrusted with the role of conducting security and stability operations throughout the country in coordination with the Afghan National Army, but they never considered ANA as their security partner. These misunderstood roles have so for badly failed as the epidemic of corruption and abuse of power spread in the ranks of coalition forces. The UN, Afghan Independent Human Rights Commission, Human Rights Watch and Amnesty International reported innumerable cases of torture, extrajudicial killing and humiliation in Afghan jails, but didn't report about the torture of American and ISAF forces.[2]

We all know what is happening in NATO and US-run prisons, but it was the first time NATO announced the suspension of the transfer of prisoners to Afghan prisons amidst widespread allegations of torture and humiliation against the country's intelligence agencies. From 2009 to 2010, some reports indicated that NATO had transferred more than 2,000 prisoners to Afghan jails.[3]

Amnesty International in its report for 2012 revealed that:

> ISAF and NATO continued to launch aerial attacks and night raids, claiming scores of civilian lives. According to UNAMA, 14 per cent of civilians were killed in ISAF, NATO and Afghan operations. On 20 February, the Governor of eastern Kunar province claimed that 64 civilians, including 29 children, had been killed during joint ground and air operations by Afghan and ISAF forces in the Ghazi Abad district over the previous four days. Senior ISAF officials disputed the account but agreed to a joint investigation. NATO officials later said that most of those killed were insurgents.[4]

The shameful story of Pul-e-Charkhi prison describes incidents of rape and humiliation where young women were routinely raped and transferred to safe houses, guest houses and government offices for sexual purposes. The police and army officers were also found involved in this business.

---

1  *Ibid.*
2  *Also see Daily Times*, 12 February 2011.
3  *The Wall Street Journal Report on Afghanistan*, 12 April. 2011.
4  *DAWN.* 2 February. 2011.

However, in US controlled Bagram prison, Afghan investigators found that US army abused detainees. The Afghan Government has no idea how many policemen and army soldiers are actually on its payroll. As the date of withdrawal approaches, the morale of the Afghan army is low. [1]

To raise morale, on 21 April, 2011, NATO announced the donation of weapon vehicles and airplanes worth more than $10 billion to the Afghan Security Forces (ASF) till 2014. Weapon and equipments would be provided to Afghan security forces, a spokesman for the International Security Assistance Force said. Some 70,000 automobiles, including armored and technical vehicles, would be purchased for ANSF.[2]

The game started when the US and NATO commanders order the destruction of sophisticated weapons instead of giving them to the Afghan army. International Security Assistance Force came under fire for its duality. This enraged the whole population of the country. In view of the impending withdrawal of foreign forces from Afghanistan, former Afghan Defense Minister Abdul Rahim Wardak visited India in 2011, asking for more military assistance. Mr. Rahim Wardak met his Indian counterpart to explore ways to improve security in Afghanistan and the region. India pledged help in strengthening the capabilities of Afghan security forces. The Indian Defense Minister, A.K. Anthony, conveyed the government of India's willingness to work with the Afghan government in building the capabilities of Afghan security forces, a statement said. Defense Minister Wardak told reporters in New Delhi, "We welcome any cooperation in the field of training and helping of Afghan national security forces."[3]

However, during his visit to Kabul, Prime Minister Manmohan Singh met President Karzai and exchanged views on bilateral relations, the war on terror, the security situation in Afghanistan and the region, and made a historical speech in the Afghan Parliament. He said that the transition to Afghan-led security meant there would be no place for Provincial Reconstruction Teams in the county. He further said that the PRTs, linked to international military bases, are a hurdle standing in the way of the Afghan Government, and that they would have to go with the start of the security transition process.

President Karzai said he plans to announce the security transition of first province that will shift to Afghani oversight in March. The government pledged to hand over the security to ANA gradually, province-by-province. Mr. Karzai said, "Had the international community focused Afghanistan at the beginning of 2002, now we would have more strong

---

1 *Daily Times*, October 20, 2011.
2 *Human Rights Watch Report*, 12 September, 2011.
3 *Daily Outlook Afghanistan*, 12 April 2011.

security force". He added that most of the problems are a legacy of the lack of focus of the international community during the first five years.[1]

The process of trust building between the Afghan army and NATO command was moving in the right direction, but the killing of US soldiers (2011) by an Afghan Air Force pilot resulted in stalemate. Prior to this incident, the national press reported that Afghan soldiers were complaining about the non-payment of their salaries. Since over ninety percent soldiers of the army and police live in rented houses, they needed their salaries on time. Afghan pilot Ahmad Gul Khan, who served in the air force for over thirty years under the communist regime, was a poor man, suffering from frustration and anxiety. He was hand to mouth and had sold his house to feed his poverty-stricken children.[2]

Afghanistan is a society where terrorism, extremism and al-Qaeda have ruined the lives of women, men and children. The present day Afghanistan presents very queer picture of anarchy, where every province is a state within state. One of the biggest challenges for foreign partners has been the effectiveness of ANA that continues to rely upon US and ISAF forces.[3]

NATO Secretary General Anders Fogh Rasmussen called upon the member states to increase their military budget and keep up their contributions to the mission in Afghanistan, in order to extend the US-led presence in the country. He claimed that a rapid exit from Afghanistan would be premature. "Afghan society is not yet prepared to take full responsibility for the security," he said, addressing a session of NATO's parliamentary assembly in Bulgaria.[4]

In his opening speech at the Kabul Conference on 20 July 2010, President Hamid Karzai said Afghanistan is "determined" to be responsible for its own security operations by 2014. "I remain determined that our Afghan National Security Forces will be responsible for all military and law enforcement operations throughout our country by 2014."[5]

After al-Qaeda leader Osama Bin Laden was reported killed by US Special Forces in Abbottabad, near Islamabad, it was widely believed that there is no reason to keep troops in Afghanistan any longer, since one of the main aims of the war on terror after 9/11 was to defeat al-Qaeda and deny it sanctuary in the country. Former Defense Minister Mr. Gates said that there are currently 200 al-Qaeda operatives left in Afghanistan. Mr. Gates said the death of al-Qaeda could be a game changer in the Afghan war.

---

1 *Times of India*, 12 June 2011.
2 *Foreign Affairs*, 2013.
3 *Times*, 05 May 2011.
4 *Long War Journal*, 01 March 2012.
5 *Khama Press*, Kabul, 31 May 2012.

The death of Osama bin Laden and growing pressure from the Congress to shrink US commitments and expenses in Afghanistan gave a new impetus to those in the Obama administration who favor a swift reduction of US forces. Military commanders were reportedly proposing President Barack Obama to begin the withdrawal by pulling out up to 10.000 troops by the end of 2014.

## CHAPTER 5. BLACKWATER, PRIVATE CONTRACTORS AND CRIMINAL MILITIAS

During the Cold War, the trend of private security companies or private militias steadily grown, security was gradually transferred to private firms to reduce some of the burdens of mounting military action. Several well-established companies developed more advanced knowledge than the state security agencies. Private mercenaries are also called paramilitaries. Most contractors have employed former members of the regular army.

The United States Special Operation Forces found a new home (Camp Integrity) in Afghanistan which is owned by Blackwater. Blackwater (which changed its name to Xe, then to the even more innocuous-sounding Academi), *The Nation* reported, is recruiting ordinary people from Northern Afghanistan to fight in the Middle East. RT News reported that the private militia Academi—formerly known as Blackwater, was the proud winner of a bigger deal which will keep its forces permanently in the country. Under this deal, Blackwater owned a 10-acre compound in Kabul.

> Pakistani Defense analyst, Brigadier Asif Haroon Raja has elucidated the basic duty of Blackwater in Afghanistan: "Most of the clandestine work in Afghanistan is being done by Blackwater. Reportedly, Blackwater in Afghanistan is training and equipping Afghan troops, who then fire on US soldiers during joint operations. Two such incidents took place in 2009 and, this practice is aimed at justifying the troop surge.[1]

Blackwater operatives help gathering intelligence information and run the secret US military drone bombing campaign. Such profitable mercenary companies operate in many states around the globe. Most private security

---

1  Asif Haroon Raja's article, *The Asian Tribune*, 07 February 2010.

companies operate under state control in the US, UK, Russia, and Israel. Many functions of security agencies were privatized in the United States, during the Reagan and Bush era, through Executive Order No 12333. Today, US armed forces rely on PMCs to maintain 28 percent of its all weapons systems.[1]

On July 2010, the Yale Undergraduate *Journal of Politics* reported the US new Afghan strategy involving an escalation of more than 30,000 additional US forces, while a Congressional Research Report revealed that President Obama's 30,000 troop surge could be accompanied by a surge in private military contractors (PMCs), numbering as high as 56,000.[2] Thus, private military contractors outnumbered American soldiers in Afghanistan by as many as 60,000.[3]

In 17 January, 2010, Mr. Colum Lynch reported that the UN General Assembly passed a resolution urging the UN to take precautions that its hiring practices do not alter the international character of the UN or endanger its staff.[4]

In Afghanistan, the UN contracted an Afghan subsidiary of a London-based company, IDG Security Ltd., to provide 169 Ghurkhas for security purposes. On 11 June, 2009, *Le Monde* reported the presence of the company in Afghanistan. "Blackwater–Xe has a visible presence with Presidential Air, which effects helicopter operations. The contract for the protection of State Department diplomats was consigned to the British company Aegis," the newspaper reported.[5]

Downsizing of the military since the end of the Cold War is one factor that has prompted the US in Afghanistan and Iraq to turn to private security companies to directly support military operations. The ranks of these mercenaries swelled by 10% percent in Afghanistan, more than two thirds of them local, which reflects Washington's desire to employ Afghans in counter insurgency operations in their country. Private military firms have been critical players in a number of conflicts. They provide staff and services of a military nature.

The hiring of professional soldiers has been a common practice throughout history. They are known as mercenaries or soldiers for hire. They carry out many jobs like guarding dignitaries, including the Afghan President, Hamid Karzai, collection intelligence information and support military operations.[6]

---

1  *Intellectual Takeout*, 30 July 2010.
2  *Congressional Report on Afghanistan*, 2010.
3  *The Yale Undergraduate Journal of Politics* July 2010.
4  Colum Lynch. *Global Policy Forum*, 17 January, 2010.
5  On June 11, 2009, Le Monde *reported the presence of the company in Afghanistan.*
6  Elke Krahmann. 2010. *States Citizens and the Privatization of Security.*

Prominent private British companies in Afghanistan and Iraq are Aegis Defense Service, Armor Group, Control Risk Group, Ervin International, Sand Line International, and International Intelligence Limited. From Iraq to Afghanistan, the United State and its allies are using private military companies to provide a range of security services commonly associated with national armies.[1]

The UK based Global Risk International is responsible for providing security to the Provisional Coalition Authority, US Department of Defense, USAID, and the UN in Iraq, employing over one thousand Ghurkha personnel. In addition to this, there are numbers of private companies involved in military and intelligence activities in Afghanistan. Their operations raised many questions and their suspicious activities, lack of transparency, and a job motivated by profit not by national interests have created misunderstanding about their real job. They have no strict regulatory regime and are not accountable to the state.[2]

These private sector intelligence and security agencies have created many problems during their operations in Afghanistan. Nobody knows what they are doing and what their business is, but one thing is clear, they have badly affected the fighting capabilities of professional armies of NATO member states. If they recruit mercenaries for war, then why are the Taliban blamed for recruitment and training of their cadets? In view of their activities, states needed to tighten regulatory provisions in domestic laws and enhance law enforcement at national level.[3]

Despite their expertise, there are many reservations about their quality of work, sincerity, and impartiality. The role of Blackwater and its involvement in many incidents have raised suspicions across the world. The role of a mercenary is often contrasted with someone who is properly employed in a security. Numerous controversies surround the continued and expanding use of the private military force. Writer Deborah Avant urged that there is a lack of legal clarity about the PMCs' role. In the United Kingdom, London recently emerged as a global security industry. Private security firms are trying to blackmail and cash in on demands for armed protection and security advice from states involved in armed conflicts.[4]

With the end of the Cold War, and the emergence of new security concepts, some military powers reduced their armies and now rely on private militias or mercenaries. Besieged by civil strife and internal conflicts, many politicians, corporations, and businessmen seek refuge and protection under the PMCs. Henry Sanchez of Rutgers University reported, over five million soldiers around the world were laid off between 1987 and 1994. Professional

---

1  *Ibid.*
2  *Ibid.*
3  *The Rise of Modern Mercenaries. Private Militia Contractors.* www.nikyan/articles/htm.com.
4  *Ibid.*

soldiers, suddenly unemployed in a hostile civilian environment, resorted to becoming mercenaries. A few became rogue and some of them joined militants, terror and insurgent groups.[1]

This happened in Iraq, Afghanistan and Pakistan. In Afghanistan and Pakistan, unemployed and disgruntled military professionals are joining the Taliban and various sectarian outfits. They are conducting military operations against UK, US and NATO forces. They fight against the national army of Afghanistan and Pakistan. States that depend on mercenaries, private military intelligence, and security companies, in maintaining law and order, military operations, intelligence gathering and police training have incapacitated themselves. They have influenced their national security and military policies, thereby compromising the state authority.

The involvement of Pakistani Blackwater in the Sunni-Shia conflict in Middle East and the Gulf region has raised many questions. The presence of Pakistan's private militias (retired army officers) in Bahrain, Yemen and Saudi Arabia, and their fight against the local Shia population has directed the attention of international community towards the new concept of the country's international jihadism in the name of a transmogrified sectarian Islam. These private mercenaries are also fighting against the US army in Afghanistan. Intelligence reports confirm that, there are militias of retired Pakistan army soldiers and other Jihadi groups in Bahrain and Yemen, involved in target killing and daylight assassination of prominent Shia leaders.

These reports were confirmed when several Pakistani Blackwater members were killed or injured by Shia protesters, in Bahrain and by the army in Afghanistan. Recently, Bahrain's Foreign Minister, Sheikh Khaled bin Ahmed Al-Khalifa discussed the role of these militias with Islamabad, where the two sides agreed to increase in the number of private militias (retired army officers) in the country. Pakistan's "Ex-Servicemen Society", like Blackwater (Xe Services LLC) is now fully involved in sectarian fight in the Middle East. Pakistani Blackwater has established a private army of 2 million soldiers, under the leadership of Lt.-Gen. (retired) Faiz Ali Chishti, the man who tortured Pakistan's Prime Minister, Zulfiqar Ali Bhutto. The army of 2 million soldiers is registered with Fauji Foudation of Pakistan.

The United Kingdom is among those states that have privatized most of the state institutions. The UK military is now reliant upon private financing of military installations and equipments. By doing this, the government ignored the basic function of the state. Management of military bases such as navy garrisons handed over to private sector. According to the author of *States, Citizens and the Privatization of Security*:

> The UK government now struggling to maintain the control of over the increasingly private provision of military services exacerbated the problem

---

1 Sam Vaknin, *Analysis of Private Armies, United Press International*. 17 July, 2002.

of executive autonomy. Owing to the proliferation of private military contractors in proportion to government personnel, the MOD not only finds
it difficult to ensure effective contract management, but also cannot count
anymore on the professional self regulation of its civil servant and soldiers
to control the action of its employees on the ground.[1]

The situation, indeed, is getting worse. It is an established fact that private military companies or security agencies work for money not for national
interests. Their illegal activities can affect a country's relations with other
states. We are analyzing here various aspects of private companies and
modern private military industry in Britain. These companies have created
misunderstandings across the globe. As far as their domestic role of intelligence gathering and security in the UK is concerned, they provide low quality information to state agencies and. In 2012, during the Olympic Games in
London, a private company G4S failed to maintain the security of the game.
Alison Wakefield revealed many things about the privatization of security
in the United Kingdom. Steven D. Gibson tells us how these private security
sector societies operate across the country:

> There are already some 60-plus private security sector associations op-
> erating in the UK who offer some sort of practitioner 'guidance' for their
> various members. Yet, their membership overlaps, their members migrate
> internally around the sector, and they belong to several such associations
> at the same time. Some of these associations are genuinely interested in
> pursuing excellence. Others are merely collections of administrative func-
> tionaries and disenchanted factions.[2]

In her paper, "Privatization of Security and Military Functions and the
Demise of the Modern Nation-State in Africa", Michelle Small urges that the
state is under an obligation to provide security to its citizens:

> [T]rans-nationalism and privatization have changed the balance of power
> between the state, corporations and the market, diminishing the state's ca-
> pacity to meet citizens' demands. The legitimization of the state through
> the core function of security provision is undermined by the use of PSCs
> and PMCs. Additionally, PSCs and PMCs decrease the need to build up
> state institutions, perpetuating state incapacity.[3]

Today, the post Saddam Hussain Persian Gulf and the entire Arab world
present an ugly picture of violent sectarian conflict, in which private militias
are playing vital role. The elimination of Sunni dominated regime in Iraq and
the Shia uprising in Bahrain, Yemen and Saudi Arabia, has shattered the balance of power in the region. Dieter Farwick questions the rapid growth of
these agencies and warns of their suspicious role in many states:

---

1  Elke Krahmann 2010. *States Citizens and the Privatization of Security.*
2  *The Privatization of security in the United Kingdom.* Vol, 15, No. 2, 02 February 2005.
3  Michelle Small. Vol, 01, No. 2, 2006. *Privatization of Security and Military Functions and the Demise of the Modern Nation State in Africa.*

All Blackwater security contractors who deploy in either Iraq or Afghanistan, regardless of whether or not they are supporting a military contract, carry U.S. Department of Defense Contractor Identification Cards.[1]

Some analysts say that former law enforcement officers, investigators and intelligence agents have become private intelligence agents. They conduct investigations and inquiries. In September 2009, there were over 100 private security and military contractors in Afghanistan compared to approximately 64,000 uniformed personnel.[2]

Pratab Chatterjee complains over the role of private military companies in Iraq and Afghanistan. He urged that the efficiency of private military companies is in doubt, as they have failed to provide security to international forces. Armed security contractors take part in combat operations, offensive and defensive, as the international law makes no distinction between the modes of participation in a military combat. Private military companies do not spend all of their funds on their projects in a particular country. They steal money and transfer it to a safe destination.[3]

The Wiki Leaks reports exposed the basic function of DynCorp in Afghanistan. In 2009, St. Petersburg Times reported the worldwide function of the company. DynCorp is one of top 25 private contractors who received $1 billion from the US government since 1995. In Afghanistan, more than 95 percent budget of the militia comes from the US military.[4]

The involvement of these companies in sex trade is more irksome. Afghan Army commanders are critical of these companies operations, as they have established close contacts with drug lords and the Taliban militia; provide them with arms and military information including counter-insurgency strategies. They even kill their coalition partners as per their instructions.[5]

In 2010, Britain's top representative warned that amid enduring suspicions over the reliability of local forces, the Afghans are turning to the Taliban for justice. Drug trafficking, corruption and the trend of alienation in the police force may delay it taking over the responsibility of law and order in 2014.[6]

Members of local Afghan police join these companies every month. A recent report, submitted to the British Parliament, warned that counter-insurgency in Afghanistan cannot succeed without two elements; essential for success a legitimate, functioning government and insurgents who are deprived of external sanctuary and support. The Transition efforts to build

1   Dieter Farwick. *Armed Forces and Private Security Companies: Partners and Competitors*, World Security Network. 24 September 2007.
2   Elke Krahmann. 2010. States Citizens and the Privatization of Security.
3   Pratab Chatterjee, *Asia Times*. 23 June 2010.
4   *World Security Network*, 24 September 2007.
5   *Reuters* 12 November 2007.
6   *Daily Outlook Afghanistan*, March 12, 2007.

Afghan forces and transfer responsibilities to them-face major obstacles and will take longer than anticipated.[1]

Recent reports indicate that some private security agencies have hired Iranian agents and Taliban soldiers. In Helmand and Kandahar provinces, the US military officials caught Afghan security guards passing sensitive security information to the Taliban. At the same time, a security firm EOD-hired two Iranian intelligence agents who were known to the US military intelligence.

An Afghan Security Council official and an aide to President Karzai, Muhammad Zai Salehi was arrested in July 2010. *The New York Times* reported that Salehi was accused of soliciting bribe to help shut down an investigation into a company suspected of transferring millions of dollars out of the country for officials, insurgents and drug smugglers.[2]

Realizing a constant threat from the corrupt officials and the nationalist elements within the Afghan National Army and the police, the ISAF, NATO and the US turned to private militias of warlords, for the protection of their military headquarters and convoys. These warlords are not only protecting the military and logistic convoys of the contributing states, but also send their soldiers for Jihad across the border into Pakistan.

Their record of criminal activities is heartrending. Their rogue armies kill men and rape women. Investigative Journalist, Bob Woodward reported the 3,000 CIA-backed paramilitary forces in Afghanistan, working closely with US Special Forces on combat operations and intelligence gathering. They are in close contact with warlords and regional commanders, and receive support from their rogue armies. Prominent journalist Mark Curtis recently reported that British and US policies in the country, that not helping but setting back development prospects. Hundreds of millions of dollars are wasted while up to 80 percent of donations return to donor countries in corporate profits or consultants' salaries.[3]

The issue of secret militias in Afghanistan has been very complicated since 2002. The United States and its allies supported Afghan warlord's criminal militias on one hand and deployed Blackwater's rogue army in various provinces on the other. Warlord's criminal militias together with the rogue soldiers of Blackwater trained several other groups, who later on challenged Afghan National Army and the police. The issue of drone attacks and the operation of US Special Forces in Eastern Afghan provinces raised many questions, when the spokesman of President Karzai blamed US forces for killing 17 people including 12 minor children in Kandahar. These illegal kill-

---

1    http:www//publicintelligence.net/afghan-contractors-hire-high-warlord-taliban-commander-iranian-spies/.

2    *The New York Times*. March 2010.

3    *Daily Outlook Afghanistan*. March 06 2010.

ings of innocent children created more problems to build confidence building measures between NATO, US and the people of Afghanistan.

After the criticism of Mr. Karzai spokesman, Afghans retaliated and
killed a CIA officer and wounded three other Americans in Kunar province.
The Americans who died were working for a secret criminal militias (established by the CIA) 0-4 unit, a so called counter terrorism team. According
to the *New York Times* report, Mr. Karzai faced criticism from both the parliament and cabinet Ministers about his weak control on National Security
Directorate (NDS). Mr. Karzai spokesman said that the 0-4 Unit maintains
the army of more than 1,200 rogue soldiers, receives direction and funds from
the CIA. "It was a joint op at most in name" he said, "but really in fact a CIA-
run criminal militia".

The United Kingdom and NATO provided arms and funds to private
militias to help maintain the security of their military convoys. The US has
spent more than $ 224 billion on defeating the Taliban and the Al-Qaeda,
while the UK government has spent £ I billion since 2001. Mark Curtis esti-
mates the worth of the arms, as 18,000 assault rifles and 800 machineguns,
supplied by the British government to Afghanistan from 2008 to 2010 at £
32.5 billion.[1]

These militias are deeply involved in child abuse and illegal arrest of
civilians in various provinces. They are free to carry out operation in any
part of the country. In Western parts of the country, people complaint that
these militias are harassing and killing locals. On 12 September 2011, Human
Rights Watch reported US-backed Afghan militias were committing serious
human rights abuses.[2]

US army trained more than 6,000 rogue soldiers but its target was 30,000
by the end of 2011. In Kandahar, *Telegraph* reported Gul Muhammad, a farmer,
was tortured to death by local militia. They kept him in their custody, killed
him, and his body was found in a stream. He was going to Helmand to buy
sheep. He had $10,000 dollars (£6,250), the newspaper reported.[3]

An Australian newspaper, *The Age*, reported Foreign Minister Kevin
Rudd saying that an Afghan local militia in Uruzgan province, loyal to war
warlord Matiullah Khan, would maintain law and order there after the withdrawal of Australian forces from Afghanistan. BBC reported Australian military close its bases in Uruzgan province of Afghanistan and its last combat
troops left the country on 16 December 2013. The Australian military maintained a permanent presence at Tarin Kot since 2005. In Kunduz province,
local residents also complained about the behavior of criminal militias.[4]

---

1  *Daily Times.* 14 July 2011.
2  *Tribune*, 03 March 2011.
3  *Daily Outlook Afghanistan,*13 March 2012.
4  *Daily Outlook Afghanistan*, 13 March 2012.

In Uruzgan province, Australian Special Forces and the US signed an agreement with a local warlord, Mr. Matiullah Khan, for protecting their convoys and military bases. He built an army of more than 3,000 soldiers, known as Kandak-e-Amniat-e-Uruzgan (Uruzgan's Protection Army). Uruzgan Protection Army is notorious for kidnapping and drug trade. Warlord Matiullah Khan receives 340,000 dollars per month for his services. This agreement confirms that the United States does not trust on Afghan National Army and the Police.[1]

The *Wall Street Journal* reported that Afghan Government officials in Northern Afghanistan have built up their own ethnic militia groups, to expand their influence in the region:

> The spread of mostly Tajik and Uzbek militias is aggravating tensions with local Pashtuns-the country's largest ethnic group but a minority in the North—some of whom say they are being driven to turn to the Taliban, a largely Pashtun group, to defend their interests.[2]

Governor of Balkh province, warlord Muhammad Atta Noor, runs two such militias, in districts close to Mazar-e-Sharif, the provincial capital and the largest city of Northern Afghanistan. He is a known criminal, drug and arms smuggler. Mr. Atta Mohammad Noor once accused the central government of distributing weapons to powerful warlords in the province, to undermine his power. The situation in the Balkh province demonstrates the weakness of the central government, to maintain security through constitutional means.

Ethnic Tajik and Uzbek warlords from the Northern Alliance still dominate the region while local citizens seek guns for self-protection because of rampant criminality. Militias are known to collect forced "taxes" from locals, create illegal checkpoints, seize property, and detain people in private jails. Killings and kidnappings now became a common practice in Afghanistan. As the situation spirals out of control, the US and the NATO turned toward the Afghan Local Police Program. US hoped that the nascent project would spark uprising against the Taliban akin to the Sunni Awakening in Iraq, in which private militias rose up against al-Qaeda. In Southern Afghanistan, Canadian forces hired a local warlord for the security of their forces in 2007. Warlord Gulalai had helped the US in driving out the Taliban from Kandahar in 2001. The Canadian military also hired another warlord, Haji Toor Jan, for the protection of its military installations.[3]

In Badakhshan, a local warlord, who is in control of a significant portion of the drug trade, provides security to the German Army's Provincial Reconstruction Team. Warlord Nazari Muhammad receives thousands of dollars as salary for his private army services. The Afghan President and his broth-

1  *Reuters* 19 November 2007.
2  *Daily Outlook Afghanistan*. 12 July 2011.
3  *Daily Times*, 02 February, 2011.

ers Wali Karzai and Hashmat Karzai, the son of Afghan Defense Minister, Hamid Wardak, Pir Gilani, Abdul Rasul Sayyaf, Rabbani, Gulbadin's son, ex-Army Chief Qasim Fahim, General Dostum, Haji Din Muhammad and some warlords from Paktia province established their own private armies, which eroded the strategic role of Afghan National Army.

According to recent reports of the UN, ISAF forces trained, armed and employed some 1,000 private security men across Afghanistan. The UN has estimated that there are 120, 000-armed individuals belonging to about 5,000 private militias in Afghanistan. The dependency of the US and NATO troops upon private criminal armies, questions the eligibility of Afghan National Army.[1]

### The Business of Private Militias in Afghanistan

Private mercenaries and their intelligence job is now a part of Western war making. The US forces cannot launch operation without the backing of the private forces. The Afghan president has long been opposed to the number of these mercenary forces as he said many of these militias disregard Afghan law. Antony Loewenstein (April 2012) discussed the function of private security companies in Afghanistan and his detailed article; intelligence is increasingly collected by these companies and given to Australia, US, and Brittan's forces. This information he says often forms the bases of the notorious, American-led night raids across the nation that have caused the death of countless civilians.[2]

A former warlord, Mr. Ruhullah, was once chairman of the Kandahar Security Group. His men were collecting taxes and shared them with the Taliban. According to the Kaleed Research Report, his criminal mafia was involved in the killing of innocent passengers. Moreover, soldiers of this security company teamed up with the Taliban in fighting the NATO forces at night. Another security firm belongs to a former war criminal, General Qasim Fahim, and his brother. Strategic Solution International collects information, protects guardians and establishes its own criminal militia across the country.[3]

Former Defense Minister General Abdul Rahim Wardak, and his son, Hamid Jan Wardak, established a security firm under the name of NCL Security Company, which is also involved in criminal activities. Former President of Afghanistan, former President, Sabghatullah Mujaddidi, established his own company under the name of Elite Security Company, collect money from local landlords.[4]

---

1  *Ibid.*
2  *Daily Outlook Afghanistan*, 12 July 2011.
3  *Daily Outlook Afghanistan*, August 23 2011
4  *Ibid*

There are hundreds of militias belongs to Afghan parliamentarians, Ministers, war criminals and religious clerics. According to a human rights report, these private militias are involved in violence, intimidation and attacks on women. The 10 pages report of Human Rights, 'Killing you is a very easy thing for us', documented human rights abuses in South-eastern Afghanistan, viz-a-viz the army and the police kidnapping Afghans and holding them for ransom in private prisons, breaking into households and robbing families is their job.[1]

In 2011, in view of the terror related activities of private contractors, President Hamid Karzai renewed his demand for the elimination of their network, claiming they are a source of corruption that undermines support for the war against the Taliban insurgency. The contractors are "running a parallel security structure in the country; they are looting and stealing from the Afghan people" and "some of them turns to terrorist groups at night time," the President revealed in an ABC TV program.[2]

The regulation of private security firms is still being debated, including their processes, staff identification, weapons use, and general requirements for their owners and staff. The criminal record of their soldiers, who are involved in human trafficking, rap, or murderers and other illegal activities, is another question raised in the Afghan parliament. Ordinary Afghans do not know about the function of these enterprises. They even do not know the multitude of security actors roaming the country.

They use government permits to smuggle weapons into Afghanistan, they dishonestly register only a part of their weapons; their sophisticated arms are not reported. They buy weapons from black market and employ those who are already armed. They arm other groups, organize violence, and create conflict mechanisms. President Hamid Karzai once accused them of involvement in robberies, malpractices and misuse of authority. Their suspicious activities, lack of transparency, and a job motivated by profit and not by national foreign policy or security interests are their negative points.[3]

President Karzai once said that the biggest source of corruption is the United States. The story began with a news report published in *New York Times*. According to the report, CIA has been sending bags of cash to Afghan President Hamid Karzai totalling tens of millions of dollars. More interesting is that the report said that the Afghan President and official of his government have been on the CIA payroll for over a decade, receiving tens of millions of dollars in cash.[4]

A *New York Times* report revealed that corruption is being encouraged by US intelligence agencies. US officials and military generals have fixed their

1  *The News*, 12 June 2012.
2  *ABC TV News*, 2011.
3  *Daily Outlook Afghanistan.* 12 July 2011.
4  *DAWN*, 14 April 2010.

own share in the corruption money. They give money to Afghan officials and receive their share.[1] This is not the first time Afghan President Karzai received massive pay-offs for his services to the Pentagon and the CIA; but in addition, he received millions of dollars from Iranian Intelligence in 2010.[2]

After the US invasion in 2001, the CIA paid huge money to warlords and so called politicians. General Qasim Fahim, Haji Din Muhammad, President Karzai, Wali Karzai, Prof. Rasul Seyyaf, Burhanuddin Rabbani, Yunus Qanooni, Dr. Abdullah, General Dostum, Atta Muhammad Noor, Ismail Khan, Prof. Mujaddidi, Pir Gailani, war criminal Sherzai and many other warlords received millions of dollars from the CIA. In 2002, the CIA essentially gave sacks of cash to Hamid Karzai to buy warlord loyalties. Generals in the Afghan National Army also received their share from the CIA and Pentagon.[3]

Some experts are of the opinion that the CIA gave money to Afghan officials to access Mr. Karzai and his inner circle, and to guarantee the CIA's influence at the Presidential palace. In all Afghan state institutions, corruption is widespread. Afghanistan ranks 174 from 176 in Transparency International's 2012 Corruption Perceptions Index. In 2010, the Kabul Bank was exposed for a financial scandal in which its owners Shir Khan Farnood, Khalilullah Fruzi and Muhammad Fahim were spending one billion dollars for their own personal luxurious lifestyle.[4]

Leaders of the Northern Alliance in and outside the government have begun to stockpile arms and take other steps to prepare for a future civil war. The Taliban will return with renewed vengeance. Bad governance or misgovernance is the main factor behind the frustration of civilian population in Afghanistan. Poor eradication management of narcotic drugs is another factor, which supports insurgency and causes alienation in the country. Al-Qaeda finances the entire network in Pakistan and Afghanistan.[5]

The war in Afghanistan has had its share of misadventures, some by Pakistani generals and some by US and Russian generals. American generals plunged into Iraq not only ignored the importance of Afghanistan, they also gave free hand to Pakistani generals to design the future direction of war in the country. Military operational mistakes, collateral damage, illegal night raids, killings, humiliation and desecration of the Holy Koran at the hands of American soldiers, created a relationship gap, between US and NATO allied forces and the people of Afghanistan.

---

1  *New York Times*, 29 April 2013.
2  *Ibid.*
3  42-*Daily Times*, April 2013.
4  *Daily Nation*, May 30, 2013.
5  *Daily Outlook Afghanistan*, April 2013.

## CHAPTER 6. THE US JOINT SPECIAL OPERATIONS COMMAND, BLACKWATER AND THE DRONE WAR

Since the US invasion of Afghanistan, the remote control robot killed hundreds of people across the Middle East, Pakistan and Afghanistan. Among the most wanted terrorists was Hakimullah Mehsud who was killed in Waziristan, Pakistan. Drone attack and military operations are part of daily life in Afghanistan and Pakistan. The United States has been engaged in remote control war in the region since 2001. Most of these attacks are on targets in Af-Pak border areas that killed many terrorist. Drones were used as guided missile by the US military in World War II. In her recent book, Madea Benjamin tells us about the use of drone in Afghanistan and Pakistan:

> Today drones are used for both lethal and non-lethal purposes. Outside the military, unmanned aircrafts are being drafted for everything from tracking drug smugglers and monitoring the US-Mexico border to engaging in search operations after earthquake and spraying pesticides on crops. In 2004, the CIA began searching Taliban and members of al-Qaeda in Afghan-Pak border region. In June 2004, in South Waziristan, a US drone killed Taliban commander Nek Muhammad.[1]

Daily Guardian reported the secret operation of Blackwater in Iraq and Afghanistan that raised serious questions, about the US secret links with the militia. Some experts in Afghanistan and Pakistan understand that the ongoing US war on terrorism is just a pretext, it is, in fact, a cover story designed to provide NATO allies with a springboard for a secret geographical destabilization campaign in both South and Central Asian regions. The main drivers behind this unending civil war in Afghanistan and Pakistan are the organizer

---

1 Medea Benjamin. *Drone Warfare: Killing by remote control*, PP-102, 118.

of US Special Forces, Blackwater and war criminals of former Mujahedeen groups. Stanley McChrystal, who fought al-Qaeda in Iraq strengthened Blackwater terror network in the country.[1]

Blackwater has been given special mission in both Pakistan and Afghanistan where the militia has constructed warehouses for weapons stock. The profitable business of murder and assassination carried out by Blackwater in both the states has raised question, that what does the militia actually want and what is its basic function? Newspapers failed to file all reports of assassinations and target killings carried out by Blackwater in Afghanistan, but the recent civil war in Pakistan's biggest city Karachi is indicative of something going wrong under the carpet. In 2009, two agents of the agency were found guilty of shooting Afghan civilians in Kabul.[2]

According to a *New York Times* report, brother of the Afghan President, Hamid Karzai, was a CIA operative and a major opium dealer, who established close ties with Taliban and Blackwater militias. On 11 December 2009, the Washington Post reported that Blackwater was operating side by side with the CIA in Iraq and Afghanistan.[3]

Some of the activities of the American "kill team" are already in public knowledge. Twelve men of the militia have been on trial in Seattle for their role in the killing of three Afghan civilians. Five soldiers are on trial for premeditated murder, after they staged the killing to make it look like they were defending themselves against a Taliban attack. On 30 May 2013, Daily Frontier Post reported the story of US soldier accused of killing innocent Afghan villagers in Southern Afghanistan.[4]

Amid reports of crimes against humanity, a debate is raging in official circles whether Americans would stay in Afghanistan or leave. If they stay, what reactions they will receive from Afghans and, if they leave what will be the nature of civil war in Afghanistan? Journalist Kathy Kelly in her recent report quoted the report of US based NGO, Save the Children, which describes the US atrocities in Afghanistan:

> The world is ignoring the daily deaths of more than 850 Afghan children from treatable diseases like diarrhea and pneumonia, focusing on fighting the insurgency rather than providing humanitarian aid." The report notes that a quarter of all children born in the country die before the age of five, while nearly 60 percent of children are malnourished and suffer physical or mental problems.[5]

1 Anthony Gregory. *What Price War? Afghanistan, Iraq and the cost of conflict.* The Independent Institute. June 2011.
2 *Asia Tribune*, 07 February 2010.
3 *Washington Post*, 11 December 2011.
4 On May 30 2013, *Daily Frontier Post* reported US soldier accused of killing 17 innocent Afghan villagers in Southern Afghanistan in March 2012.
5 *Save The Children* (NGO) Report, 03 March 2010.

Pakistani newspapers reported secret operations of the US Joint Special Operations Command (JSOC), in major cities like Karachi, Peshawar and Lahore. The notorious private contractor, Blackwater, has been at the center of target killings and assassinations in both Afghanistan and Pakistan, since 2001.[1]

A well-known Pakistani journalist, Musharaf Zaidi, reported the concerns of Afghans and Pakistanis about the illegal activities of Blackwater. According to well-placed military sources in Pakistan, Blackwater operatives gather secret information to help direct drone attacks in FATA and Waziristan. The militia not only controls drone strikes but also gathers intelligence for JSOC in Pakistan. There is an ongoing debate in the Pakistani press about Blackwater and military operations of JSOC, asking under what law they have the license to kill.

Without going into the details of the story, the case is simple. On 9 May 2001, *The Guardian* reported a secret agreement signed between the Pakistani President, General Pervez Musharraf, and the US President, George Bush, which allow US Special Forces, the CIA and the JSOC to carry out secret operations and drone attacks inside Pakistan.[2]

This agreement was renewed in February 2008 by the former President Asif Ali Zardari government. Both sides agreed that Pakistan would ostensibly protest incursions, the newspaper reported. Referring to the recent Abbottabad operation, a government official in Islamabad told this author that the US just implemented the agreement.[3]

Before signing the deal, General Musharraf agreed to convince Pakistani nation about the US secret operation inside Pakistan, without the consent of the regime. Of course, the JSOC was allowed to continue its mission. Moreover, Blackwater was also directed to deny its presence in all major cities of Pakistan. The deal is still secret, but the recent operation in Abbottabad exposed the intentions of US forces in Pakistan. Political parties criticized the army and the ISI for their connivance, while some demanded the resignation of the ISI chief.

At the government level, in his address to the National Assembly, Pakistani Prime Minister expressed concern over the US operation in Abbottabad district. He complained that the US forces violated the sovereignty of his country. The killing of Osama bin Laden in Abbottabad created many doubts and misunderstandings among politicians, the ISI and army generals. Prime Minister Gilani, in fact, wanted to keep Pakistani nation in dark. His government and Army were in contact with US Special Forces during the killing of Osama bin Laden in Abbottabad.[4]

1 *Save the Children* (NGO) Report, 2010.
2 *The Guardian*, 09 May 2011.
3 *Huffington Post*, 02 May 2011.
4 *The New York Times*, 03 September, 2010.

One of my friends from the Interior Ministry of Pakistan told me that Osama was killed with the consent of armed forces. This authorized operation further deteriorated relations between politicians and army generals. The Army chief warned, "Any similar action violating the sovereignty of Pakistan will warrant a review on the level of military intelligence cooperation with the US." Some people questioned the ability of Pakistan Army to protect the country.[1]

Opposition parties raised the issue of the presence of CIA contractors in Pakistan, while Interior Minister, Rehman Malik, offered his resignation and said, "if the presence of the private contractors is proved he will resign the same day". Sources within Blackwater circles confirmed operatives work for the CIA and the JSOC in Pakistan. The militia established various facilities in Karachi, Lahore and Peshawar and has deployed personnel throughout Pakistan.

In April 2002, the CIA paid Blackwater more than $5 million to deploy a small team inside Afghanistan, in the early stages of US operations in the country. The Nation reported that Blackwater continues to operate on the US government payroll both in Iraq and Afghanistan, where it works for the State and Defense Department. On 03 September 2010, *New York Times* reported that Blackwater has created a web of more than 30 shell companies or subsidiaries to obtain millions of dollars in American government contracts, after the security company came under intense criticism for reckless conduct in Iraq.[2]

The murderous business of Blackwater developed not only in Iraq and Afghanistan, but it has also established a secret network in the United Arab Emirates. Press TV reported that the founder of the militia has been hired by the crown prince of Abu Dhabi to form a secret mercenary army in the UAE. According to *The New York Times*, billionaire Erik Prince who relocated to the UAE in 2010, in the wake of mounting legal problems in the United States, received over $500 million to organize an 800-strong battalion of foreign troops in the UAE.[3]

Another report in the *New York Times* revealed the secret directive signed by General David Petraeus, former Chief of the US Central Command, which ordered the expansion of covert military operations throughout the Central Asia and the Middle East. It further revealed that the US Government wants to target hostile countries with which it has maintained diplomatic relations.[4]

---

1  *Ibid.*
2  On September 3, 2010, the *New York Times* reported that Blackwater created a web of more than 30 shell companies or subsidiaries to obtain millions of dollars in American government contracts after the security company came under intense criticism for reckless conduct in Iraq.
3  *Ibid*
4  *DAWN*, 27 January 2011.

Potential targets include Iran, Saudi Arabia and Somalia. *The New York Times* disclosed that despite concerns over its legality, the US military still runs a secret network of private spies in Afghanistan and Pakistan. The newspaper noted that the US military is "largely prohibited from operating inside Pakistan." On 01 March 2011, Mark Mazzetti reported that the spy network, managed by Duane R. Clarrldge, a former top official at the Central Intelligence Agency, procures agents from the Federal Bureau of Investigation in Kabul.[1]

The secret operation program of the JSOC started in Pakistan during the Musharraf regime in 2007, under the leadership of William McRaven, who took over the post from General Stanley McChrystal, who headed the JSOC from 2003 to 2008. As a private military and intelligence force, Blackwater operates under the instructions of the JSOC in Karachi and coordinate every plan with the task force based in Bagram Air Base in Afghanistan. US military intelligence says that Blackwater classified contracts keep being renewed at the request of the JSOC.[2]

Sources in the Afghan Defense Ministry once told this author, that the Blackwater signed its first contract with the CIA for operations in Afghanistan in 2002. Afghan intelligence sources disclosed that the JSOC operation in Karachi is referred to the base in Qatar, which acted as the planning center for the US invasion of Iraq. Blackwater makes strategies for drone attacks in Waziristan, FATA and Afghanistan. In August 2010, *New York Times* reported Blackwater's clandestine operations in covert bases in Pakistan and Afghanistan. In underground hideouts, Blackwater operatives assemble and load Hellfire missiles and 500-pound laser-guided bombs on remotely piloted Predator aircrafts.[3]

In September 2010, Pakistani newspapers disclosed a secret ISI report about the suspicious activities of Blackwater and a federal Minister who provided them with houses and helped those clear shipments of weapons and vehicles through Port Qasim in Karachi. The arrest of Raymond Davis in Lahore in 2011 further exacerbated pressure on government by opposition parties, which demanded a thorough investigation into the secret deal between the Musharraf regime and the CIA. Print and electronic media in Pakistan quoting various politicians, alleged that the government and the military establishment know about the secret activities of Blackwater on Pakistani soil.[4]

A spokesman for the US-led International Security Assistance Force (ISAF) told journalists that there are, at present, nearly 400 US and coalition

---

1  *The New York Times*, March 1, 2011.
2  *Daily Times*, 26 May 2001.
3  In August 2010, *the New York Times*, "clandestine Blackwater operations in covert bases in Pakistan and Afghanistan."
4  *Ibid.*

bases in Afghanistan, including camps, forward operating bases, and combat outposts. In addition, there are at least 300 Afghan National Army (ANA) and Afghan National Police (ANP) bases, most of them having been built, maintained, or supported by the US.[1]

On 27 May 2013, Daily Dawn reported US Secretary of State John Kerry, defending US uses of drone against the people of Afghanistan and Pakistan. "Let me be very clear...first of all there have been very few drone strikes in the last year. Why? Because we have been so successful in rooting out al-Qaeda in Pakistan", John Kerry said. The drone attacks against the innocent civilians are inhuman and the most controversial aspect of US fights against Taliban militants. In Addis Ababa University, John Kerry told students that the US has a very fair program. "Each target was carefully monitored and, sometimes it takes a year to build the authority to know that you're correct.... We do not fire when we know there are children or collateral, we just don't. We have absolutely not shot at high level targets when we have seen that there are people there. I will tell you that the extremists who put bomb in those mosques never engage in the kind of clear discretion we have used in this program," John Kerry said.[2]

In 2013, *The Financial Times* reported President Obama defended drone strikes in Pakistan in a public discussion in New York. On 30 May 2013, prominent columnist Dr Muhammad Taqi highlighted some aspects of Obama's speech and International Crisis Group Report:

> President Barak Obama delivered an extraordinary a speech at the National Defense University at Fort McNairy, Washington DC. The speech that addressed an array of issues from the post 9/11 hunt for al-Qaeda to the concerns regarding the civil liberties in the US has drawn flak from both the left and the right..... President Obama discussed the US drone campaign, but bulk of which has been in the FATA between Pakistan and Afghanistan, at length.... Mr. Obama qualified in position with expressing concern about the occasional collateral damages and the civilian causalities and pledged to minimize both in future by seeking 'near certainty' that no civilian are harmed.[3]

In June 2013, the newly elected Pakistani government protested over the killing of Wali-ur-Rehman by US drone in Waziristan region. Pakistani journalist Imtiaz Gul reported foreign Office, summoned US Ambassador to protest over the killing of al-Qaeda terrorist in Waziristan.30 It was tenth time that an American official had to listen to Pakistani "Umbrage" over the 353rd predator strike into Pakistan territory at the Ministry of Foreign Affairs.

1 On 27 May 2013, *Dawn*, "US Secretary of state John Kerry defending US use of drone against the people of Afghanistan and Pakistan."
2 On January 2013, *Financial Times*, "President Obama defended drone strikes in Pakistan in a public discussion in New York."
3 Dr Muhammad Taqi. *Daily Times*, 30 May 2013.

On 02 November 2013, US drone killed Pakistani Taliban leader, Hakimullah Mehsud in North Waziristan agency. Mr. Hakimullah Mehsud was leaving a meeting in a mosque in Dande Darpkhel village when the drone missile targeted his vehicle he was travelling in. Before his death, his close friend, Latif Mehsud was arrested in Afghanistan. Pakistan's Foreign Office condemned the attack and said these attacks are violation of the country's sovereignty. Mr. Mehsud is believed to have been behind Times Square, New York bombing. Senior Pakistani journalist and analyst, I.A Rehman in his article suggested, that the renewed debate on drone attacks in FATA and the response from the Pakistan authorities deserve due attention:

> Meanwhile, powerful voices continued to be raised against what was de-scribed as killing by remote control. The American lawyers for civil lib-erties renewed their call for the cessation of drone attacks. Amnesty In-ternational again condemned such attacks for causing extra-legal killings and for violating international law. And now the UN High Commission for Human Rights has taken exception to the drone attacks.[1]

As the US army cannot fight in a mountainous regions, therefore, it use drone to kill the enemy from a long distance. The United States and NATO never faced any difficulty in targeting the Taliban insurgents in both Afghan-istan and Pakistan, but this remote control war raised many questions. After the killing of Taliban commander, Wali-ur-Rehman in Waziristan, Paki-stan's Foreign Ministry denounced drones in general, maintaining that the drone strikes are counterproductive, entail loss of innocent civilian lives and, moreover, it violates sovereignty of the country.[2]

Pakistani press published numerous stories on drone war in FATA but the Obama Administration never considered the death of innocent Pashtuns in this brutal war. Daily Nation in its editorial comment criticized the illegal drone war:

> This backlash apart, it bears stressing again and again, the drones violate the inherent principle of independent state; its territorial sovereignty and integrity. It was for this reason that the Foreign Office without even assess-ing the merits or demerits of the event, came out protesting that the missile strike was in violation of the country's sovereignty and an open abuse of human rights.[3]

Journalist Dr. Raza Khan views the new shift of drone control from the CIA to Pentagon as a good development in US policy towards Pakistan. The Obama Administration realized and accepted that the CIA is killing inno-cent civilians in both Pakistan:

> Although tens of al-Qaeda commanders and fighters of TTP have been killed in these drones strikes, but a large number of non-combatants have

---

1  I.A Rehman, *Dawn*, 30 May 2013.
2  Death of Waliur Rehman. *The Nation*-May 31, 2013.
3  Dr. Raza Khan. *Obama's new doctrine on war*. Weekly cutting edge. Volume 08 Issue, 41May 30 to June 05 2013.

also perished in these lethal attacks. Due to the loss of innocent lives, Washington has been facing extreme pressure from human rights groups, both within the US and outside, as well as political circles, particularly, in Pakistan. . . .The most important issue regarding terrorism which the US faces right now is the issue of home-grown terrorists. President Obama said the end of the global war on terror is necessary to preserve the traditional American values of freedom.[1]

Under the new guideline signed by the President, the Pentagon took control of drone strikes. Journalist Nasim Ahmed views this shift a big policy shift of the Obama administration towards Pakistan:

> The most important speech of president Obama's speech was where he redefined the overalls US policy on the war on terror. Making direct reference to Pakistan, the American President acknowledged the cost of US-Pakistan relationship.[2]

Debates in Pakistani press intensified over the drone and its fatalities when the US administration refused to stop killing innocent Pashtuns by remote control bombs. Pakistani analyst Talat farooq raised the question of drone legality in his recent article:

> The Geneva Convention developed in 1949 codified general principles for aerial bombardment, in particular the need to discriminate between combatant and civilians and for attack to be proportional to their expected operational gain. The additional protocol of 1977 developed these principles further.[3]

The present illegal drone attacks against the innocent civilians of Afghanistan and Pakistan in which one side has an ever increasing global reach, while the other has no possible means of computable retaliation. Pakistan Tehreek-e-Insaf (PTI) (a political party) submitted a resolution against drone attacks in the country parliament in June 2013, terming this illegal war against innocent civilians a violation of the country's sovereignty and urged the government to respond militarily.[4]

PTI representative Dr. Shirin Mazari submitted the resolution and said: "Today we, the newly elective representatives of National Assembly express deep distress over the death of more than 3000 Pakistani civilians due to the drone strikes since their initiation in 2004." The drone attacks have created an uneven situation in Pakistan, while it violates the International Convention on Civil and Political Rights (ICCPR). Article 6 of the convention states that every human being has the inherent right to life and this right should be protected by law.

---

1   Nasim Ahmed. *A shift in the US security paradigm*, Weekly cutting edge, 31 may 2013.
2   Talat Farooq, Drone Speak, the News International, 12 June 2013.
3   *Daily, Times*, 11 June 2013.
4   *The Frontiers Post*, 11 June, 2013.

In Pakistan and Afghanistan, suicide bombers and drone are the new facets of modern war. Print and electronic media in south Asian region warned against the consequence of this illegal warfare:

> The irony is that while resentment increase against the drones among Pakistani citizens and internationally, a handful of pro-US journalists in Pakistani media, politics and military circles continue to defend the attacks using the strategic logic that foreign terrorists also violate our sovereignty, Khalid Iqbal reported in daily the Nation.

DRONE ATTACKS IN PAKISTAN FROM 2005 TO 2013

| Year | Attacks | Killed | Injured |
|---|---|---|---|
| 2005 | 1 | 1 | 1 |
| 2006 | 0 | 0 | 0 |
| 2007 | 1 | 20 | 15 |
| 2008 | 19 | 156 | 17 |
| 2009 | 46 | 536 | 85 |
| 2010 | 59 | 831 | 85 |
| 2011 | 59 | 548 | 52 |
| 2012 | 46 | 344 | 37 |
| 2013 | 12 | 85 | 18 |
| Total | 274 | 2521 | 299 |

Sources: *South Asia Terrorism Portal, Long War Journal, 2013, and the Bureau of Investigative Journalism.*[1]

---

1 *South Asia Terrorism Portal, Long War Journal, 2013, and the Bureau of Investigative Journalism.*

# CHAPTER. 7. STATE-OWNED CRIMINAL MILITIAS
## AFGHAN NATIONAL POLICE, VILLAGE STABILITY OPERATION FORCE, PUBLIC PROTECTION FORCE AND LOCAL POLICE FORCE

In 2001, divergent groups of Afghan warlords and political circles signed the Bonn Agreement to design a strategy for political, security and social development in the country. Since 2001, US and NATO allied forced established a number of armed forces in Afghanistan, each with stated intention of bringing security to the country. After the fall of Dr. Najeebullah regime in 1992, the police force of Afghanistan disintegrated. With the collapse of the Taliban regime in 2001, there was no police force across the country; only private criminal militias were in control of their respective provinces. In 2006, Afghan government and Combined Security Transition Command Afghanistan (CSTM-A) established Afghan National Auxiliary Police force (ANOPF).

In March 2009, General David McKiernan established Afghan Public Protection Program (PPP) in Wardak province to support the police and army in restoring peace and stability in the province. In July 2009, another local militia force, Local Defense Initiatives (LDI) was also established under the supervision of Afghan Interior Ministry.

After the Bonn Conference, Germany became the leading nation responsible for the re-establishment of Afghan National Police in 2002. The US began to support ANP in 2003. From 2002 to 2003, German police officers trained a few hundred Afghan police but in 2005, when Taliban started attacking government installations, the recruitment process was expedited.

Up until 2008, Germany spent more than 12 million Euros a year on training the ANP.[1]

Germany set up a police academy and entered with full involvement into the process of training Afghan police. The force it had prepared from 2003 to 2004 was not sufficient to strengthen the structure and senior command levels of police force. As the reach of Germany was limited in the North, the US department in 2005, decided to shift the implementation of the police training program to the Office of Security Cooperation–Afghanistan, under the authority of the commanding general, combined forces command. In 2006, the performance of Afghan police was considered on priority bases. In 2007, 2008 and 2009, Afghan police became a bigger force and established its branches across the country. In 2010, President Hamid Karzai authorized the establishment of Afghan Local Police (ALP) program through Presidential decree.[2]

In 2007, Euro Police Mission was set up in Afghanistan, to train and support Afghan police force in maintaining law and order. This office is, in fact, the European Union commitment to Afghanistan and a coordinated Euro approach that includes local political guidance provided by the Euro Special Representative and reconstruction efforts, managed notably through the European Union delegation in Kabul. Europol is stationed in capital Kabul, while its reconstruction teams are existed in various provinces. In this mission, there are 350 international and 200 local staff is on duty.

In 2011, CNN reported US Special Operations Commander Admiral William H. McRaven saying that the program needs to be extended beyond its original mandate, and to exceed 30,000 ALP members by 2015. Afghan Police was entrusted the following responsibilities:

Ensure law and order and individual security, take preventive actions to stop crime, arrest criminals, counter moral deviations, protect public and properties, fight against narcotic cultivation and smuggling and fight against terrorism and organized crime".[3]

NATO and the European Union states tried to increase the capacity of ANP and its sphere of operation. They think that the growth of ANP is on track to reach the target set to November 2012. The issue of literacy rate still needs attention as there are complaints from the local population against the treatment of the police. The police agencies falling under the Ministry of Interior of Afghanistan consisted of four pillars and two sub pillars. These pillars are comprised on Afghan Uniform Police, Border Police Force, Afghan National Civil Order Police (ANCO) and Anti Crime Police Force ACPF). Anti Crime Police (ACP) also includes General Directorate of Police

1  Cornelius Friesendore. *Paramilitarization and Security Sector Reform: The Afghan National Police, International Peace Keeping,* Vol. 18, No. 1, February, 2011.
2  Cornelia Schnelia, Afghan police through the ages: 250 years of change, October 2012.
3  *Ibid.*

Unites (GDPSU). The two sub pillars are Afghan Public Protection Force and Afghan Local Police.

We have four forces operating under the Ministry of Interior:
1 Afghan Uniform Police
2 Afghan Border Police
3 The Afghan National Civil Order Police
4 The Afghan anti Crime Police

Other Forces operating under the Interior Ministry are:
1 Crisis Response Unit – a national level counter terrorism police force.
2 Investigative and Surveillance Unit – a human intelligence based on human policing, countering improvised explosive devices.
3 Commando Force 333 – a counter insurgency police force.
4 Afghan Territorial Police Force 444 – also a counter insurgency police force.
5 Judicial Security Unit – a VIP protection force.
6 Afghan Public Protection Force – a force that takes responsibilities of private security agencies step by step.
7 Afghan Local Police
8 Afghan National Police "enablers", comprised of logistics, training general command, recruiting, medical, directorate of intelligence and fire fighting.
9 Provincial Response Companies are special police units.

Moreover, the police have several private partners on community level that counter insurgency and guard government installations. With the help of NATO, US and Germany, Afghanistan has now established a strong police. The strength of the ANP reached in April 2012, by 149,642 while more than 7,000 were undergoing training process. In 2012, trainees of the Afghan police were more than 1,000 while Primary Afghan National Police organizations include (March 2012): Afghan Uniformed Police (AUP): 84,000, Afghan Border Police (ABP): 22,200, Afghan Civil National Order Police (ANCOP): 16,500 and other forces comprised of 18,200 personnel.[1]

The United States and Afghanistan understand that building a capable force is important task to counter insurgency in the country. According to the department of defense report; the joint work of Afghanistan and the United States on building an effective police force:

> The United States and Afghanistan have worked to correct longstanding deficiencies. Other US commanders credit a November 2009 raised in police salaries (nearly doubled to about $240 per month for services in high

1 Lisa Saum-Manning, *Comparing Past and Current Challenges to Afghan Local Defense*. RAND Corporation, December 2012.

combat areas)-and the streamlining and improvement of the payments system for the ANP-with reducing the solicitation of bribes by the ANP. The
raise also stimulated an eightfold increase in the number of Afghans seeking to be recruited.[1]

The failure of building an effective police force in Afghanistan, international community proposed the strategy of establishing of local police
force to protect their communities. American commander, David Petraeus
supported and funded this force. Middle East Affairs specialist, Kenneth
Katzman in his report on post-Taliban governance in Afghanistan has analyzed the efforts of International community:

> The village stability operation concept began in February 2010 in Ar-
> ghandab district of Kandahar province. US Special Operations Force or-
> ganized about 25 villages into an armed neighborhood watch group, and
> the program was credited by US commanders as bringing normal life back
> to the district. The pilot program was expanded and formalized into the
> joint Afghan-US Special Operations efforts in which 12-person teams from
> these officers live in communities to help improve governance, security and
> development.[2]

A report published by an Afghan research and media organization funded
by the United Nations Development Program (UNDP) has some interesting
insights into how the people perception of Afghan National Police (ANP)
has changed over time. The torture of the local populace by the Local Police
and the use of the LPC to settle old enmities created more problems.[3]

Katzman described a different story about the function and performance
of Afghan Local Police:

> An outgrowth of the Village Stability Operation is the Afghan local Police
> Program in which the US Special Operations force conducting the Village
> Stability Operation set up and train local security organs of about 300 mem-
> bers each. These local unites are under the control of district police chiefs
> and each fighter is vetted by a local shura as well as Afghan intelligence. As
> of September 2012, there are about 16,000 ALP operating in over 60, differ-
> ent districts. There are three LPC centers in Helmand province. A total of
> 99 districts have been approved by the program, each with 300 fighters,
> which is expected to bring the target size of the program to about 30,000
> by the end of 2014.[4]

The controversial issue has been the Afghan Local Police (ALP). The ALP
program was approved by the government of Afghanistan in 2010 and since
then thousands of local people have been organized as local police forces at

---

1  In 2011, CNN, "US Special Operations Commander, Admiral William H. McRaven saying that
   the program is to be extended beyond its original mandate, and to exceed 30,000". ALP
   members by 2015.
2  "Allied Command Operations is a unified command of NATO forces based in Brussels,
   Belgium, is a political headquarters of the alliance." *Daily Outlook Afghanistan*, 2005.
3  *Afghanistan: Post Taliban Governance, Security and US Policy*, September-2012.
4  Kenneth Katzman. Afghanistan: *Post Taliban Governance, Security and US Policy*, September
   2012.

the village and local levels within a program being run by the US government and US-led NATO allies under the name of Village Stability Operation.[1]

In early 2012, people from various provinces protested against the Taliban attacks on their houses and shops. Due to a weak response of local authorities, they formed local militias to counter the Taliban insurgents in their districts and villages. Local groups like ALP played very important role in bringing stability to the villages.[9] The legal powers of ALP is limited compared the ANP powers. The ALP does not have power to arrest people but can detain people. ALP, no doubt, has been the hotbed of controversies. The Afghan Local Police does not operate alone; it works with other forces like US SOF (Special Operations Force), Afghan SOF, the ANA and ANP.

### REGIONAL COMMAND STRUCTURE OF THE AFGHAN NATIONAL POLICE

Afghanistan has been divided into North South, East, West and Central regions. These entire regions have regional command under the control of Interior Ministry of the country.

Commands:
1   Regional Command of Kandahar
2   Regional Command of Gardez
3   Regional command of Kabul
4   Regional Command of Mazar-e-Sharif.

Regional Training Centers:
1   Bamyan regional training center,
2   Jalalabad regional training center.
3   Gardez regional training center.
4   Kandahar regional training center,
5   Herat regional training center,
6   Mazar-e-Sharif regional training center,
7   Konduz regional training center,

In the above mentioned provinces, Afghan instructors provide training to the Afghan police including border police and highway police in order to protect civilian from criminals and Taliban attacks. The following courses are being taught in the centers of the above mentioned provinces:

1   Basic Course-1 (BCI): this is a nine month course which trains newly recruited police officers in the field of human rights, community policing, reporting, legal procedure, arms, defensive tactics, patrol, drug recognition and criminal investigation.

2   Basic Course-2 (BC2): This is a five week course which trains students in the same way.

---

1   *Daily outlook Afghanistan*, 4 June, 2013.

3   Basic Course-3 (BC3): This is a thirteen weeks teaching reading and writing course (how to read and write). Ministry of Education of Afghanistan helps these student in improving there abilities.

4   Transition Integrating Program: This a two week course which trains students in human rights, police tactics and policing.

5   Afghan Border Police: This is comprised of nine weeks. In this course, police operation and check point operation are being taught.

6   Highway Police: The highway police course is comprised of nine weeks. This course provides training in highway operation and defensive driving. Another course is comprised of five weeks where highway police operation and checkpoint operation are being taught.

THE OATH OF AFGHAN NATIONAL POLICE

I (swear by Almighty Allah/do solemnly and sincerely declare) that I will well and faithfully serve the government of Afghanistan, according to law as a police officer, that I will obey, uphold and maintain the law of Afghanistan, that I will perform the power and duties of my office honestly, faithfully and diligently, without fear of or favour to any person and, with malice or ill-will towards none, and that, I obey without question all lawful orders of those set in authority over me.

*(Ministry of Interior Affairs, Afghanistan).*

## CHAPTER 8. MARKETING TERRORISM AND THE IMPORT/EXPORT OF SUICIDE BOMBERS

Since our era is that of the fear market, where ignorance drives our thoughts and responses, every day we observe auctions in terror markets across the globe. These fear markets are exploited successfully because we do not do our homework. We have no specific counter-terrorism strategies, religious research and awareness in Afghanistan and Pakistan. We fight without planned strategies and gain nothing. Our children are being kidnapped, sold and used — dying in order to kill.

In 2013, a new video touting the appealing career of the suicide bomber appeared in Saudi Arabia that introduced a new trend of terrorism marketing in the Middle East. The video focused on a Saudi father selling his young son as a suicide bomber for the sectarian war in Syria. In a conference room of a hotel in Jeddah, Saudi Arabia, Mr. Abusaleh sold his son for just $40,000.

In Pakistan and Afghanistan, poor parents are also offering their children to die in order to kill. The way the Afghan Taliban designs their strategies for training and brainwashing suicide bombers is no different from the suicide techniques of Saudi and Pakistani Mullas in Waziristan regions. They peddle fear and terror, according to the market demand. If we deeply consider the terrorism marketing techniques of both the Afghan and Pakistani Taliban, we will observe a similarity in their way of killing.

In 2013, a suicide terrorist killed 81 people in Khyber Pakhtunkhwa province of Pakistan. They were gathered for prayer in church, when a suicide bomber attacked their ceremony early in the morning. In that incident, the Pakistani Taliban successfully marketed terrorism and fear. Moreover, in 29 December 2013, a female terrorist armed with explosives blew herself up at

Volgograd railway station in Russia. These suicide bombers were success-fully used as weapons of modern warfare.

In Pakistani madrassas, clerics belonging to the Salafi and Deobandi school of thought market terrorism in South Asia and the Middle East. They train young people and market them across the Asian continent. They sold their bombers in Syria and Afghanistan. During the last 12 years, thousands of children were kidnapped or recruited by the Taliban networks. They are being sold like commodities; a secret arms deal is no longer about a shipment of black market Kalashnikovs, but children.

Violence, extremism and radicalization have taken deep roots in Paki-stan, due to a mistaken set of beliefs about the true message of Islam. Poverty and the lack of freedom of expression are responsible for the growing num-ber of radicals. Politicization of religion, influence of the Arab religious cul-ture, and the institutionalization of sectarianism has developed a new form of religious belief.[1]

Radicalization of Pakistani students in universities, colleges and reli-gious schools poses a big challenge to the security of the state. Socio-eco-nomic conditions in Southern Punjab and FATA region forced poor parents to send their children to sectarian schools. This extremist infrastructure, widespread terror network of militant groups, and poor governance, have created the climate of fear and harassment in the country.[2]

Foreign and domestic investment has stopped. Investors are on the run and industrial firms are being shifting to Bangladesh. According to a recent report of the National Crisis Management Cell of the Interior Ministry of Pakistan, the province of Punjab is home to 400 extremist groups, who have gained a foothold in all major cities of Southern Punjab. They have deployed their forces in Southern Afghanistan for fight against the US and Afghan forces.[3]

Terrorist attacks carried out by Punjabi and Pashtun Taliban in broad daylight in Afghanistan, show that radicalization has fully gripped their minds and souls. They receive psychological satisfaction from the killing of non-Muslim or member of a rival sect. This violent method of practicing reli-gion has raised many questions in Pakistani society, as illegal and unauthor-ized fatwas issued on sectarian and political basis, have endangered the lives of writers, men of letters, political and religious leaders.

However, there are distinctive political, social, economic and geographic factors, including limited political institutionalization, ethnic, linguistic and sectarian divisions and, the slow process of national reconstruction,

---

1  Randy Borum. *Radicalization into Violent Extremism-II: A Review of Conceptual Models and Empirical Research.* Journal of Strategic Security.Vol-4, Number-4 Winter-2011.
2  *Daily Times*, 10 March 2010.
3  *Ibid.*

which fuel extremism and terrorism in a failed and dysfunctional state like Afghanistan.[1]

Prior to the Taliban years, the so-called Mujahedeen militias undermined the political, economic and national critical infrastructure of the country. Warlords tightened their control over the regional criminal market. The state was no longer fully functional. Poor and unemployed citizens lived without shelter. Terrorist groups carrying out attacks from safe havens within Afghanistan and Pakistan killed innocent people and recruited young children. Thousands of orphans children fallen prey to insurgent groups. Waziristan, FATA and parts of Afghanistan became terror-training centers.[2]

Pakistani extremist groups and the Taliban are increasingly relying on suicide attacks, to achieve major political objectives. Their members are willing to die to accomplish the mission and cause of maximum damage to the target. It is notable that most of the suicide bombers are teenagers, carrying out attacks against military targets.

The Taliban are targeting primary and secondary schools of boys and girls. Analysts believe that one of the reasons behind sabotaging schools is, keeping the children away from modem education. They use children in their terrorist attacks, seduce young people, and invite women to martyrdom. Once recruited and trained, they are threatened with dire consequences, if they refuse to blow themselves up. This is an established fact, that Taliban insurgents use human missiles and train young children for mass murder in Afghanistan.[3] On 17 May 2011, Guardian reported the arrest of an Afghan young man Noor Muhammad by the Taliban forces:

> The Taliban put a simple choice before him—either they would cut off his hands for stealing or he could redeem himself and bring glory on his family by becoming a suicide bomber, the newspaper reported.[4]

However, on 14 November 2010, Digital Journal reported German Brig. Gen. Joseph Blotz, (Spokesperson for International Security Assistance Force) about how the Taliban recruit 8th graders to become suicide bombers.[5] On 16 September 2011, Xinhua News Agency reported that the Taliban were recruiting young people for suicide attacks.[6]

---

1  T, Azeem Ibrahim. "Tackling Muslim Radicalization: Lesson from Scotland." *Report of Institute for Social Policy and Understanding*, June 2011.

2  *The Guardian*, 17 May 2011.

3  *Telegraph*, 01 January 2012.

4  *Xinhua News Agency*, 16 September 2011

5  On January 01 2012, *Telegraph*, "Afghan police arrested 9, 12 and 14 years old boys in Eastern Afghanistan. All the three boys were to be used in suicide attacks." *Digital Journal* also reported on 14 November 2010.

6  On September 16 2011 *Xinhua News Agency*, "Taliban recruit young people for suicide attacks. However, On 14 November 2010, *Digital Journal*, journalist KJ. Mullins reported German Brig. Gen. Joseph Blotz (spokesperson for International Security Assistance Force) about how the Taliban recruit 8th graders to become suicide bombers". *Daily the Sun* also reported on 04 February 2011.

---

On 4 February, 2011, the *Sun* reported about Taliban commander Qari Hussain, who brainwashes young children for suicide attacks within thirty minutes. On 18 April 2011, journalist Ashfaq Yousufzai reported the Taliban way of recruiting children aged 12 for suicide attacks.[1]

Moreover, in July, *Washington Times* reported Taliban men were buying children as young as seven years as suicide bombers to attack police and army targets: "The going price for child bombers ranges from $7,000 to $14,000, depending upon how urgently the bomber is needed and how close the child is expected to get to the target," the newspaper reported.[2]

On 01 January, 2012, *The Telegraph* reported Afghan police arrested 12 and 14 years old boys in Eastern Afghanistan. All the three boys were to be used in suicide attacks. Moreover, Afghan Interior Ministry admitted that some 25 more failed suicide bombers were under the custody of the police. According to a nine-year-old, Ghulam Farooq, his instructors told him that when they carried out suicide attacks, all the people around them would die but they would stay alive.[3]

On 2 December 2012, *The Wall Street Journal* reported Taliban coordinated attacks on key coalition base in Jalalabad, detonating series of car bombs. The attack began when Taliban set off three suicide car bombs outside the Forward Operation Base of International Security Assistance Force. On 04 March 2013, Bakhtar News Agency (State owned news agency) reported the arrest of six suicide bombers in Jalalabad-Torkham Highway. A 13-year-old suicide bomber was among them. The child told reporters that he was trained for suicide mission in Pakistan. Moreover, on 03 August, 2013, Express Tribune reported a powerful bomb blast occurred outside the Indian Consulate in Jalalabad city, killing 9 people and injured 22. This is not a single terror-related incident in the city; terrorist have reached everywhere in the province.

Well-trained suicide bombers explode themselves in mosques, imambargahs, (Shia mosques) churches, markets, military installations, police centers, public places, shrines and government offices. Suicide terrorism against political leaders, security forces or civilians has strategic as well as tactical objectives. Several suicide 'factories' in Pakistan and Afghanistan 'manufacture' suicide bombers for import and export purposes. In 2013, several suicide attacks on government and military installation were reported in local and international press.

*Radio Free Europe*, in October 2013, reported two police officers and one civilian were killed, when a suicide car bomber detonated his vehicle at the police station in Jalalabad. Officials confirmed the death of several

---

1  On 4 February, 2011, Daily the Sun, "Taliban commander, Qari Hussain, who brainwashes young children for suicide attacks within thirty minutes."
2  *Xinhua News Agency reported* on 16 September 2011.
3  *The Washington Times*. July 2009.

police officers and civilians. On 29 May 2013, AFP reported two terrorists attacked the Red Cross office in Jalalabad, who, later on killed one secu-rity guard inside the office. The attack came on the same day Afghanistan security forces killed six militants who stormed the Panjshir provincial governor office in Northern Afghanistan. On 04 January 2014, Associated Press reported Taliban attack on NATO base in Jalalabad. Taliban killed one soldier. NATO spokesman said a services member died following a sui-cide bomb attack, but did not identify the nationality of the soldier. Taliban spokesman, Zabihullah Mujahid claimed responsibility for the attack in an email to local newspapers.

The sacrifice of a suicide bomber is played out on the stage of political the-atre to an audience. Terrorist and Taliban forces in Pakistan and Afghanistan represent no specific ideology, sect or religion, other than killing innocent people. According to Centralasiaonline.com report, a young boy Zakaullah Khan was picked up by Taliban militants to their military based, showed him a video films of the training for suicide attacks. Khan, Centralasiaonline.com reported to be among 140 young militants who recently completed a de-radicalization course in Pakistan.[1]

The Taliban groups in Afghanistan disrupted every reconciliatory effort and infiltrated into Southern Pakistani Punjab as well. They received train-ing from Waziristan and, increasingly rely on suicide attacks to achieve major political objectives. Their members are willing to die to accomplish their mission and to cause maximum damage to military and civilian targets. These acts of suicide terrorism, whether directed against political leaders, security forces or civilians, have strategic as well as tactical objectives.

The business of import and export of suicide bombers in Pakistan is not a new thing. A police officer in Punjab province once told this author that the business of suicide bombers had recently flourished. In 2008, in Bhakkar dis-trict of Southern Punjab, he said a suicide bomber was purchased and used in a family dispute. In Tank district and in South and North Waziristan, several suicide-bombing academies recruit young people and export them to Afghanistan, Middle East and Gulf region.

In one incident, a teenager suicide bomber arrested in Karachi revealed information about the Taliban suicide schools for brainwashing of young men. Taliban teachers deliver lectures on religious issues to brainwash young men to join their ranks and carry out suicide attacks. These terror-ists are looking for young boys day and night. When they kidnap teenagers from schools, streets or parks, they start bargaining with the parents of the kidnapped children. They pay them three to ten thousand pounds sterling for one child.

---

1  *Centralasiaonline.* 2012.

Recent confirmed reports revealed the recruitment of more than 5,000 to 6,000 young suicide bombers, waiting for their turn in Waziristan and FATA region. *Long War Journal* revealed some terror centers have been established in eight districts of Kunar province. Afghan and Pakistani teenagers who were kidnapped by the Taliban for recruitment purposes, reached Karachi and Peshawar to carry out target killings and suicide attacks.1

Today, the trend of violence in Afghanistan that spans from suicide attempts to targeted attacks on Coalition forces and governmental installations, have now graduated into the political assassinations. The last series of such attacks that involved the killing of Afghan Peace Council's Chief, former President Burhanuddin Rabbani and the President's brother, and the other well-known officials are quite worrisome.

In the past, we have seen many instances in which soldiers and security personnel were arrested extending assistance to members of Taliban and other militant groups. As Dawn reported more than 50 children and men were found, shackled in the basement of a seminary off Super Highway in 2012. Senior Superintendent told reporters, that police raided Jamia Masjid Zakriya Kondali and recovered people whose ages ranged between 15 and 40.[2]

The Senior Superintendent of Police said they were drug addicts while the seminary's administration was running a detoxification unit. A signboard at the seminary said that drug addicts were treated there. Taliban groups in North Waziristan claimed they are running three secret camps close to the Afghan border, training potential suicide bombers numbering more than one thousand. "We have three facilities exclusively for suicide bombers. Each one has more than 350 men being trained in it," a Taliban instructor told Express Tribune.[3]

Recently, a Taliban-motivated terrorist killed the Kandahar police chief in an attack on the police headquarters in the provincial capital. In another incident, a Taliban suicide team attacked an Afghan police training facility in the east, killing three policemen and wounding five. Both civil and military officials in their statements to the press said that Baitullah Mehsud used to pay families up to one million rupees to get children as young as seven to serve as suicide bombers for the TTP or its subsidiaries.

In addition to those running and working for the seminary — who should have cases filed against them immediately — any parents who knew what was being done to their children and still consented to that treatment should also be charged. One US official went a step further and said, "The Taliban

---

1  *Daily Times*, 12 April 2011
2  As *Dawn*, "More than 50 children and men were found shackled in the basement of a seminary off Super Highway last year." *Long War Journal* also reported this incident on 21 April 2011.
3  *Dawn*, 13 December 2011.

leader has turned suicide bombing into a production output, not unlike [the way] Toyota outputs cars."

In April 2011, a suicide bomber killed 42 people in the settled district of Kohat, situated in Pakistan's insurgency infested northwest. Before this attack, two suicide bombers had killed 41 and wounded more than 65 in an attack outside a Sufi shrine in central Pakistan. Massod Ashraf Raja discusses both the mission of suicide bomber and drones attacks in Pakistan: "Suicide bombers and drones are products of dollars of tax payers' money that are deadly accurate and hit their targets very accurately and never miss; while the drones are directed by Sims that are planted by human Intelligence to direct the smart bombs".[1]

Afghan police in the border town of Spin Boldak, captured three suicide bombers (two Pakistanis and one Afghan), who were trained in Quetta. A top provincial security official in Kandahar province said, that they would be suicide bombers were around 15 years old, and were trained in Pakistan. In Afghanistan, the future of sectarian clashes or violence totally depends on how the people and the religious and political figures respond to this particular attack, and to any future ill intentions. The role of the neighboring countries will also have an important impact — especially the role of Pakistan and Iran, in this regard, will be crucial — and above all the role of the Afghan law enforcing agencies, is going to be very much crucial as well.

It is important that culprits behind such attacks should be found and they should be countered through strict measures. At present, Afghanistan is going through a very crucial period of its history. This period is going to decide the future developments in the country, to a large extent. A culture, that perceives martyrdom as a virtue, has the potential to incite people to do almost anything in certain situations. Terrorist organizations reap multiple benefits at various levels, without incurring significant costs. A successful suicide attack demonstrates complete dedication of the bomber to the cause of his group. He inspires others and adds legitimacy to the organization. Self-induced as well as externally induced motivation by an organization or its leader plays equally important roles in the making of a suicide bomber.

He commits suicide in retaliation, killing maximum number of people and motivating Afghan children to carry out a suicide attack against US forces. Leaders of the Taliban and Hezb-e-Islami motivate insurgents in the name of "Afghanistan's occupation" and the obligation to perform "Jihad." A Punjabi Taliban, arrested in Dera Ghazi Khan District in April 2011, revealed that more than 350 suicide bombers are trained in Mir Ali District of North Waziristan every year. In future, rival states may use suicide bombers in their import and export business.[2]

---

1  *Express Tribunes*, 18 April 2011.
2  *Indian Defense Review*, 03 April 2011.

Like Pakistan, Afghanistan has the same gory narrative of suicide terrorism, which started with the fall of the Taliban regime in 2001. The Afghan Taliban has set up several suicide training centers in North Eastern, Western and Southern parts of the country. They receive money from business communities based in Pakistan, Saudi Arabia and Dubai and kill people in Afghanistan and Pakistan.[1]

Warlords and criminal mafia, who run the illegal business of black market, have become formidably strong with the capture of political power in Afghanistan. Poverty and unemployment allow the Taliban to recruit young children. The Independent Human Rights Commission of Afghanistan (2008) reported the Taliban abuse of Afghan civilians. IRIN also reported the hardships faced by the poor Afghan children.[2]

Talking to a JRIN reporter, an Afghan child said, "I abandoned my education because there is no one in my house to work and support my family, after the death of my father. I have to work hard. Otherwise, I will be forced to beg on the streets, as there is no one to help us."[3]

Innocent Afghans are increasingly being targeted as part of an anti government struggle for control over population. The Human Rights Watch (2010) reported the brutalities of warlords, exerting their power on various Afghan communities.[4]

In 16 October 2009, Afghan TV AINA reported the concern of the people of Afghanistan over the political uncertainty in the country: "If we review the eight year war in the country, we reach to the conclusion that there is no change, whatsoever, in the fortunes of the citizens of Afghanistan. In fact, the Taliban and other anti government groups have stepped up attacks against the civilians, including attacks on schools and clinics, across the country".[5]

### MARKETING TERRORISM AND THE BUSINESS OF FEAR

The generators of fear are very strong in South Asia and Middle East. In Afghanistan, the marketing of terrorism is a profitable business. This business and terror market now flourishes in the Arab world, where parents offer their young children for suicide attacks. Terror market is run in different ways. If we deeply study the news stories of only one month suicide terror related incidents, we will find out that terrorists use different techniques of killing in the region.[6]

In print media, some stories appeared about the Pakistani, Afghani and Somali teenage suicide bombers who were captured during the military

---

1  *Daily Times*, 03 April 2011.
2  *The Independent Human Rights Commission of Afghanistan.* 2008.
3  *Ibid*
4  *Xinhua News Agency, and Time Magazine*, 03 May 2009.
5  In 16 October 2009, *Afghan TV AINA* "reported, the concern of the people of Afghanistan over the political uncertainty in the country".
6  *Ibid.*

operation in Swat, Bajaur and Somalia. They revealed an interesting story about the way suicide bomber is honored in mosques. While their training is completed, in the tail end, according to journalist Peter Chamberlin, suicide bombers are taken to mosques for congratulation for being chosen by God. On the day of the planned attack, they are heavily drugged which made them forgetful and stop crying for mother, brother and relatives. In Somalia, Sudan and Nigeria, young children are threatened when they refuse to carry out suicide attacks.[1]

Parents of such children are involved in the business terrorism marketing and fear. The cumulative effects of all these fear-generating mechanism, Terrell E. Arnold says, is a human condition closely akin to superstition. There is no proper strategy to deal with the caused suicide terrorism. The goal of marketing terrorism is tom create immediate change, instill panic and chaos.[2]

Terrorist organizations like al-Qaeda, Al Shabab, Boko Haram, the Taliban, Arab extremists and Takfiri Jihadists in Britain, Europe, Pakistan and Afghanistan, marketing fear and terrorism through Facebook, YouTube and Twitter, invite young people to join their networks and use various marketing techniques. These terror groups are marketers as well as consumers to a degree, and the recruiters, marketing young boys in the market. They supply suicide bombers across Asia and Middle East just for $20.000. Religious and political vendettas are being settled by using suicide bomber against rival group or family in Pakistan. This generation of fear and panic is controlled by extremist elements and non state actors, in Waziristan, Kabul and Quetta. Fear and terror marketing systems are updated every year and, new techniques are introduced time to time.[3]

Prominent American scholar Philip Bobbitt elucidated the way terrorism is marketed and says non state actors can be best described as terror marketers. On 17 February 2013, Dawn newspaper reported, Pakistani suicide bombers killed 90 innocent Hazaras in Quetta while Afghan suicide bombers attacked Afghan intelligence headquarters in Kabul. In these two incidents, terrorism was marketed in the same way.[4]

In Britain markets, videos and CDs of suicide terrorism are available and cheap—young Britons are the main customers. In these CDs, the way of suicide attacks, techniques of killings, religious zeal, accounts of events, explosion and the importance of time and distance have been described in detail. These CDs are being imported from Pakistan, Somalia, Algeria, Nigeria and Afghanistan, and sold in the streets of the country. Incidents in the past ten years indicate that Britain has long been an island under siege from terrorists, who believe they can advance their aim through acts of violence.

---

1 *The Human Rights Watch Report*, 2010.
2 *Aina Television of Afghanistan.* 16 October 2011.
3 Terrel E. Arnold. *Terrorism and the Fear Market*, Rense.Com.
4 *Dawn* 17 February 2013. Dr. Muhammad Taqi article. *Daily Times* on 29 January 2013.

The involvement of British citizens in ethnic and sectarian conflicts across Asia, Africa and the Arab World, raised many questions, when these young Britons are arrested by local counter terrorism police abroad. Recently, in such a case, on 10 January 2013, Scotland Yard arrested four Syrian British men, trying to join opposition forces in Syria, BBC reported. This is not the only case, official figures show that arrests for suspected terrorism offences rose by 60% in 2012. [1]

The competition of marketing terrorism among ISI, RAW and Afghan intelligence (NDS) has entered a crucial phase, as all intelligence and counter insurgency measures of international community failed to defeat Taliban insurgents in Afghanistan. In a recent report, Pentagon accepted intelligence failures and warned that without sweeping changes to intelligence gathering practices in Afghanistan, military success is impossible. Unfortunately, American and European intelligence agencies collect information about insurgents and their movements, through weak sources. The CIA and Pentagon are not satisfied with the cooperation of ISI's intelligence sharing, as the agency is not willing to help NATO, ISAF and Pentagon in countering the Taliban insurgency across the Durand Line. There are pro-Taliban and anti Taliban elements within the ISI networks that run the agency on adverse directions.[2]

---

1   *BBC*, 10, January 2013.
2   *Daily Times*, 29 January 2013.

## CHAPTER 9. AN INCOHERENT APPROACH TO THE WAR

After the fall of the Taliban government in Afghanistan, the United States did not focus on war against violent extremism, terrorism and al-Qaeda, the US and its allies instead focused on occupying Afghanistan. The US created international coalition to build Afghanistan under the mistaken assumption that al-Qaeda and its associated groups had been defeated and, it will contain China and control Pakistan and its proxies. These serious mistakes were, later on, felt by the Pentagon policy maker in Washington.

The US and NATO established an artificial state, which is unable to build a durable peace and extend its writ to the whole of the country. Their generals failed to bring stability, defeat Taliban and contain China. Their mission has had a lot of mistakes such as the killing of women and children in night raids. On 27 July 2010, ZNews reported the disappointment of experts in National Security Council of Afghanistan, about the incoherent approach of international community to the war against Taliban. Thousands of secret files released by WikiLeak backed Afghanistan's stance, that ISI provide safe haven for the terrorist outfits that kill innocent civilians in the country. In October 2013, Afghan President said the United State and UK had done little more than cause suffering, loss of life and no gains.

Pakistani scholar Syed Iftikhar, in his research paper posted at the FATA Research Center, has also urged that the approach of all stakeholders to the conflict in Afghanistan is incoherent. Syed understands that before the US invasion in 2001, the war in the country was confined within the border of Afghanistan, has now spilled over into the entire neighborhood. Now, the United States is fighting two Taliban groups; Afghani Taliban and Pakistani Taliban.

Afghanistan also understands that NATO and its allies approach to the war on terror is an incoherent. The Obama administration is changing its war strategies time and again, but all have failed. White House unveiled five strategies for Afghanistan in 2008, 2009, 2011, 2012 and 2013, to disrupt, dismantle and defeat the Taliban insurgency, but none of these proved successful.[1]

In March 2008, Obama announced his first strategy to win the hearts and minds of the people, but failed and met its defeat at the hands of 100 al-Qaeda terrorists and a few Taliban insurgents. Misunderstandings emerged between the US and NATO allies over the way the Taliban insurgency ought to be tackled. US President Barack Hussian Obama was in hot waters. He promised to improve governance and security, provide weapons to Afghan forces, make the forces self reliant, and press Hamid Karzai to expel corrupt officials from various ministries and departments in Afghanistan, but nothing changed.

In December 2009, the second strategy announced for defeating the Taliban militants in Afghanistan also failed. However, differences between the US, Pakistan persisted. Afghanistan welcomed the announcement of new strategy, but Pakistan opposed the deployment of more troops, claiming it would fully "convert the country into a battlefield.[2]

President Obama expressed concern over the emerging terror threats in both Pakistan and Afghanistan, but did not prefer any reasonable solution. "We will act with the full recognition that our success in Afghanistan is inextricably linked to our partnership with Pakistan," President Obama told cadets at the US military academy at West Point. All NATO and US efforts to modernize economy, industry and agriculture are doomed to fail without a strong security network. President Hamid Karzai should not be solely blamed, as the international community is equally responsible for the misadventures of Afghans, ill-prepared policies and military strategies.

Lack of concordance among the international coalition prevented the development of a unified strategy. Dr. Antonio Giustozzi has also pinpointed some sign of incoherent approach to the Afghan conflict in his recent report: "Much has been said on the role of opium in fuelling the conflict over the years. While it is evident that insurgents tax the drug trader their involvement in it is likely to have been overstated."[3]

Notwithstanding the propaganda of international community on the police success story, police building efforts encountered significant problems. The Coalition and ISAF are not following the rules and principles of post war reconstruction paradigms. They still rely on the support of war-

---

1  *The New York Times*, 02 December 2009.
2  *Daily Times*, 02 December 2009.
3  Antonio Giustozzi with Niamatullah Ibrahimi, *Thirty Years of Conflict: Drivers of Anti Government Mobilization in Afghanistan. 1978-2011,.* January 2012.

lords and their private armies. They protect warlords and provide funds to their soldiers, even it has established it own criminal militias in Afghanistan, use it in the Middle East and Persian Gulf region. Throughout 2013, Afghan Shias fight Afghan Sunnis in Syria. They fought in Libya and ruined the critical infrastructure of the country. In a post conflict society like Afghanistan, militancy, sectarian and ethnic loyalties pose grave threats to security. Common Afghans wonder, how peace can prevail if paramilitary forces are patronized, black-market economy flourishes, and the existing fragile state is not strengthened.[1]

A coherent approach was needed for the reorganization and reorientation of Afghan state institutions. Unfortunately, foreign aid has been politicized and some states are vying for their interests. Military and political interests of NATO and US, on the one hand, and of India and Pakistan, on the other are in clash. India trains Afghan forces, while US doesn't want a strong Afghan army. Reluctance of some European states to follow the US-led military policy further affects peace-building efforts. Some Afghan experts predicted a ten-year time frame for bringing the whole territory under government control, but how and who will do this? Afghan government needed an effective security apparatus, including an efficient police force for controlling its territory, but desertions fade away all hopes. Public finance should have been used for channelling both internal and external resources effectively, and spent accountably through a strong and organized accountability system.

In case of administrative control, the level of governance could be easily defined and coordinated. Some experts suggested market building and job availability for young unemployed Afghans, to prevent them joining the insurgency, or the narcotic industry, this was a good idea. International scholars often debated centralized vs. decentralized system of government in Afghanistan. The idea of a centralized state is applicable to a country where the government is in full control of its territory; therefore some warlords of Northern Alliance suggested de-centralized system of government for Afghanistan.[2]

In Afghanistan, the idea is easily implementable after a long civil war. The power vacuum enabled the warlords and the criminal mafia to control major state resources. Due to the lack of financial resources, writ of the Afghan state does not exist in half of the country. Civil war of 1990s and the present Taliban insurgency devastated large regions of Afghanistan. Settlement areas, agricultural and pastoral lands, and roads were laid with land mines. There are over one million land mines in parts of the country. An ordinary Afghan is now dependant on foreign aid. Afghan economy has shattered; criminalized and its statehood ruined. In such circumstances, economic reconstruction is impossible without the reconstruction of state institutions.

1 *Daily Times*, March 2011.
2 *Ibid.*

NATO and the US have not been able to provide protection to industrialists and the business community in Afghanistan. No one is willing to bring or transfer his/her assets into the country. Afghan nationalism ceases to exist. A minor political change in the country is sufficient to jeopardize the fake national unity. Ethnic violence is exacerbated in both the South and the North, and relations with neighboring states needed drastic improvement.[1]

Pashtuns feel more safe and respected in Pakistan than in Afghanistan. This is a big mistake on the part of the Afghan leaders, who have lost the confidence of their own people. Afghans needed an intelligent system of government, with its own revenue generation, legal economy and trade, and an indigenous army and police force. They needed to weed out warlords from the government and the state institutions. Main factors behind the present insurgency are high unemployment rate, poverty, and inhuman treatment of common citizens by American criminal private militias, who raid houses in nights and kill women and children.

Young, unemployed, starved, oppressed and humiliated people with no legal source of income join the Taliban force in the North and South. All dreams vanished and all hopes undermined as Taliban insurgents continued their war against foreign forces. According to some statistics, over forty percent people in Afghanistan are jobless. This high unemployment rate and poverty forced thousands of young people to cross border illegally into Iran and Pakistan. Other factors include al-Qaeda, narcotics, transport mafia, merchants and landowners, who regularly pay taxes to insurgents every year.

War study experts warn that continued violence and insurgency, will force peacekeepers to abandon political and economic ventures in Afghanistan. Uzbekistan, Iran, Turkey, Pakistan and Russia interfere through nonstate actors. Many Afghans believe that if the international community had not lost interest in 1990s, the present insurgency could have been avoided. The concept of building strong national institutions was not supported and, no rehabilitation program was facilitated. Internal migration increased and no specific housing strategy was outlined. Poverty increased and drug trafficking became the major source of income.[2]

Consequently, the Taliban insurgency took strong roots in Afghanistan. Insurgents challenged the writ of the state. The government lost control of most parts of the country. Afghan army leave several districts to Taliban insurgents every year, due the shortage of financial resources. The US, the NATO and their partners failed to establish a strong central government. This failure promoted the concept that, there is no legal enforcement mechanism to support the processes of democratization, peace and stability, and the reorganization of state institutions.

---

1 *International Crisis Group Report*, 02 November 2006.
2 *Afghanistan, Post Taliban Governance, Security and US Policy.* 2012.

A major decisive factor behind the undefeated insurgency is Pakistan's refusal to fight the Afghan Taliban. According to the *Wall Street Journal* report, Pakistani officials declared that their first priority was to consolidate the control of South Waziristan and FATA. Pakistan fears that the US may further destabilize the country, by enraging the 27 million Pashtuns in NWFP and FATA.[1]

A recent Critical Threat Project of the American Enterprise Institute for Public Policy Research revealed that Pakistan is unwilling to attack or destroy the headquarters of Haqqani networks in North Waziristan, Quetta Shura in Baluchistan, and the Gulbuddin terror network in NWFP. NATO military command has taken seriously the close association between the Pakistan and the Afghan Taliban. *Dawn* reported US General David Petraeus alleged that Pakistan provides military assistance to the Afghan Taliban. The US General urged, in the MANAMA discussion of December 13, 2009, that Pakistan needed to put pressure on the leadership of the Afghan Taliban. The US is in trouble. It has lost the confidence of the people of Afghanistan. While skills of Taliban fighters in the South have improved.[2]

President Karzai accuses Pakistan army and its intelligence agencies for supporting the Taliban with money, military supplies and strategic planning guidance. General Stanley McChrystal, highlighted the increasing clout of the Taliban after eight years of continuous struggle. In his comprehensive report The General, has accepted his failure:

> Mullah Omar has appointed shadow governors in most provinces of Afghanistan, levies taxes, establishes Islamic courts there and conducts a formal review of his military campaign each winter.[3]

*The New York Times* reported that Mullah Omar was in permanent contact with his troops. Taliban launched a website in various Asian and European languages. Despite American criticism, Pakistan army refused to open a new front against the Afghan Taliban in Pakistan. Misunderstandings between these two states portend troubles for the Obama government. Disagreements over military action against the Afghan Taliban and surveillance of American citizens in Pakistan cities, further exacerbated distrust between the two states. General Stanley McChrystal said, he had evidence of Pakistan's support for the Afghan Taliban.[4]

Pakistan has reservations about the Indian presence in Afghanistan, but Kabul and Washington refused to hear it. The military establishment and religious circles in Pakistan are worried at the growing Indian influence in

---

1  *Wall Street Journal*, 16 December 2009.
2  *Dawn*, "US General David Petraeus alleged that Pakistan provides military assistance to the Afghan Taliban". 10 September 2011.
3  *The New York Times*, 23 September 2009.
4  *New York Times* reported that Mullah Omar was in permanent contact with his troops and launched a Taliban website in various Asian and European languages. 3 September 2009.

Afghanistan. They repeatedly accused India for using Afghanistan as a terror base against Pakistan. In a recently published article, Pakistan's former army Chief, Gen Mirza Aslam Baig, called Afghan Taliban the military strength of Pakistan. He totally rejected the involvement of the Afghan Taliban in terror incidents in Pakistan and, contended that they are friends of Pakistan. Pakistan is satisfied that the Afghan Taliban is fighting for a great cause. They are Mujahedeen (Holy Warriors) and occupy an important place in the foreign policy of Pakistan.[1]

The *Times of India* reported Taliban's letter sent to the Shanghai Cooperation Organization demanding the intervention of member countries, in resolving the Afghan conflict. The letter, written in Pashto language, was an attempt by the Taliban, who run their government in Southern Afghanistan, to exploit the US differences with China and Russia. The letter, published by the Chinese official media, requested, "We count on the SCO to assist countries in the region against colonialists and adopt a stance against the occupation of Afghanistan."[2]

Another jolt to the US strategy in Afghanistan was the news of Britain's possible withdrawal from Afghanistan, which caused deep concern among policy makers in Kabul and London. In November 2009, Prime Minister Gordon Brown hinted at the possible withdrawal, but did not fix a specific date for it. Some organizations in the UK started surveying various cities to know how a common citizen views this decision. BBC reported most people supported the UK withdrawal from Afghanistan.[3]

The United Kingdom hosted an Afghan Conference on January 28, 2009 in London, which highlighted the previous achievements of the international community, and took stock of what Britain lost and gained in the war on terror in Afghanistan.[4]

On January 28, 2010, delegations of over sixty countries attended the London Conference on Afghanistan. The conference was co-chaired by Prime Minister Gordon Brown, President Hamid Karzai and the UN Secretary General. Old promises were renewed and new hopes raised. The conference, however, like its predecessors, could do little more than repeated gory stories of the sick, unemployed, poor, oppressed and vulnerable people of war-torn Afghanistan.[5]

What about the pledges of the previous London, Tokyo, Paris and Bonne conferences to eradicate poverty, insecurity and unemployment? Poverty and unemployment are on the rise and, Territory is being lost to the Taliban, cold war between US and the Karzai government has intensified and the

---

1   *Dawn*, December 13, 2009.
2   *Times of India*, 16 October.2009.
3   *South Atlantic News Agency*.05 September 2009.
4   *Spiegel Online*, 29 January 2009.
5   *The Guardian*, 28 January 2010.

process of the partition of the state has begun. What happens then, ultimate failure? The conference discussed security, governance, reconstruction and narcotics. They vowed to improve governance but failed. They promised to bring stability but failed. Instead of carrying out the process of reconstruction, they destroyed critical infrastructure in various parts of Afghanistan.[1]

The US presence in Afghanistan and its drone attacks in Waziristan and FATA are deemed a major security threat. The London Conference repeated old promises and agendas. It couldn't change the fate of Afghanistan. In Tokyo, Paris and London in the past, commitments were made, funds were allocated, and strategies were prepared to establish peace, security and the writ of the government across the country. All the above mentioned failures were the consequences of incoherent approach to the Afghan conflict. The US military strategy suffered from serious internal contradictions. Its military success becomes a fiction.

Currently, the Afghan National Army is facing weapon shortage holding territory on their own, to say, nothing their ability to capture new territory independently. Worse still, Afghan army is abandoning their posts shortly after US forces leave them in Afghan hands. Afghan president disagreed with the key pillars of the COIN campaign. Once Afghan Security Forces became strong in number and get sophisticated weapon, their first priority would be to fight the occupation forces in near future.

---

1  *Daily Outlook Afghanistan*, 17 January 2010.

# CHAPTER 10. WAR ON TERROR IN A FAILED AFGHAN STATE

Throughout its history, state building efforts in Afghanistan were doomed to failure. The state also has no history of self-sustained development; it never depended on revenues generated by its own ownership class and remained a *rentier* and a tribal state having conflicting legal, cultural and political systems.[1]

In 2001, after the terror attack in US, a perception developed that failed and rogue states are a danger to world peace. Some scholars warned that state failure can cause serious security threats and rise to non state actors. State failure, according to Paul D. Miller, typically causes neighboring states to increase spending on their defense, which can trigger regional arm race. This happened in Pakistan due to the failure of state in Afghanistan.

In political science, there are three categories of states: fragile states, crisis states and failed states. Fragile states are susceptible to crises in one or more of their systems. Crisis states are under acute stress where institutions are unable to manage conflicts and economic crisis, and failed states are considered to be collapsed states at all levels — states that cannot perform their basic duties with no control on their territory. Failed states are tense, deeply conflicted and contested by warring factions. Afghanistan can be fixed into the third category of states.[2]

Author Robert I. Rotberg has defined failed states in a few words:

> Civil war that characterized failed states usually stem from or have roots in ethnic, religious, linguistic, or other inter-communal enmity. The fear of

---

1  Robert I. Rotberg, *Failed States, Collapsed States, weak States, Causes and Indicators*.
2  *Tribune*, 17 December, 2010 and also see, *Xinhua*,, March 27, 2009.

the "other" that drives so much ethnic conflict stimulates and fuel hostilities between regimes and subordinate and less favored groups.[1]

In failed states, like Afghanistan, revenues retrieved from criminal trade and the containerized market economy fosters several ethnic and sectarian non-state actors. Later on, these groups challenge the authority of the state, defeat the state and establish their own states within the state. Today in Afghanistan, the state is divided in three parts; the Taliban-controlled provinces, The Northern Alliance warlords-controlled provinces in Northern Afghanistan, and Kabul-controlled (by President Hamid Karzai and his friends).

On the issue of state and nation building and US foreign policy, a Cambridge scholar, Jeremy Allouche (2009) has stressed "nation building", not "state building", or more precisely, the combination of state building and nation-making missions. Anyhow, coming to the basic argument, we need to highlight some aspects of the Afghan government and state institutions.

Though the present Afghan government comprises a wide range of formal bodies at the presidential, municipal, community, provincial, district and parliamentary level, all these bodies have conflicting roles and duties. One of the key compulsions to strengthen the present administrative system is, the absence of a professional policy network regarding the institutional structure. Moreover, weaknesses in the human resource system, an absence of functioning systems and a reliable national critical infrastructure caused stagnation.[2]

Administratively speaking, the present Afghan government has divided the country into 34 provinces, 364 districts and 40,000 villages, but the administrators of most of the provinces and districts have their own designed administration, which does not accept instructions from the central government. In districts and municipalities, no election has yet been held for formal government offices at village level. Many of these villages are instead self-governed by a combination of village elders and local councils, who act as intermediaries between the communities and governors.[3]

The present way of state building at sub-national level has been characterized by the lack of a sub-national governance policy. Some experts understand that state building as an effort to increase the value of state actors in governance systems and, to shift governance towards government. This will give the government strength to reform institutions, but the case is different here; government has lost control of most parts of the country, it lost the trust of citizens and international partners. Most the administrators are illiterate and have no basic knowledge of governance. The low level of

1 Robert I. Rotberg, *When States Fail: Causes and Consequences*, Princeton University Press.
2 Antonio Giustozzi with Niamatullah Ibrahimi, *Thirty Years of Conflict: Drivers of Anti Government Mobilization in Afghanistan*. 1978-2011. January 2012.
3 *Ibid.*

Afghan bureaucratic capacity is being addressed in different ways, but those are mostly misguided.[1]

There are approximately 500,000 government employees in Afghanistan, but most of them have no basic or formal education. As there is no civil services academy in the country: key appointments are being made on political bases. Warlords and war criminals have their own share in government institutions. In 2011, government decided to implement a merit-based policy for senior posts, but internal and external power players sternly opposed it. The state is now ultimately shrunken, defeated and in retreat, due to a tenacious resistance from non-state actors.[2]

In 2012, Juma Khan Humdard, the Governor of Paktika province, complained against the discriminatory policies of the central government. A lack of loyalty to the central government by some provincial governors and ethno-sectarian non-state actors has left a significant impact on all state institutions. The above-mentioned alleged war criminals and the present state-sponsored mafia groups have mostly been loyal to regional power brokers, drug mafia, terrorist bands and sectarian forces since 1992.[3]

Afghan society had to collect its shattered pieces during the last three decades without the presence of a legitimate and functioning state, but internal migration, power games and foreign interference faded away all dreams. Civil war has destroyed the state, its institutions, and devastated economy. The mujahedeen and Taliban in the 1990s did not discriminate between innocents and criminals in the course of fighting in Kabul. From 1992 to 1994, Gulabuddin Hezb-e-Islami and Ahmad Shah Massoud killed over 60,000 men, women and children in Kabul alone. The rise of the Taliban in 1994, kept the war going on as they started their business with a new strategy of killing, abduction and humiliation. The criminal structure that fuelled the civil war is still in place.

War criminals and factional leaders remain in positions of power within society and continue to maintain criminal militia networks. A source from the Afghan Defense Ministry informed this author, that leaders of the Northern Alliance in and outside the government have begun to stockpile arms and take other steps to prepare for a future civil war. Some experts understand that after the withdrawal of foreign forces from Afghanistan in 2014, the US-backed regime will collapse and the civil war might be worse than that in the 1990s, when the Soviet army left the country. Kabul will be dominated by violence and torture. The Taliban will return with renewed vengeance.[4]

The issue of the adjustment of various ethnic colors in the tribal structure of the country has never been discussed on government level. The Dur-

---

1 Elizabeth, Sellwood, *State Building and Political Change*, New York University.2011.
2 *Revolutionary Association of Women for Afghanistan*, 2008 and 2001 Reports.
3 *BBC*, 05 February 2013.
4 *MANAMA Conference* 13 December,2009 report.

ranis ruled the country for centuries, but brought nothing to the lives of poor Afghans, therefore, the only solution to the century's old conflict was a fair election. The Durranis denied elections and kept the country poorer, illiterate and divided. Warlords in Northern Afghanistan and some elements in the Karzai administration, demand decentralization system of power, but suggest partition on ethnic lines will bring stability to the whole region.

In May 2012, the United States signed a strategic agreement with Afghanistan and proposed the removal of the Durand Line between Pakistan and Afghanistan. US General David Petraeus proposed the elimination of the international boundary between Pakistan and Afghanistan. The Durand Line divides Pashtuns between Pakistan and Afghanistan. When Pakistan became independent in 1947, it declared Durand Line its international border.[1]

In the past, Afghan rulers tried to settle the issue by offering Pakistan some sort of secret recognition of the border as an internationally recognized border. President Daud in a Shalimar Bagh ceremony gave Zia-ul Haq the same offer. The recent Plans B and C for the ethnic division of Afghanistan began a new debate in both US and Europe. Plan C, worked out by Tory MP and Foreign Office aide Tobias Ellwood, proposed the partition of Afghanistan into eight kingdoms (Kabul, Kandahar, Heart, Mazar-e-Sharif, Kunduz, Jalalabad, Khost and Bamyan). This plan enraged some elements in the corrupt Afghan administration.[2]

Mr. Ellwood warned that Afghanistan would face a bleak future after the withdrawal of NATO forces. According to newspapers reports, this plan was presented by the British Foreign Minister William Hague and discussed with US administration. On 9 September, Mr. Ellwood shared his plan with Pakistani officials in London. In Kabul, US ambassador to Afghanistan denied the plan to break up Afghanistan as part of a peace deal with the Taliban, but some of my friends in both the Defense and Foreign Ministries in Kabul confirmed the plan and said the game has started.[3]

Former Indian diplomat and writer M. K. Bhadrakumar in a recent article doubted the security transition process in Afghanistan and said thing have come to a pass that the NATO can no longer trust the Afghan army. A British film maker warned:

> I think that various warlords will once again have their fiefdoms and that this will be exacerbated by the reduction in foreign aid. I think Afghanistan will disappear from our newspapers.[4]

1   Bob Woodward, *World Security Network. McChrystal, More Forces or Mission Failure.*21 September,2009.
2   *Dawn*, October 26, 2001.
3   http//www.veteranstody.com/2010/06/18/general-mirza-aslam-beg-america-and-the-future-of-afghanistan-and-Pakistan/
4   Indrani Baghchi, *Taliban Political Ace: A Letter to Shanghai.* TNN-16 October, 2009.

Security situation is volatile across the country. Stability in a country necessitates the people accepting the state authority and trusting its institutions. Unfortunately, Afghan nation is fragmented and scattered. There is no national consensus on security issues. Propaganda machinery starts working when the government tries to engage the Taliban in peace talks. National concordance disappeared. There is a dire need for nation building in the country. Nation building barely materialized.

In December 2013, the removal of two words, "Afghan" and "religion," from the National ID Card, caused ethnic conflagration across the country. Pashtuns rejected the plan while some minorities supported it and said they are not Afghans, they are Khurasanis. Some televisions channels screened anti state programs and interviewed ethnic minority leaders who urged the division of the state on an ethnic basis, while some criticized the discriminative behavior of the Karzai regime towards minorities. The flames are now slowly spreading out from the North and spread to South and West.

Peace building is normally conducted as a single, undivided mission. At one time, the coalition forces were fighting the Taliban and al-Qaeda simultaneously, yet strived for a long-term peace process. These are two conflicting strategies in a war-torn country. Consequently, there is neither a real war nor a real peace effort. Most peace building efforts help re-build a state that has collapsed due to civil war. In Afghanistan, however, the case is different; the US removed the Taliban government by force, and is now trying to install a government of its choice by force.[1]

Bad governance or mis-governance is the main factor behind the frustration of civilian population in Afghanistan. Poor eradication of narcotic drugs is another factor, which supports insurgency and causes alienation in the country. Al-Qaeda finances the entire network in Pakistan and Afghanistan. Corrupt governance is now going to cost both NATO and Afghans. The lives of Americans, Europeans, Pakistanis, Indians and Afghans are in constant danger.[2]

In fact, the Bush and Obama regimes never devised a clear-cut military strategy for Afghanistan. Bush worked in many different directions; teaching a lesson to Pakistan, undermining al-Qaeda, containing China and empowering war criminals in all provinces of Afghanistan. An uneasy balance was created between counter terrorism and counter insurgency. There were many alliances between the US and warlords on the one hand, and warlords, war criminals, narco dealers and corrupt Afghan mafia, on the other.

Military experts warned that the former Jihadist leaders, who have their own private armies supporting either the International Coalition or the Taliban, are controlling a major portion of Afghan army and the police. Afghan army lacks discipline and organization of a regular army. At the same time,

---

1  Telegraph, 19 July 2008.
2  *Telegraph*, February 2011.

it has none of the good qualities of a tribal army. The US army is doing its own business. Some 30% of army soldiers are doing civilian jobs. That is why General McChrystal called repeatedly for help to improve the security situation in Afghanistan. He called for a unified strategy.[1]

To pressure Pakistan, the Chairman of the US Joint Chiefs of General Staff, Admiral Mike Mullen, visited Islamabad and asked General Kayani to 'do more'. Newspapers reported Admiral Mullen's visit to Pakistan as a growing US impatience with Pakistan. He complained of the inability of the government, to clear insurgents from safe havens bordering Pakistan from where they carry out lethal attacks against American and Allied forces, in neighboring Afghanistan. Admiral Mullen told General Kayani, "We all have a sense of urgency about this. We are losing people."[2]

Later on, General Kayani and General Pasha brought new proposals to Kabul. Fighting insurgencies on their respective soils, leaders of both the states realized that political and military confrontation is not in their interest. Realizing Pakistan's importance in the reconciliatory process in his country, Afghan President visited Islamabad and returned home with a new message. The visit of Afghan President to Islamabad was being viewed as a great success to revive Loya Jirga for evolving a common strategy on supporting the Kabul Reconciliation Plan.

Karzai gave concrete assurance to Pakistan that his country will not be used as a terror training ground against Pakistan, who has a genuine concern over the presence of India in Afghanistan.

To keep Pakistan safe and end the ongoing Taliban insurgencies in both the states, Islamabad reacted speedily to the peace efforts in Afghanistan. Discussions between the two in Islamabad and Kabul reflected a thawing of relations between them. Pursuing the efforts for a permanent settlement, Mr. Mullen met President Hamid Karzai, while General Pasha and General Kayani were trying to prepare an effective prescription for curing the economically ill Afghanistan.[3]

The cost of the Afghan war is getting increasingly prohibitive. At present, the US spends about $ 120 billion a year with an internal deficit of one trillion dollars, while government in Afghanistan is widely seen as corrupt. People do not trust either the US-led forces or the Karzai regime.[4]

Non-Pashtuns are wary of any deal between Karzai and the Taliban that might strengthen the Pashtun hegemony. Warlords in the North have gone filthy rich. They run black market economy and criminal trade across the country. They have established their own private armies which provide security to the coalition forces. Many in Afghanistan are skeptical of the progress

---

1  *The Guardian*, January 28, 2010.
2  *Daily Outlook Afghanistan*, 30 January 2010.
3  *Daily Mail*, January 31, 2013.
4  *The Washington Post*, 04 March 2011.

cited by the US military commanders. The level of violence in the country, which usually dips in the winters, remains higher than the previous years. Rampant government corruption persists that undermines public support.[1]

Afghanistan's six neighbors and its regional partners, all have a stake in the country's future after 2014. Pakistan is the most influential country. Regional and neighboring states have often tried to create problems for Afghanistan. They helped various ethnic and sectarian groups for their own national strategic interests. Without finding an acceptable balance between the interests of all ethnic and sectarian communities, internal power politics will continue in future.

1  *Ibid.*

CHAPTER 11. AFGHAN INTELLIGENCE, THE INTELLIGENCE WAR
AND INTELLIGENCE FAILURE

Normally, good intelligence management begins with a professional way
of intelligence gathering and analysis and, proper determination of what
needs to be known. When data is collected, that is evaluated and transformed into a practical form; this is the way professional intelligence works.
Unfortunately, CIA and NATO intelligence management has badly failed as
they could not recognize the major causes of the resentment of Afghan army
towards their forces in Afghanistan. Afghan intelligence agencies are suffering the same disease. They have no proper information analysis center where
collected information is analyzed, processed and specified.

In the past 30 years, no intelligence reforms have taken place in Afghanistan. During the cold war, intelligence community in the country witnessed
no changes in gathering and processing intelligence information. KHAD still
uses the KGB way of intelligence collection. The basic function of Afghan
intelligence is to protect the country from terrorism and foreign aggression.
But unfortunately, the way Afghan intelligence function is neither traditional nor professional. NDS, KHAD and RAMA have never tried to improve
the professional capabilities of their networks.

Afghan secret agencies disseminate disinformation and provide different
kinds of intelligence to ethnic and sectarian leaders. They also leak secrets
of the state, cabinet meetings, Presidential palace and ANA quarters. Most
workers in these agencies have come from minority ethnic groups based in
Northern Afghanistan. There are people within the agencies who have no
knowledge of intelligence—they just passed a primary test in KGB training centers in 1980s. Afghan intelligence agencies, specifically, military intel-

ligence has only focussed on the activities of Pashtun commanders, officer and soldiers on the pretext that they may have established close links with Taliban insurgents. This is a dangerous trend in a country where civil war has already disintegrated the state.

The failure of these intelligence agencies in the war against terrorism and their ethnic and sectarian affiliations and loyalties, have badly affected military strategies and counter insurgency measures of NATO and US intelligence infrastructure. Secret political and military reports are being sold into the hands of war criminals, regional states and the Taliban insurgents. Because, the significance of recent developments in intelligence practice areas is still not fully understood by Afghan officers, working in police and intelligence departments. The secret war in Afghanistan brings to light the full role of the CIA in arming Afghan Mujahedeen. American intelligence still uses the services of war criminal militias in collecting intelligence information in the country. Private security firms comprised of US, UK and Afghan warlords are now natural part of the war game in Afghanistan.

International terrorism remains a vital threat to national security interests. The Taliban insurgency and al-Qaeda and their intelligence organizations are too advanced in retrieving secret information about the enemy. Author of "Intelligence and Intelligence Analysis", Mr. Patrick F. Walsh has analyzed intelligence cooperation between five most powerful states:

> The greater achievement of British intelligence and their domination around the world gives us new information about the collection of intelligence in war and peace. Britain has the most advanced intelligence network operates on different directions. Wartime intelligence cooperation between the five allies (Australia, Canada, New Zealand, the United Kingdom and the US), particularly between the America and the UK, set the stage for common approaches and cooperation during the cold war period. Wartime technological advancement such as signal intelligence (sigint), overhead imagery and counterintelligence also produced greater modernization, specialization and cooperation between the national security intelligence communities in the five countries. These intelligence arrangements became even more formalized in the cold war period, starting with 1946 UK/US communication intelligence agreement, where the five countries agreed to share their sigint collection efforts with each other. This agreement stipulated the following sigint agencies would share intelligence: the National Security Agency (US), Government Communication Headquarters (UK), Communications Security Establishment (Canada), the Government Communication Security Bureau (New Zealand and the Defense Signal Directorate (Australia).[1]

Former Director General of Indian Intelligence Service (RAW) Major General VK Singh (2007) in his recent book has termed intelligence the second oldest profession, while Professor Sir David Omand views intelligence

---

1 Patrick F. Walsh, *Intelligence and Intelligence Analysis.*

as a tool required by state policymakers to further their national interests. In his well-written book on intelligence, Michael Herman has defined intelligence as a set of permanent institutions dating back to the 19th century.[1]

Writing on traditional intelligence mechanisms in Afghanistan is a difficult task, as there is little information in the public domain. In this chapter, an addition to philosophical and technical argument, I will try to elucidate some facts about the way intelligence operates in Afghanistan. A prominent British security expert and former Director General GCHQ, Professor David Omand views intelligence differently:

> "Intelligence as a trade has been gradually becoming a profession over the last 100 years." About the UK and US intelligence community, he warns, "The cry has gone up that intelligence analysts lack imagination. They failed to connect the dots that could have provided warning of terrorist attacks."[2]

National interests are more important for an intelligence man in the field. Every spy agency goes outside the law in reaching its goal, but author Edward Lucas views it from different perspective:

> Espionage involves breaking laws, perhaps of your own country, more often of its allies and certainly in the country being spied upon. The reason is simple. Secret information may come through dedication and inference or from exploitation the other side's carelessness by bluff and subterfuge. But the blunt fact is that for the most part secrets must be stolen. This means instigating treachery, using bribery, burglary, blackmail or outright violence as necessary.[3]

As we have experienced the failure of intelligence in the Afghan conflict in the past, we also experienced the failure of KHAD and NDS in countering insurgency in the country, because most of the provincial chiefs of Afghan intelligence are illiterate, who have no basic knowledge of counterinsurgency, and intelligence information process. In 2006, once I met a mullah in Kabul, who later on, became an intelligence chief of three Eastern provinces (Jalalabad, Kunar and Nooristan), who told me that the main source of his networks to collect intelligence information is farmers. Because, he said, his agent were unable to travel to villages and district headquarters The rate of corruption is very high while there is no accountability system to control the unaccountable rogue elements within the intelligence infrastructure. Every intelligence chief, before leaving NDS and KHAD offices, transfers large sums of money into their personal accounts from secret funds and purchases properties in US, Europe and Dubai.

---

1  General VK Singh, *India's External Intelligence*. Manas Publication.2007.
2  Sir David Omand, *Securing the State*, 2011.
3  *Daily Times*, 18 December 2012.

In her *Foreign Policy* article, Candace Rondeaux gives some details about the failure of Afghan intelligence in countering Taliban and foreign intelligence networks:

> Meanwhile, growing concern among NDS leaders about increased infiltration of insurgents and Iranian and Pakistani double agents within their ranks has resulted in the reported arrests of little more than a dozen NDS officials in the last year. These problems have been known for some times but only really started turning heads at the headquarters of the International Security Assistance Force (ISAF) when in April 2012 the NDS failed to accurately analyze scads of tips about an impending attack on Kabul that was billed as one of the largest in the entire year. Conflict between Pashtuns and primarily Panjshiri Tajik dominated officer corps of the NDS has been cited as among the main reasons that information about that attack did not reach the right people in the right time in Kabul.[1]

In all democratic nations, intelligence agencies are under the control of government and accountable to law, but in Afghanistan, intelligence is out of control and above the law. Lack of accountability, institutional and parliamentary supervision in Afghanistan has done more harm to the state. Unfortunately, in parliament level or at any other political and governmental forum, the issue of torture and atrocities of intelligence agencies, against the citizens have never been raised.[2]

Director General Indian Intelligence (RAW) Major General VK Singh describes the check and balance system in intelligence infrastructure of a country:

> Intelligence and security agencies exist in all nations. However, they suffer from peculiar diseases. After sometimes, they become so big that they after devour their creators. This phenomenon occurs more often in totalitarian regimes or military dictatorship than in democracies, when the other organs of the state — legislature and judiciary — and the fourth estate act as a check on the executive. Without this system of check and balance, there is a great danger of intelligence and security agencies becoming a law into them.[3]

In his report about the failure of intelligence operations in Afghanistan, Major General Michael T. Flynn urged that intelligence analysis play vital role in fighting insurgency in Afghanistan. We have numerous stories of intelligence failure and successes in peace and war, but the recent stories of intelligence failure in Afghanistan need to be highlighted in detail. As we all know, the way of operation and concept of intelligence has ultimately changed after the 9/11 and US invasion of Afghanistan, but National Director-

---

1 *Ibid*
2 Major General VK Singh, Director General RAW, *India's External Intelligence.*
3 Major General Michael t Flynn, Pentagon Report: "Fixing Intelligence: A Blue Print of Making Intelligence Relevant in Afghanistan". *Daily Times*, 29 December 2012.

ate of Security (NDS) and its sister agencies still follow the traditional Russian models of intelligence mechanisms, information gathering and analysis.[1]

Afghan intelligence agencies and their way of operation, way of investigation and information gathering is no more working effectively in countering the Taliban insurgency. They have never been able to collect reliable military information from the Southern and Eastern parts of the country. They have no access to information in Pashtun provinces like Kunar, Nooristan, Logar, Paktia and Khost, as most of their members are non Pashtuns and are confined to their headquarters. They have no access to remote areas, to collect intelligence information and establish close contacts with local population.[2]

National Directorate of security (NDS) operates in Kabul and parts of Southern and Northern Afghanistan. It is comprised of more than 30 departments mostly based in Northern provinces. People working in all intelligence agencies of the country including NDS are more than 35,000 while its private informers are thought to be over 50,000. NDS enjoys full legal powers; it investigates, detains and prosecutes and judges suspects. Intelligence officials in Kabul say they are aware of ethnic and sectarian loyalties within the agencies, but trying to improve the operational capabilities, information process and ethnic concordance.[3]

In the case of NDS and KHAD, we have experienced the same thing in the past and, at present, they are free to arrest, kill and torture any Afghan citizen if they want. Media is under their control, while from 2010 to 2012, on several occasions, they banned media from broadcasting live images of tortured Afghans in their private secret prisons. Editor in Chief of a major Afghan daily newspaper (*Daily Outlook Afghanistan*), Dr. Yasa Hussain was called to the NDS office in 2013, harassed, abused and forced to leave the country. He his family was threatened of dire consequences. His brother, Mr. Kazim Ali Gulzari was also forced to leave the country. The issue of missing journalists still needs to be investigated. KHAD and NDS forcefully make disappear innocent Afghans, keep them underground and torture them to death.[4]

The influence of foreign intelligence agencies, warlords, war criminals and ethnic and sectarian leaders in Afghan intelligence is matter of great concern. Foreign influence in their ranks and file raises many questions; while it is on the record, that intelligence agencies of neighboring states fund their favorite officers within the NDS. Experts say that this unlawful interference caused the failure of US and NATO forces to undermine insurgency and terrorism in Afghanistan. *Wall Street Journal* recently quoted an Afghan official in Presidential Palace saying that Iran has truly influenced a considerable

---

1  *Ibid.*
2  *Daily Times*, 29 December 2012.
3  *Tolo TV News*, 8 December 2012.
4  *Daily Telegraph*, 16 April 2012.

number of influential Afghans in different ways, which is more risky than suicide terrorism. Iran provides funds to various projects and expands intelligence networks across Afghanistan, moving to fill the gap after the NATO withdrawal from the country by the end of 2014.1

Iran has also increased its military and intelligence influence within the ranks of the Afghan intelligence agencies. Iranian intelligence has established several networks across Afghanistan and fixed salaries for the NDS's double agents. In Northern Afghanistan, Iran's various intelligence activities, including signal intelligence, human intelligence and counterintelligence, are operating under the auspices of the ministry of intelligence and security (MOIS), known as VEVAK.

Intelligence officials have purchased expensive houses in major provinces of the country. Another secret agency, RAMA, which was established under the auspices of Indian intelligence agency RAW in 2009, is working in an adverse direction. The National Directorate of Security (NDS) works for the CIA while Pakistani intelligence agency, ISI, is doing different businesses.

Another source of intelligence collection must be social media in Afghanistan, but, unfortunately, 90% people intelligence official in various province have no access to social media. As we all know, social media has changed the concept of intelligence gathering. Facebook, Twitter, YouTube and other networks are useful sources of intelligence collection. A recent report of Facebook newsroom revealed that more than 800 million people use Facebooks across the world while some 900 million interact with various groups, friends and communities. On Facebook, according to the report, more than 250 million photos are uploaded per day. The report further revealed more than 500 million users use app on Facebook and about 7 million apps and sites are connected with the mobile of Facebook.

Several intelligence agencies of developed nations use social media for spying. In Afghanistan, the case is different, as the use of social media for collecting intelligence information is limited. Two percent people use internet, mobile phone and Facebook and more than 90% Afghans have no access to electricity. Intelligence officials and workers are facing the same problem; therefore, gathering intelligence information through social media is impossible.

THE INTELLIGENCE WAR AMONG 50 NATIONS IN AFGHANISTAN

Technologically strong western and European intelligence agencies have badly failed to gather high quality information about the Taliban networks in Afghanistan. The recent suicide attack on Afghan intelligence chief, Mr. Assadullah Khalid, is the worse example of intelligence failure. This attempt came just as the Afghan president said that the US-led military was respon-

---

1  Anthony H. Cordesman. *Report of the Centre for Strategic and International Studies.* 17 June 2011.

sible for instability in his country. Afghan parliamentarians criticized the National Directorate of Security (NDS) for its non-professional manner of intelligence gathering: "If NDS cannot secure itself how can people expect anything from these security organizations?" MP Nazifa Zaki asked.[1]

Intelligence war has now intensified in Afghanistan as intelligence agencies of Chinese, Russian, ISI, RAW, Germany, Italy, Canada, Australia, Europe, Arab and African nations are trying to penetrate each other networks. Every intelligence agency is well-organized. We cannot accommodate Afghan intelligence in any of the above mentioned categories. NATO, US and UK intelligence agencies have often criticized the way Afghan intelligence operates. The NDS in its turn criticized international community for failing to intercept the bomber reaching their intelligence Chief. They sharply criticized all foreign intelligence agencies for their lack of long-term coordination and intelligence sharing with the NDS.

President Hamid Karzai blamed NATO for the intelligence failure and said that its intelligence system was not working properly. "The terrorist infiltration in Kabul and other provinces is an intelligence failure for us and, especially, for NATO and should be seriously investigated," the president warned. In response to his allegations, the NATO chief warned against descending into a blame game. Afghan parliamentarians raised the question of political influence in the Afghan intelligence infrastructure.[2]

Most Afghanistan-based intelligence agencies like the CIA, MI5, MI6, Government Communication Headquarters (GCHQ), RAW, ISI, Australian Intelligence Secret Service (ASIS), Canadian Forces Intelligence Branch, French Directorate of Military Intelligence (DRM), German Intelligence (BND), MOSSAD, Chinese and Russian FBS, Iranian Ansarul Muslimeen, Al Quds Brigade and Saudi Intelligence (GIP) collect, process and retrieve low quality information from their illiterate and non-professional sources, about the military and political tactics of Taliban insurgents. They are confined to Kabul and have no access to remote areas where the Taliban operates.

On 22 April 2013, newspapers reported suicide attack on MOSSAD intelligence Unit in Jalalabad. In Jalalabad, 14 MOSSAD agents were working. In the Taliban attack, 12 MOSSAD agents were killed and 2 critically injured. Now from this incident, we can guess how professional foreign intelligence agencies failed to protect their networks in Afghanistan.

General McChrystal also raised the same issue, and warned about the US intelligence failure. As a mountainous country, Afghanistan is a big challenge for civil and military intelligence agencies, therefore Afghan government and international community has never been able to gather intelligence information from all parts of the country. Most parts of the country are controlled by the Taliban and are inaccessible. Intelligence agencies of rival powers have

---

1  Anthony H. Cordesman. *Report of the Centre for Strategic and International Studies.* 17 June 2011.
2  WikiLeak.org. *Global Intelligence files.* 19 October 2012.

failed to collect the exact data of population movement inside the country. They cannot move out of their embassies and headquarters, therefore, they mostly depend on intelligence information gathered by journalists and their private informers. They have employed non-professional and illiterate Afghans who never experienced the taste of modern intelligence war in Afghanistan.

A recent report of the Center for Strategic and International Studies revealed some facts about the intelligence failure in Afghanistan:

> Intelligence also did not address the growing unpopularity and failure of the Afghan government, the impact of power brokers and corruption, and role of Pakistan and insurgents sanctuaries in that country." Recently, Deputy Chief of US military intelligence in Afghanistan, Major General Michael Flynn complained about the low quality intelligence information gathered by US intelligence on the insurgents' military tactics. The recent report of German intelligence (BND) has also revealed about the US and NATO failure in Afghanistan.[1]

Three years ago, the Taliban attack on the CIA camp in Khost province is also considered a clear proof of the US intelligence failure in Afghanistan. Some recent reports indicate that the struggle between nations with double agents and their intelligence, international spy networks, arm smugglers and the Taliban has entered a crucial phase. In 2012, Afghan intelligence announced that an Afghan army officer was arrested on charges of cooperation and his secret link with a neighboring state. The intelligence war in Afghanistan causes many problems, not only for the US, NATO and ISAF, but for Afghanistan as well. President Obama finally accepted that the basic problem in Afghanistan is, the intelligence war among nations:

> We argued that establishing an effective Afghan army would be extremely difficult, if not impossible, because the Americans and their NATO allies lacked knowledge and sophistication in distinguishing friends from foe among those being recruited into the army.[2]

In his recent report about the US intelligence failure in Afghanistan, Major General Michael T. Flynn, has criticized the way intelligence operates in Afghanistan:

> What lies beyond them is another issue. Lacking sufficient number of analysts and guidance from commanders, battalion S-2 shops rarely gather, process and write up quality assessment on countless items, such as census data and patrol debriefs; minutes from Shuras with local farmers and tribal leaders, after action reports from civil affair officer and Provincial Reconstruction Teams (PRTs); polling data and atmospherics reports from psychological operation and female engagement teams, and translated

---

1   Major General Michael T. Flynn, Captain Matt Pottinger and Paul D. Batchelor.  In their recent report about the US intelligence failure in Afghanistan, have criticized the way intelligence operates in Afghanistan. 2012.

2   *Daily Times*, 18 December 2012.

summaries of radio broadcasts that influence local farmers, not to mention the field observations of Afghan soldiers, United Nations Officials, and non-governmental organizations (NGOs). This vast and underappreciated body of information all most all of which is unclassified, admittedly offer few clues about where to find insurgents, but it does provides elements of even greater strategic importance—a map for leveraging popular support and marginalizing the insurgency itself.[1]

In a divided nation like Afghanistan, a single ethnic group leads the intelligence community and military in wrong direction. The roots of Afghan intelligence are in the Northern Alliance or in Northern Afghanistan not in the South and East. NDS does not have a successful intelligence networks in Kandahar Jalalabad, Khost, Paktia, Kunar and Paktika provinces. When Washington set up Afghan intelligence (NDS), a majority of its ranks were recruited from Panjshir province. According to *The Christian Science Monitor's* recent report, "the NDS officials accept that the agency knows nothing about the Southern and Eastern parts of their country".[2]

AFGHAN INTELLIGENCE: FOREIGN INFLUENCE AND ALLEGATIONS OF TORTURE

Michael Herman (2011), in his well-written book (Intelligence Power in War and Peace) has described intelligence analysis and intelligence cooperation in detail. In the case of Afghan intelligence agencies, we observed that they never adopted effective measures of intelligence and counterintelligence to lead the government in positive directions.[3]

As per the nature of their controversial work, Afghan agents belong to a single group and ethnicity. Like the Afghan police and army, intelligence network has also been divided between states, warlords, NGOs and foreign intelligence agencies. On July 13, 2012, Khaama Press reported that intelligence organizations of neighboring states had acquired Afghan intelligence ID-cards to operate independently.[4]

Former Pakistani President Musharraf once alleged that Afghan intelligence was being used by the RAW against Pakistan. "Afghan intelligence, the Afghan president and the Afghan government don't talk of them. I know what they do. They, by design, mislead the world...The Afghan intelligence is entirely under the influence of Indian intelligence. We know that."[5]

After the US intervention in 2001, General Hamid Gul said that Afghan government along with the CIA, RAW and FBS formed a new intelligence agency (RAMA) to use it against regional states. Russia, the US and India

1 Michael Herman. 2011.
2 *Khaama Press*, July 13, 2012.
3 Alhaj Gulam Jilani Wahaj, *The role of MI6, CIA, ISI and Iran in Afghanistan.* Khaama Press, 19 March, 2013.
4 Nikita Mendkovich, "A brief survey of NATO's intelligence services in Afghanistan", *Oriental Review.org*, 3 January, 211.
5 *New Eastern Outlook*.

provide training to its members. Intelligence operations of Afghan, NATO, US and UK intelligence agencies have badly failed as they started bribing Afghan President, army generals, police commanders and intelligence officials. The war among various intelligence agencies is on the peak as NATO, India, Pakistan Arab states, Iran, Russia, China and UK's secret agencies intensifies their efforts to monitor each other in a war zone state. MI5 and MI6 have often depended on law quality intelligence information, retrieved from their operatives in UK. The way British intelligence works is too complicated.

The intelligence activities and under-cover operations of NATO, US and the United Kingdom in Afghanistan, has long been the subject of conjecture and supposition, and that has sometimes made it difficult to properly analyze events in war zone. Writer Nikita Mendkovich analyzes the NATO, US and UK intelligence presence and their activities in Afghanistan:

> Despite the fact that the ISAF has an independent intelligence analysis staff (CJ2) at its disposal, most of the operational work in the country is carried out by the national-level intelligence agencies of individual NATO countries. The CIA plays a leading role in providing intelligence support for coalition forces in Afghanistan; the intelligence services of Great Britain and Germany are also active there. The regional unit's head office is located in Kabul. The CIA has a total 18 local stations, located in most of the country's provinces. Those in the west and in the south are especially active. The stations usually operate under the cover of various coalition force support unites, western firms and humanitarian organizations.[1]

German intelligence agency, BND is active in Northern Afghanistan but never been successful to understand ground realities through its secret glasses. The BND operations in Afghanistan are mostly electronic intelligence information collection. BND also monitor internet trafficking in various provinces of the country.[2] The coalition led Afghanistan Intelligence Transition Directorate (AITD) is responsible for collecting intelligence information for ISAF and still conforming to Afghan national intelligence protocol to protect sources, methods and capabilities. The Coalition-led Afghan Intelligence Transition Directorate (AITD) was responsible for expediting the development of an effective information and intelligence capability for the ANSF while still conforming to Afghan national intelligence protocols to protect sources, methods, and capabilities.[3]

The distribution of Iranian weapons across Afghanistan raised many questions as its intelligence agencies are bringing into list, former Mujahe-

---

1  *Inspector General of the United States, Department of Defense Report* No DODIG-2013-058 March 22 2013.

2  Joe Pappalardo, Popular, *The Pakistan, Iran-Afghanistan intelligence war*, Mechanis.com, 04 August 2011.

3  Loannis Michaletos, *The era of the private intelligence agencies.* World Security Network.com, 23 February, 2009. 23-Feb-09.

deen commander for the future civil war. Afghan TV (TOLO) reported the distributed Iranian weapons in 2011. Iranian intelligence has established its networks across Afghanistan, gives money to informers, religious leaders and sects.[1]

The failure of US intelligence in Afghanistan resulted in the deployment of private intelligence companies to collect intelligence information, for the CIA and NATO intelligence agencies. As we understand that private intelligence agencies are non state actors, they normally collect and analyze intelligence information. At present, a large number of companies have established their intelligence networks in Afghanistan, to collect information about the Taliban activities.

Pakistani secret service, Inter Services Intelligence (ISI) has established a strong network in all Afghan institutions. In the Defense and Interior Ministry of Afghanistan, ISI have a successful access to their policymaking decisions. ISI support the Taliban, in signal intelligence and intelligence gathering. Dr. Adrian Hanni has painted an interesting picture of ISI game in Afghanistan:

> The great double game soon proved to be an institutional difficulty for the ISI. Under the watchful eyes of Western intelligence agencies, at was almost impossible for them to help the CIA on the one hand and on the other to lead the Taliban. This challenge was overcome through privatization; especially the construction of a new secret organization that was to operate outside the military and intelligence operates. Former ISI coaches of the Taliban as well as retired Pashtun officers of the army and, especially the Frontier Corps were rehired on contractual bases. Logistics and funding no longer went directly via the ISI but the less closely observed Frontier Corps.

Moreover, in Washington, a well informed American commander said that the Afghan Taliban and the Haqqani network have sanctuaries inside Pakistan and there are intelligence reports about their links with the spy agency ISI."There have been intelligence reports that link the ISI, particularly, to the Haqqani network," the commander said.

The activities of Inter Services Intelligence (ISI) in Afghanistan have created a lot of confusion in Afghanistan. ISI helps Taliban and other groups to target Afghan forces, but US military command refused to endorse the claim of the Afghan President that Pakistani spies have infiltrated their security forces and, were attacking foreign forces. "It's our understanding that these attacks aren't the work of foreign intelligence service". A US military commander told the *Wall Street Journal* that: "they're typically Afghans who decided to conduct them, and some Afghans from insurgents networks might have helped on occasion."[2]

---

1  *Daily Dawn*, 27, 08, 2012.
2  Octavian, Dumitrescu, *The intelligence and security services of Iran*, 20 November 2010, Worlds Security Networks.com.

Once the Director General of Counter Terrorism in Afghanistan told this author that more than 400 agents of the Iranian intelligence agency (Ansa-rul Muslimeen), were operating across the country. The active role of Ira-nian intelligence agencies in Afghanistan is evident from the fact, that Iran has been recruiting Afghans for its intelligence and political purposes since 1990s.

CHAPTER 12. SOCIAL MEDIA, CYBER TERRORISM AND THE
TALIBAN'S TACTICAL INTELLIGENCE

During the last 12 years, the use of internet and communications promoted information war in the cyberspace. Wireless system, radio and television networks developed in Afghanistan, while the use of social media for
the purpose of intelligence information collection introduced new changes
in the mechanism of intelligence. Ministry of Communication in Afghanistan
signed a $64.5 million agreement with a Chinese company, ZTE, to establish
a fiber optic cable network across the country. With the establishment of
the network, the quality of Internet and telephone will improve.[1]

In Afghanistan, Neda Telecom, Insta Telecom, Rana Technologies, IO
global, Caretechs, New Dunya, Netzone, Asix and Afghan Telecom, are the
bigger and effective Internet Services Provider companies. Now there are still
limited number of people using mobile phones and benefit from the services
of Etisalat, Roshan, Afghan Wireless and MTN companies. The number of
televisions and radio channels also in increased.[2]

In 2002, Internet cafes became centers of social interaction. These cafes
also created awareness among young Afghans. During the Taliban regime, all
social media networks were banned; even watching television was a crime.
After the fall of the Taliban regime, Afghanistan was given legal control of the
"Af" domain in 2003, and Afghanistan Network Information (AFGNIG) was

---

1  "Installation of new equipment communication expands throughout the country." *Bakhtar
   News Afghanistan*, September, 2012.
2  MCIT. "*Annual Achievements Summer.*" Summary Reports 2006.

established to administer domain name. A new Telecommunications Ministry was now in operation that controlled all services of Afghan Telecom.[1]

The adoption of mobile applications and social media use for intelligence purposes, and the worldwide web have changed our traditional way of life. We live in an evolving world with an ever-changing situation, trying to stay competitive in dynamic markets. A new revolution of social media in the field of intelligence information collection about al-Qaeda, Taliban insurgents, terror groups and foreign espionage networks, opened a new chapter in the history of intelligence mechanisms in Afghanistan.[2]

We are living in the age of social media, and now Facebook, Twitter, Google, Yahoo, LinkedIn and YouTube play an important role in intelligence collection. Most Afghan insurgents and terror groups are largely dependent on social media to retrieve secret information from the field. Recent research in Europe has warned that social media is going to change the traditional concept of intelligence gathering. The concept of security and intelligence gathering changed after the fall of the Taliban regime in 2001, while the use of social media for intelligence purposes directed the attention of intelligence and counterintelligence experts to the new business of information warfare.[3]

Professor Sir David Omand has also emphasized the use of social media for intelligence gathering, because it is now significantly relevant to security. On many occasions, Facebook has been used for contract killings and other legal and illegal activities. In the case of YouTube, we often heard that it gives users the ability to instruct others on many tasks. In a poor country, like Afghanistan, access to Facebook, YouTube, twitter and other social media instruments is limited. Most important, members the Afghan secret agencies also have no specific training in the use of social media for intelligence gathering, which elsewhere is viewed as a vital source of intelligence collection.[4]

The Center for a New American Security in its report for 2010 quoted General McChrystal as saying that the way intelligence information is gathered in Afghanistan is no more effective. Major-General Michael J Flynn in his report has raised the same question:

> The Intelligence community is preoccupied with gathering a flood of highly detailed information on insurgents and has thus failed to provide vital general information on the environment in which the Taliban operates... The central problem with intelligence gathering in Afghanistan is the great emphasis placed on detailed information on insurgents. The intelligence community's standard mode of operation is surprisingly passive about ag-

---

1  Sir David Omand, *Facebook Newsroom, 2004. Also see, The Future for Intelligence*, 21 September, 2012.
2  Sir David Omand, *Securing the State*, 2011. Also see, *Daily Times*, 18 December 2012.
3  *Face book Newsroom*, 2004.
4  *The Centre for a New American Security* "General McChrystal as saying that the way intelligence information is gathered in Afghanistan is no more effective."2010.

gregating information that is not enemy-related, and relaying it to decision makers or fellow analysts further ups the chain. The US intelligence community has fallen into the trap of waging an anti-insurgency campaign rather than a counterinsurgency campaign. Capturing or killing key mid-level and high-level insurgents is without question a necessary component of successful warfare, but far from sufficient for military success in Afghanistan.[1]

The issue of double agents is more irksome while from 2009 to 2012, dozens of intelligence collectors were killed by the sources, which were playing as double agents in Afghanistan, and FATA region of Pakistan. The US Combating Terrorism Center in its research report on intelligence and counterintelligence has revealed about the Afghan Taliban intelligence network, which conducts numerous functions, such as advance information and warnings about the patrols of the NATO forces. They also provide US forces with misleading information. A former US intelligence analyst says that the Taliban are fighting a political war:

> The Taliban are fighting a political war while the United States and its allies are still fighting a tactical military war. We remain focused on terrain, and they are focused on attacking the transition process and seizing the narrative of victory.[2]

The way the Taliban intelligence operated before 9/11 is very queer. Their Ministry of intelligence and Ministry for Promotion of Virtue and Prevention of Vice were the main centers of intelligence information collection. The Taliban Ministry of intelligence had employed 20,000 spies and 100,000 informers. At present, the Taliban conduct counterintelligence activities by infiltrating into Afghan government institutions to retrieve important information.

In October 2012, Taliban used Afghan intelligence agents in a suicide attack against the US forces. A uniformed member of the NDS detonated a suicide vest in Kandahar killing an American soldier and a former US military officer and four Afghans civilians. According to an Afghan private TV Channel, Tolo, the Interior Ministry immediately issued a directive to all police forces, to be vigilant against Taliban infiltration.[3]

The post-9/11 Taliban intelligence now operates in professional ways and, it uses a wide variety of human intelligence. Their intelligence networks at district and village level continue to collect information about the enemy's movements. In their tactical intelligence and counterintelligence ways, they use human and signal intelligence to identify suspects. Moreover, sometimes they force cell phone companies in the southern districts to shut down their networks. In March and April 2011, in some districts of Helmand and Pak-

1  *Washington Post*, 18 September, 2012.
2  Khaama Press. 13 July, 2012.
3  Muhammad Hassan Kakar, *Afghanistan: The Soviet Invasion and the afghan Response, 1979-1982,* 1997, University of California Press.

tika provinces, they often forced private cellular companies to shut down their networks. To retrieve information about the NATO and ISAF tactics, the Taliban use radio codes, throwaway phones and shorter range radio communication.

There can be no disagreement that reforms and the intelligence mechanism in Afghanistan need urgently to be upgraded, because the recent stories of torture and killing of innocent political workers and ordinary people in KHAD-run secret detention centers raised many questions. The international community has also voiced the need for urgent reforms, and demands a thorough investigation into the Afghan spy networks, to find out who is who, and who is working for whom. On 20 January 2013, New York Times published a report released by the United Nations about the torture and humiliation of Afghans, at the hands of their country intelligence agencies. The report, titled "Treatment of Conflict Related Detainees in Afghan Custody" revealed that in Afghanistan's detention facilities, young people are abused and tortured.[1]

The unnecessary political and military influence of western intelligence agencies, within the Afghan intelligence agencies, including the CIA, is considered an obstacle to mending the problem. This influence has always caused frustration as most KHAD agents want to work independently. At present, the Afghan spy agencies are not free of foreign influence and the Afghan government does not have full control over their networks.[2]

For example, President Hamid Karzai once ordered the release of journalist Hujattullah Mujaddidi, arrested by KHAD to recruit him as an informer; the agency refused and said it knew better than the president. In reality, the leadership of the Afghan secret services has undergone no reforms since its inception, and as such orders from the president hold no importance for them.

The US military machine understands that its successes in the war on terror depend on the cooperation of Afghanistan's controversial spy agencies. CIA understands that Afghan spy agents provide them with low quality disinformation about the Taliban and other terror groups inside Pakistan. Lack of professional leadership is another phenomenon.[3]

## CYBER TERRORISM

Cyber war among Asian and European nations in Afghanistan has intensified as Taliban members are trying to get secret information through different means. Intelligence information is being collected through social media

---

1 American CIA has been paying a lot of money to Afghan intelligence to buy the loyalties of warlords and politicians. *Press TV*, 29 April 2013.
2 Eric Beidel, Sandra I, Erwin and Stew, *Technologies the US military will need for the next war.* Magnuson. National Defense,2011.
3 Mark A. Stokes, Jenny Lin and L.C Russell Hsiao, "The Chinese People's liberation army. Signal Intelligence and Cyber Reconnaissance Infrastructure." Project 2049 Institute, 2011.

and human intelligence across the country. As we understand, communications are critical to everyday life, therefore, Afghan Governments rely on communications to receive information, develop policies, conduct foreign affairs, and manage administrative affairs. Businesses also rely on communications for financial transactions, conducting trade, and managing supply chains.[1]

Cyberspace has become decisive arena of modern information warfare. It opens up new dimensions to conflict. Cyber terrorism and hacktivism is the art of fighting without fighting; of defeating enemies without spilling their blood.[2]

Hackers break rules to retrieve information. They are breaking the law of targeted country. These techniques are varying time to time and amended as well. Technological advance has also enabled cyber-espionage to reach sensitive data or reach sophisticated level. Computer worms and drone attacks have been relatively successful in responding to perceived threats. These attacks are facilitated by powerful software, which is easily available from thousands of websites on the Internet. The emergence of cyber terrorism tactics are changing ways every year that can make it more dangerous and difficult to counter. Hackers retrieve secret information from exploiting the other side's carelessness. They are given the task to stolen information. Daily Tech News recently reported that China is building one of the world's largest drone fleets aimed an attacking the United States in the event of a war.[3]

In Afghanistan, cyber war has entered a crucial phase when hackers of China, Russian and Pakistan started targeting each other websites. Pakistani hacker received training in China while India is planning to train Afghans for cyber war in their country. US Marine Lt. Gen. Richard P. Mills recently revealed at the TechNet Land Forces conference, that that he used cyber operations:

> "I can tell you that as a commander in Afghanistan in the year 2010, I was able to use my cyber operation against my adversary with great impact." Mills said, according to the *Washington Post*. "I was able to get inside his nets, infect his command–and–control, and in fact defend myself against his almost constant incursions to get inside my wire, to affect my operations."[4]

Mills was in charge of International Security Assistance Forces (ISAF) in Afghanistan, from 2010–2011. On 27 August 2012, Press TV reported Pentagon's cyber war in Afghanistan and said, Pentagon cyber war is compelling evidence, that the US military is using everything at its disposal, to save face and avert a debacle in the country. "If we look at the war in Afghanistan, the

---

1   R Heickero, *Emerging Cyber Threat and Russian view on information warfare*, also see, Royal college of Defense studies paper on *cyber warfare*, 2012.
2   *New York Times*, 25 January 2012.
3   *Huff Post*, 28 May 2013.
4   *Press TV*, 27 August 2012.

United States and its allies are definably not winning, and the US strategy to put ANA and police in their role has failed" Richard Becker told Press TV.[1]

The United Kingdom is using drone technology in Afghanistan, which has become under severe criticism. In fact, drone not only targets the military bases of militants but collect information as well. The UK drone technology in Afghanistan use the technique of electronic warfare, to jam communication and radar, guide missile strike on carriers, fire missiles at Taliban targets. Inflammatory war propaganda and diplomatic tension between US and China indicates, that world war III scenario between the two states has developed. The issue of cyber terrorism has become a testing relationship between China and America, prompting President Barack Hussein Obama to raise concern over the expanding Chinese cyber networks around the globe. China and Russia have trained thousands cyber warriors and use them against the west.[2]

The United States and Britain are locked in a tight race with the cyber intelligence networks of China, Russia and India, but all sides including the Peoples Liberation Army (PLA), the US Army, the CIA, GCHQ and Pentagon have been unable to defeat each other in cyberspace for a decade. To retrieve information about advanced technology, each side exploits security flaws in software and email attachments to sneak into the networks of various institutions and companies. According to recent reports, hackers for the US and China are the most expert and successful cyber warriors.[3]

Russia is part of the game. It has also developed a strong cyber warriors networks. The case of Russian cyber operation is indicative of the potential pattern of cyber intelligence operations in near future. There is a wide range of differences between Western and Russian cyber security concepts. Russia holds a broad concept of cyber warfare, cyber intelligence, and cyber counter intelligence, degradation of navigation support, psychological pressure and propaganda. Secret agency (FSB) recently received directions from President Putin, to develop a new system, to ensure Russian networks can detect cyber threats. Western cyber war experts are of the opinion that Russian cyber network is stronger than China. As we have already experienced an intelligence war among China, US, UK, European states, India, Pakistan and Russia in Afghanistan, during the last 12 years, the same game is being played among these states in cyberspace.[4]

---

1  James A Levis, *Assessing the risk of cyber terrorism, Cyber war and other cyber threats.* Center for Strategic and International Studies. Washington, 2002.

2  *The United States and Britain are locked in a tight race with the cyber intelligence network of China.* Daily Mail. London, 7 May 2013.

3  David J. Smith, *Russian Cyber operations.* Potomac Institute for Policy studies, July 2012.

4  Tang Lan, Zhang Xin, Harry D. Raduege, Jr. Dmitry, Grigoriev, Pavan Duggal and Stain Shulberg, edited by Andrew Nagorski, *Global Cyber Deterrence: View from China, the US, Russia, India, Norway.* The East West Institute, US, 2010.

New cyber weapons, technologies, modernization of signal intelligence technology and means of attacks against each other national critical infra-structure, and institutions are, the most recent development in Asia, Europe and America. India has developed modern technology, attacking Pakistani institutions, while Pakistan's army (with the help of China) has developed its own cyber technologies. China is striving to retrieve US and UK's tech-nology by attacking their institutional networks, military industry and financial sectors, while Russia is also doing business in the same way. The United Kingdom and American are not in position to effectively counter Chinese and Russian cyber networks, because techniques used by Chinese secret services to recruit and train new cyber warriors are quite different from the West and Europe.[1]

This new industry of information theft now sends its trained members across the world. They are not tanks and guns; they are missiles, which target the institutional assets of many countries from safe distances. As Western societies have become totally dependent on information technologies; there-fore, attacks on computers have increased. Recently, Britain's security agen-cies started coping with the emerging threat of cyber terrorism and cyber attacks, but the result of countering Chinese and Russian cyber attacks have so for been unsatisfactory. This is a new chapter in the security policy of the United Kingdom. Though new strategies, allocation of huge funds to the fighting force in cyberspace, and hectic efforts to protect private sector is the main objective of the country's cyber security strategy, the GCHQ and its cyber force need more time to improve its countering strategies.[2]

The emergence of violent technological forces in China and Russia, Iran, India, North Korea and, their day to day increasing attacks on security com-puters in UK and Europe, has created the climate of fear. Britain is an easy target of cyber terrorism, as various institutions recently reported, the vul-nerability of their computer data. Government and private sector is under threat, while cyber espionage has created the climate of fear in investment sector. GCHQ and its experts are in trouble and think what to do and how to respond to the growing fear of cyber terrorism.

During the last ten years, the Ministry of Defense, FCO, Border Agency, Home Office and Metropolitan Police, experienced numerous cyber attacks, which ranged from terror attacks to hacktivism, professional criminals and terror groups, or those that they sponsor. National security, private sector, economic security and market economy, have come under attack from these groups time and again, but response from counter terrorism department has been very regrettable. In April 2013, Britain's Cabinet Office Minister Smith

---

1  "As we have already experienced an intelligence war among China, US, UK, European states, India, Pakistan and Russia in Afghanistan during the last 12 years." *Policing in Multicultural Britain.*

2  *Independent*, 23 April. 2013.

warned that government faced around 33,000 cyber attacks each month from state sponsored groups.[1]

Cyber attacks remain one of the top four threats facing national security. Terrorists have moved into cyberspace, to facilitate traditional forms of terrorism, such as bomb attacks. Britain has a well-established office of cyber security and information assurance (OSCIA), which supports the Minister for Cabinet Office, and the National Security Council, but it failed to respond to the present cyber threat positively. As a poor state, Afghanistan does not have any kind of cyber center, technology or trained hackers.

LICENSES ISSUED TO INTERNET SERVICES PROVIDER COMPANIES IN AFGHANISTAN

1   Neda Telecom: license type, national, based in Kabul, issue date 2004.
2   KBI: license type: national, based in Kabul, issue date 2004.
3   Cereteches: license type, national, based in Kabul, issue date 2004.
4   New Dunya: license type, national, based in Kabul, issue date 2004.
5   Insta Telecom: license type, national, based in Kabul, issue date 2004.
6   IO Global: license type, national, based in Kabul, issue date 2005.
7   Rana Technologies: license type, national, based in Kabul, issue date 2005
8   Multi Net: license type, national, based in Kabul, issue date 2005
9   Liwal: license type, national, based in Kabul, issue date 2006
10  AWCC: license type, national, based in Kabul, issue date 2006.
11  Atlas Telecom: license type, national, based in UAE, issue date 2006
12  Ariana Network Service: license type, national, based in Kabul, issue date 2007
13  Pactec: license type, national, based in Kabul, issue date 2007.
14  AFSAT: license type, national, based in Kabul, issue date 2007.
15  Asix: license type, national, based in Kabul, issue date 2008.
16  Afghan ICT Solution: license type, national, based in Kabul, issue date 2008.
17  MTN: license type, national, based in Kabul, issue date 2008.
18  Net Zone: license type, national, based in Kabul, issue date 2008.
19  Stream Link Feb — 2009 National Based in Kabul
20  Universal Telecom Service: license type, national, based in Kabul, issue date 2008.
21  Asia Consultancy Group: license type, national, based in Kabul, issue date 2009.
22  Nashita: license type, national, based in Kabul, issue date 2009.
23  Etisalat: license type, national, based in Kabul, issue date 2009.
24  Melat Networks: license type, national, based in Kabul, issue date 2009.

---

1   *Economist*, 5 September 2011.

25  Stan Telecom: license type, national, based in Kabul, issue date 2009.

26  Arya Sat Ltd: license type, national, based in Kabul, issue date 2009.

27  Quality Net: license type, national, based in Kabul, issue date 2009.

28  Wasil Telecom: license type, national, based in Kabul, issue date 2010.

29  Afghan Cyber: license type, national, based in Kabul, issue date 2010.

30  Global Entourage: license type, national, based in Kabul, issue date 2010.

31  Connect Telecom: license type, national, based in Kabul, issue date 2010.

32  Afghan Yar Technologies: license type, national, based in Kabul, issue date 2010.

33  Cast Global: license type, national, based in Kabul, issue date 2010.

34  Giga Noor: license type, national, based in Kabul, issue date 2010.

35  Kaynat Technologies: license type, national, based in Kabul, issue date 2011.

36  IDIL: license type, national, based in Turkey, issue date 2011.

37  Aryan Technologies: license type, national, based in Kabul, issue date 2011.

38  Vital Telecommunication: license type, national, based in Kabul, issue date 2011.

*(Sources: Ministry of Communication of Afghanistan, Kabul).241*

---

1  *Ministry of Communication of Afghanistan, Kabul.*

## Chapter 13. The US–Afghan Strategic Partnership and the Pentagon's China-Phobia Policy

The US president, Barak Obama, and Afghan President Hamid Karzai, signed the enduring strategic partnership agreement in 2 May 2012. According to the agreement, the United States will strengthen the country's sovereignty, stability, prosperity and continue cooperation to defeat Taliban and al-Qaeda terrorist networks. At the initial stage, this agreement increased in the confidence of Afghanistan, but after a year, when US Special Forces started killing Afghan women and children, in villages and towns, Afghan President warned US commanders, that unless the killings of innocent people is stopped, Afghanistan will not be in position to implement the agreement.

The long awaited strategic partnership agreement between the United States and Afghanistan sparked a harsh reaction in neighboring states like Pakistan and China, demanding the withdrawal of foreign forces from Afghanistan. Pakistani military experts warned that this agreement will widen distances between Afghanistan and its neighbors. They warned that the US could use Afghanistan for creating instability in Pakistan. President Obama in his statement said:

> Today, we are agreeing to be long-term partners in combating terrorism with the Afghan security forces, strengthening democratic institutions, supporting development and protecting human rights of all Afghans.[1]

Afghans from all walks of life termed this agreement as a long-term enslavement of their country, because the US and its allies neither strengthened democratic institutions, nor trained the Afghan army or protected

---

1 *Huffington Post*, 1 March, 2012.

human rights. The Obama administration and its intelligence agency, the CIA killed, humiliated and severely tortured innocent Afghans, destroyed their country, sectarianised and ethnicized state institutions, specifically the army and police.

The US and NATO failed to bring peace and stability to the country while distrust between the two states further caused problems in the days to come as the Taliban have already infiltrated into the ranks and file of the security forces and the police.[1]

Recently, four US senators demanded the downsizing of the Afghan security forces after 2014. Mr. Obama and his Pentagon friends want to heavily downsize the ANA to reduce the burden of military expenses on the US and NATO allies. Prominent Pakistani military analyst Brigadier Asif Haroon Raja in his recent article warned:

"The US military supported by the armies of 48 countries, including 27 of NATO, swooped upon heavily sanctioned, impoverished Afghanistan, devoid of regular armed forces, technical and technological means.[2]

The recent Pentagon China-phobia policy, its containment of China, the emergence of a new military intelligence agency, and the US hegemonic designs in South and Southeast Asia, received wide-ranging courage in electronic and print media in Europe. The increasing Chinese influence in Pakistan, Afghanistan and Central Asia, its influence on European and African markets, together with the improvement of Russian economy and military, have caused an unending torment for the US commanders in Afghanistan. The Pentagon authorities did not sleep a wink since the commencement of the last year joint Russia-China naval exercise in the Yellow Sea, between the east coast of China and the Korean Peninsula, and their stance on the Arab Spring.[3]

These new developments and the recent US policy in Afghanistan, negotiations with Taliban insurgents and the deterioration of Pak-US relations signal new military challenges for China, Afghanistan and Pakistan. The clouds of a new war are about to spread, while either Afghanistan or Pakistan might become the battlefield of this intelligence game in near future. This is the beginning of a new economic war as the former US Defense Secretary; Leon Panetta declared that his country was at a strategic turning point after a decade of war in Afghanistan and Iraq. Having realized the sensitivity of the recent political and military developments in the region, the Pentagon established a new military intelligence agency to strengthen its control over the region.[4]

---

1 *Daily Times*, 08 March 2012.
2 *Ibid.*
3 *Rupees News*, 08 March 2012
4 *Daily Times*, 09 March 2012.

Many experts view Afghan–US partnership agreement and peace in Afghanistan as two different things. The agreement gives US the right to establish permanent military bases, but the restoration of peace needs winning the mind and heart of Afghan population, which is probably impossible in the presence of US forces. As the US intensified its military domination on Afghanistan, regional and international opposition increased. The proposed plan of the Obama Administration to reduce the size of the Afghan National Army in 2015 is quite understandable as the United States wants Afghanistan's long-term military dependency on it. American generals decided to reduce the Afghan army from 352,000 to 230,000.[1]

Author Vanda Felbab Brown in her recent book has analyzed the inability of Afghan Security Forces and NATO false commitments:

> Despite ISAF's announcement that special support operations, such as medevac, would not be affected by the new rules of engagement, the restriction could in fact hamper such ISAF support. Yet for many years to come, certainly well beyond 2014, the ANSF will continue to be deficient in several critical domains. These include command, control and intelligence, air support, medical evacuation, logistics and maintenance, contractor management, battler space integration and other especially enablers. Currently, the Afghan National Security Forces frequently know how to fight and win battles at the tactical level, but they have yet to learn how to fight and win campaigns.[2]

The NATO allies' states urged that ANA cost more than $10 billion every year, while the reduced size might cost them $4 billion every year. Double deep recession in Europe and US put their war on terror efforts in trouble. The US is no more in position to support Afghanistan alone while Germany, France and the UK want to settle their own problems.[3]

With the implementation of this plan, the story of a strong Afghan army will become more complicated as various sections of civil society have already expressed apprehensions about the vulnerability of the security forces, after the withdrawal of foreign forces from Afghanistan towards the end of 2014. During the last 12 years, they trained hundreds of thousands of Afghan soldiers; now they want to reduce the size of the rogue army. I think there is no need to reduce the size of Afghan Army, the day-to-day desertion of Afghan soldiers is doing that quickly way to down-sizing the ANA.

The United States and NATO understand that in the presence of a larger rogue Afghan army that hates its partners, their existence might be a bigger problem in Afghanistan. The attitude of the Afghan security forces has further become a bigger challenge for the US, NATO and their allies.

---

1 *China Daily*, 24 April 2012.
2 *Daily Outlook Afghanistan*, 08 March 2012.
3 Vanda Felbab Brown, *Aspiration and Ambivalence, Strategies and realities of counterinsurgency and state building in Afghanistan.* PP-14, 15, 16. 2013

Author Vanda Felbab Brown highlighted some important points of the process of rebuilding ANA and the police. She has directed the attention of her readers to the false promises and commitments of international community:

> Worse yet, Afghans have become disconnected and alienated from the national government and the country's other power arrangements. They are profoundly dissatisfied with Kabul's inability and unwillingness to provide basic public services and with the widespread corruption of the power elites. They intensely resent the abuse of power, impunity and lack of justice that have become entrenched over the past decade. The initial post-Taliban period of hope and promise did not last, as governance in Afghanistan became rapidly defined by weakly functioning state institutions unable or unwilling to uniformly enforce law and policies. Characteristically, official and unofficial power brokers issue exceptions from law enforcement to their network of clients, who are thus able to reap high economic benefits and even get away with major crimes. Murder, extortion and land-grabbing, often perpetrated by those, in the government have gone unpunished.[1]

There are reports in international press that the post 2014 mission has been divided in two parts; one will be implemented by Iran and the other by Pakistan. Iran will try to create a federal system of government in Afghanistan, while Pakistan will try to bring back the Taliban and Mr. Gubuddin Hekmatyar into power. The main problem in Afghanistan is to create a balance among all ethnic players. Internal power politics will continue in the future and will never end. The Pashtuns' alienation from the state is a greater danger.

The issue of security transition has become more complicated as more than 20,000 Afghan soldiers defect to the Taliban or leave their service every year. In London and Kabul conferences, NATO affirmed support for and focused on the sustainable transition of security responsibility to the Afghan army, but NATO also understands that ANA will not be able to maintain security in a single province of Afghanistan. In 2010, Britain warned that amid enduring suspicions over the reliability of local forces, Afghans are turning to the Taliban for justice.

Drug trafficking, corruption and the trends of alienation among the police force may delay the force's ability to take over the responsibility of law and order in 2014.[2]

Russia and NATO still view each other with suspicion over what is going on in Afghanistan and Pakistan. Moscow now rises and the emergence of militarily and economically strong Russian will restore the balance of power in the region. President Putin mission is to bring Russia back to its previous place in international politics. Iran has also expressed concern over the

---

1  *Daily Times*, 02 February, 2011,
2  *The Washington Post*, 23 April, 2012.

Obama-Karzai agreement and came up with an irrational diplomacy. Iran warned before signing the agreement that if Afghan government endorsed the agreement, it would expel all Afghan refugees from the country. Karzai got his job done but put his nation in an ordeal. Afghans mostly consider him as a second Abdur Rahman, who sold half of the Pashtun land to Britain in the 19th century. Now, most Afghan parliamentarian consecutively criticize him and don't want to dance to his tune.

### THE PENTAGON, THE CIA AND THE DEFENSE CLANDESTINE SERVICE

The United States has established another new intelligence agency, the Defense Clandestine Service (DCS), positioned to focus Chinese activities in South and Southeast Asia. The agency will also focus on non-proliferation issues related to Pakistan, Iran and North Korea. US intelligence circles understand that there are similarities between the Defense Clandestine Service and the CIA's National Clandestine Service. Recent research reports have documented armed conflict between the United State and China and the re-emergence of Muslim resistance movement in China. The present conflictual situation in South China Sea which joins Southeast Asian states with Western pacific and functioning as a global sea routes, has exuberated diplomatic tension between China and the United States.[1]

Interestingly, more than fifty percent of the world's annual merchant fleet tonnage passes through these routs, and a third of all maritime traffic. Most oil transported through Malacca strait from Indian Ocean, enrooted to the whole East Asia through South China Sea [2] Since the Afghan peace and reconstruction process kicked off in 2002, the Chinese enterprises actively devoted themselves to the cooperation and exploitation in fields of mining, energy, infrastructure, telecommunication, etc. Among them, Aynak copper mine project in Logar province, which is by now the largest Chinese overseas direct investment in Afghanistan. Chinese security interests in Pakistan are, to contain India and built Pakistan's conventional military, as well as nuclear missile capabilities, to keep military balance in South Asia. Pakistan supported Chinese Muslim uprising in 1990s, which resulted in mistrust. Some recent reports indicate that China has complained over several of its Muslim dissidents living in Pakistan.

Moreover, in July 2011, terror attacks in Xinjiang that killed more than 20 people, prompted Chinese criticism of Pakistan for failing to crackdown the training camps of Uyghur extremists in Waziristan region. Chinese authorities understand that terror activities of Chinese separatist groups

---

1 *Daily Outlook Afghanistan*, Oct 2011.

2 "Defense Clandestine Service and CIA's National Clandestine Service". *Daily Outlook Afghanistan*, 01 March 2012, Telegraph, 02 January, 2012.

have increased in Pakistan, while a Chinese writer recently complained that China has been disappointed by Pakistan's response.[1]

The names published on Chinese government website (www.mps.gov. cn) are of Uyghur suspects. The current Muslim extremism in Xinjiang has clearly been inspired by some changes in Central Asia, Pakistan and Afghanistan. Some Chinese officials understand that Chinese militants are being trained in Pakistan's FATA and Waziristan regions. To intercept militant attacks inside the country, Chinese government is trying to establish close cooperation with Pakistani and Afghani extremist groups. Having secured economic privileges in Afghanistan, China is paying huge amount of bribes to the Taliban. In a recent report, Hindustan Times claimed that China is helping the Taliban in fight against foreign forces.[2]

US has recently expressed concern over the PLA activities in Pakistan, and warned Pakistan not to give on lease the disputed Gilgit and Baltistan region to China. China has special interests in this region. Having realized expected US invasion on Pakistan, China ordered thousands of its soldiers to enter Gilgit Baltistan, construct Karakoram Highway and save the region. Northern areas of Pakistan connect some important economic zones in the region like Central Asia, South Asia, China and Middle East. Moreover, connection between Central Asian and South Asian market can be established, while Uzbekistan and other states can establish trade relations with Pakistan. In future, the oil and gas pipeline from Iran to China will also pass through this region, because this region is playing important role in connecting China to Middle East.[3]

No doubt, Chinese involvement in Gilgit does not change the disputed status of Gilgit and Baltistan claimed by India. Pakistan lacks state control over Gilgit-Baltistan, therefore, it has no right to allow China to establish military bases here. According to Lawrence Ziring, China has assumed the de-fecto control of Gilgit-Baltistan. To find new enemies, US want to bring some long-term changes in Pak-Afghan policy, watch China and Russia closely and facilitate the Taliban in their dealing with Afghanistan. The recent intelligence reforms together with the wide-ranging differences between the CIA, Pentagon and Obama administration raised many questions. Their differences on several issues like the publication of US soldiers pictures with suicide bomber in Afghanistan became the central debate of American think tanks.

The recent establishment of a new military intelligence agency, Defense Clandestine Service and, its focus on South East Asia, emerging economic

---

1  *Daily Times*, 08 March 2012. *The Guardian*, 24 April 2012.
2  *Daily Outlook Afghanistan*, "In July 2011, terror attacks in Xinjiang that killed more than 20 people prompted Chinese criticism of Pakistan for failing to crackdown the training camps of Uyghur extremists in Waziristan region", 01 March 2012.
3  *Ibid.* 17 April, 2012.

and military powers means that Pentagon wants to contain and confine both China and Russia, to specific regions. The Defense Clandestine Service, according to Pentagon's report, will work closely with both Pentagon and the CIA, recruiting spies from Defense Intelligence Agencies and deploying them in most part of South Asia, to closely watch the military and economic movements of communist China in South and Southeast Asia.[1]

According to new revelations of the US military news website "Inside defense", Pentagon and ministry of defense asked Congress for authority for spies to work undercover posing as businessmen when conducting covert operations abroad? [2]

The US policy towards China involves a strategic design to keep it a global power. The only force that can play an instrumental role in spreading the Pentagon's intelligence war inside China is the Uighur Muslim Movement. Uighur Muslims are being trained in Pakistan and Afghanistan. In China, the government is already under increasing pressure from Muslim separatist and extremist groups seeking independence from the country. In Xinjiang province, the Uighur Islamic Movement and other minor ethnic and political groups have established secret networks, recruit and invite young people to their groups. Beijing is already facing constant threats from Tibet and Taiwan, the low-key conflict which has been simmering in the region long since.[3]

These ethnic and religious challenges are very significant for China's expanding economic and military role in both Asia and Africa. The Obama administration wants to switch US national security focus away from the Middle East to address long-term issues such as the rise of China, Russia and North Korea. Xu Feihong, current Ambassador of the People's Republic of China to Afghanistan, said the system of political consultation fully embodies the democracy and diversity of China's politics ensures full rights and channels of expressing ideas and suggestions by people from all walks of life.[4]

Ambassador told newspaper about the Chinese government policy about the ethnic autonomous regions and said: "The system of regional ethnic autonomy refers to the system whereby regional autonomy is practiced in all areas where ethnic minorities live and organs of self-government are established for the exercise of that autonomy. In order to allow ethnic minorities to govern on the basis of their historical, regional and cultural characteristics, the Chinese government adopted the system of regional ethnic autonomy in accordance with the realities and the will of ethnic minorities. To date, China has established five ethnic autonomous regions which are Inner Mongolia Autonomous Region, Xinjiang Uyghur Autonomous Region,

---

1  *Express Tribune*, 13 March 2013.
2  *Daily Outlook Afghanistan*, 1 May 2012.
3  *Daily Guardian* 24 April 2012.
4  *Daily Times*, 1 May 2012.

Guangxi Zhuang Autonomous Region, Ningxia Hui Autonomous Region and Tibet Autonomous Region."[1]

China's relations with neighboring states have been in strain. The Sino-Vietnamese flair-up, Philippine policy towards China, and the current turmoil in Xinjiang, may further create problem for the country. There are reports, which in near future, guerrilla war in China would disrupt its economic process. Suicide attacks in various Chinese provinces cannot be ruled out as extremist groups of Muslim dominated region recruit their young member for suicide attacks in neighboring states.[2]

According to some research reports, the future of China would be at stake if Uyghur Muslim extremist received weapons and financial support from outside the country. There are apprehensions that Uyghur members will radicalize other minority groups, whether ethnic Tibetans or Muslim Hui. All states in the region are under threat from Uyghur violent operations, specifically, those with sizable Uyghur minorities. According to some reports, Southeast Asian states are also worried about the growing extremist tendencies and terror training camps, specifically in Afghanistan and Pakistan, but they also understand that conflagration in China would destabilize the whole region. Pakistan's indirect involvement in Chinese Muslim province may further deteriorate relations between the two states.[3]

1 *Daily Outlook Afghanistan*, 26 April 2011.
2 *Annual Report*. "Congressional Executive Commission on China", 2005.
3 *Daily Outlook Afghanistan*, "China's relations with neighbouring states have been in strain". *Daily Outlook Afghanistan*, 1 May 2012. Also, Elizabeth Van Vie Davis, *Uyghur Muslim Ethnic Separatism in Xinjiang, China*. 2008. Asia Pacific Centre for Security Studies.

## Chapter 14. The Pakistan Army War on Pashtuns

In 1947, when Afghanistan refused to recognize Pakistan as an independent state, the country adopted a hostile policy towards Afghanistan. Cross border attacks started in 1949. In 1960s, Afghanistan openly supported an independent Pashtunistan. In 1971, during the Bangladesh war for independence, Afghanistan helped Pakistan in securing its borders. In 1979, after the soviet invasion of Afghanistan, Pakistan helped Afghans in their struggle for independence. During the 1980s, the mujahedeen received support from US, Saudi Arabia, Iran and Pakistan.

After the Soviet withdrawal from Afghanistan in 1989 and, when aid dried up on Afghanistan in 1992, civil war began. From 1992–2001, Pakistan was a dominant power in Afghan politics. The country distributed sophisticated weapons among various Mujahedeen groups. The presence of Pakistan army in Afghanistan was evident from the fact, that retired military men were conducting civil war on different directions.[1]

Pakistan army and ISI played a very negative role in the Afghan conflict in 1980s and 1990s. Army provided arms to Mujahedeen who destroyed Afghanistan. The army supported Taliban and various other groups to widen ethnic and sectarian slots and maintain its influence in Afghanistan. The army ordered the flocks of sectarian jihadist to enter Afghanistan support the Taliban and kill minorities. Pervez Musharraf's regime openly supported the Taliban, trained them and armed them. These extremist forces, unfortunately, looted museums, libraries, houses, shops, markets, kidnapped women and killed ethic Hazaras and Tajiks.

---

1  *Pajhwok Afghan News*, 2011.

According to the Afghan Ministry of Defense, Pakistan army still main-tains its secret networks within the ranks and file of ANA and the police forces of the country. In this chapter, I want to discuss the secret ethnic war within Pakistan army units and the impact of Pashtun and Baluch insurgen-cies in the country. The army, that killed and forcefully disappeared thou-sands innocent Pakistani citizens from Baluchistan, Khyber Pakhtunkhwa and Sindh provinces, has now fighting internal ethnic war within its mili-tary barracks. Military operations in Waziristan and FATA regions caused resentment, alienation and despondency. The army killed, humiliated and tortured both Pashtuns and Balochs and destroyed their houses. In Swat, Dir, Mohmand and Bajour, dozens of young women were kidnapped.

Relations between Pakistan and the ANA have never been friendly due to Pakistan's interference in the internal affairs of Afghanistan. Pakistan's Inter Services Intelligence (ISI) support to the Taliban and its recruitment of disgruntled Afghans has created a lot of misunderstanding between the two nations. In 2003, just a year after the establishment of the Afghan National Army, Pakistan started firing missiles inside Afghan army posts in Khost province, in 2004, 2005, 2007, 2011, and 2012. Pakistan's army violated inter-national law and entered Afghan territory time and again.[1]

In Kunar and Nuristan provinces, cross border shelling intensified with many reports from different occasions claiming that Pakistani missiles hit areas inside Afghanistan's Nuristan, Kunar and Jalalabad provinces.[2]

Pakistan's internal turmoil continues as the country is undergoing numerous crises. Army is in trouble due to the international isolation and shortage of fund. The election of Mr. Nawaz Sharif as Prime Minister for the third time created an alarming situation, as generals' fear that Nawaz Sharif might once again target the army by bringing its size down. Army is not ready to allow Nawaz Sharif to trim its command structure and its ranks and file. Violence and illegal killings of innocent Pashtuns in the hands of Pakistani forces in FATA and Waziristan, drone war and Pakistan's deterio-rating relations with both India and Afghanistan, has put the army on a long ordeal. The army killed thousands in Swat, Bajaur, Waziristan, Baluchistan and Sindh and forcefully disappeared more than 18,000 Pakistani citizens during the last 12 years.[3]

Pakistan army supports Taliban, sends them to Afghanistan and trains them on its own soil. From 1990s to present, Pakistan's military establish-ment never accepted Afghanistan as an independent state. They captured it in 1997, ruined, looted and annexed it as a fifth province to its geography. The army tightened full control over Afghanistan from 1997 to 2001. Afghanistan was considered as a fifth province of Pakistan and, every year, specific bud-

---

1 *Huffington Post*, 6 June 2011.
2 *Afghan TV Tolo News*, 4 July 2011.
3 *Daily Times*. 1 May 2013.

get was being allocated to the province (Afghanistan). Gen Musharaf was the real Mullah Omar of Afghanistan. To bring the Afghan security forces under its political and military influence, Pakistan army has long been offering to train the Afghan National Army, but, until now, Afghans have shown little interest, largely due to Pakistan's atrocities in 1990s.[1]

The army is in a state of deep crisis as it fights on different fronts against the Taliban and sectarian forces unwillingly. Thousands of its soldiers have so for denied to fight against the Taliban or kill innocent people in FATA and Baluchistan. From Peshawar to Karachi, hundreds of soldiers and officers of the army have been incarcerated when they refused to fight in Waziristan. War on terror and army's reluctant participation in it created ethnic slots in its ranks and file. Officers of various corps are suffering frustration, tired and do not want to fight this useless war in which they kill their own brothers. The army was equipped for conventional war against India, not to fight insurgency, therefore, at present, the way military commanders fight insurgency with non-professional way has alienated the people of two provinces from the state.[2]

Journalist Shuja Nawaz has pinpointed some weaknesses of the armed forces in his recent report:

> The Pakistan army currently, though large and ubiquitous, is ill-equipped and untrained for low intensity conflict and has suffered heavily at the hands of well-trained guerrillas that melt into the population. And increasingly, its association with the American superpower that is driving the war against the Taliban in Afghanistan pits the army against its own population...The army is not yet fully equipped for that war. Many army officers recognize the situation clearly. But the change will take time and will be affected by the composition of the army itself.[3]

Research scholar Dhruv C Katoch (2011) has described the role of armed forces in state politics during the last 65 years, and says that Pakistan has remained consistently dependent on its armed forces to create a nation state from an entity divided by ethnic, religious and social fault lines. Renowned scholar Dr Pervez Hoodbhoy (2013) has warned that the army is getting weaker and its morale is diminishing:

> Why is the army getting weaker? The problem is not the lack of material — guns, bombs and money. These have relatively easy fixes. Instead, it is the military's diminished morale power and authority, absence of charismatic leadership and visible evident accumulation of property and wealth...Recent revelations has brought this contradiction into stark relief. More than anything else, the Army has sought to please both the Americans as well as their enemies.[4]

1  *The Hindu*, 12 April 2013,
2  Shuja Nawaz, *Pakistan army: Fighting the wars within.*, Oxford University Press, 2008.
3  *Daily Times*, 1, May 2013.
4  Shuja Nawaz, *Pakistan army: Fighting the wars within.* Oxford University Press, 2008.

The smell of ethnic and sectarian hatred within the army command structure is now felt outside the GHQ. Sectarian role of some brigades have also
affected the professional and counterinsurgency capabilities of the armed
forces. This unending war entered a crucial point when Pashtuns attacked
Punjabi officers in GHQ and killed high ranking officers. An army broken
within its inner fabric, according to military observers, is unable to defend
itself from an outside enemy. Of much greater consequence the army is being asked to attack its own citizens. The tribesmen, they are currently at
war with army inside the FATA region are, the same heroes they supported
throughout their history. Our elders, Maliks, and tribal chiefs have been
severely tortured in public. They were humiliated and tortured in front of
their relatives. Many have been dragged on roads to unknown places, torn
their bodies with bullets.[1]

In 2012, one of my journalist friends told me that soldiers of the Pakistan army arrested an eighty-year-old Pashtun in Swat and tortured him to
death. The most important thing is the crisis of confidence and the army's
continuing inability to defend its own leaders, troops and assets from its
trained jihadist brothers. In January 2013, former Army Chief Ashfaq Kayani
announced a new doctrine to review its war strategy and sternly deal with
sectarian terrorists across the country.

The Green Book, consisted of 200 pages, defines the new counterinsurgency strategy of the armed forces. This new strategy means that previous counterterrorism strategies were wrongly designed and based on misunderstanding. Some analysts understand that Pakistan Security Forces
now believe that the Tehreek-e-Taliban Pakistan (TTP) and other militant
groups are a bigger security threat. Prime Minister Nawaz Sharif announced
that India is no more Pakistan's enemy, but in November 2013, when army
revised it Green Book, the stance abruptly changed. Army declared that the
US-India nexus is a bigger threat to its existence.[2]

Operations in Swat, Baluchistan and Waziristan suggest that the military establishment remain largely unwilling to hold itself accountable to the
public. Army is reluctant to be more transparent to civilian authorities.[3]

Operations in Swat, Bajour, Mohmand, Tirah Valley and Waziristan
have done nothing to raise the credibility of the armed forces. The issue of
extra-judicial killing still needs to be settled as world's human rights groups,
the HRCP and newspapers reported human rights violations in Swat. People
were killed in groups, women were raped in groups and children were kidnapped and killed in groups. On January 16, 2013, BBC reported hundreds of
protesters in Khyber Pakhtunkhwa displayed the bodies of at least 14 people, who they said were victims of extra-judicial killings outside government
office in Peshawar. Military leaders should think that the present attacks

1 *Ibid*
2 *Guradian*, 2 October 2012.
3 *Pakistan Affairs*, 5 January 2013.

on military convoys are revenge attacks of Pashtuns whose houses are being targeted by army gunship helicopters.[1]

In Baluchistan, the army used helicopter gunships, bombarded villages, raped and kidnapped women and destroyed the houses of the poor Balochs and Pashtuns. Asian Human Rights Commission in its recent report (2013) recorded army's atrocities in Baluchistan: "The main military sweep took place in Awaran, Panjgur and Makran districts of Baluchistan. Hundred of villagers were rounded up and interrogated. Many since have disappeared. Some were later found dead, with their mutilated bodies showing signs of torture."[2]

Pakistani security forces followed the same tactics learnt in Bosnian war on those Pashtun officers and their relatives who refused to fight against their own brothers in FATA and Waziristan. They also killed numerous people in Bosnia and Afghanistan by providing arms to Taliban, Mujahedeen and Bosnians to fight the Serbs.

The army trained Afghans, Bosnians, Somalis, Sudanese, Kashmiries, Chechens, and Arabs, Philippines, Tamil, Muslim groups of Chinese Turkistan, Iranians, and Islamic Movement of Uzbekistan in Central Asia, Nigerians and Americans. The military became a radicalized jihadist groups and started sending young jihadists to Chechnya, Bosnia, Kosovo, Kashmir and Afghanistan. Various Arabs marooned in Afghanistan were identified as Afghan Arabs, while the Pashtun fighters were described as Taliban – a name that had been adopted by Mullah Omar's organization. General Javed Nasir, a former ISI Chief accepted the allegations in Lahore High Court, that he breached arms embargo of UK to Bosnia.

The new shift in US hegemonic policy, alliance with the Taliban insurgents and the deterioration of Pak-US relations signal new military challenges for China, Afghanistan and Pakistan, if India and Iran become part of US military adventurism in the region. This is the beginning of a new cold-bloody war as US Defense Secretary Leon Panetta declared that his country is at a strategic turning point after a decade of war in Afghanistan and Iraq. Having realised the sensitivity of the recent political and military developments in the region, Pakistan's army chief recently went to China to discuss the strategic turning point in US policy with the Chinese leadership.

His abrupt visit to China immediately after the announcement of the US Defense and Strategic Plan raised many questions, including the concern of the Chinese and Russian leadership about the American military preparation for future military confrontations in South and Southeast Asia. Pakistan and China vowed to support each other and strengthen long-term military cooperation. Beijing gives a lot of importance to peace and stability in the region and understands that peace in Afghanistan is in its interest.

---

1  *Daily Times*, 1, May 2013.

2  *Daily Times*, "The Asian Human Rights Commission report", 2013. *The South Asian Tribune*, Issue No 54, August 10-16, 2013, *Daily Times*, 01 May 2013.

## Chapter 15. Afghanistan's Future and the Blueprint for Civil War

This is an irrevocable fact that the United States and NATO allies are not scheduled to withdraw their forces from Afghanistan in the end of 2014. If they withdraw, Afghanistan will lose a large portion of US military aid and after a new phase of civil war, the Taliban and al-Qaeda will success-fully return to the country. A new US intelligence assessment report also predicted that the gains US and NATO allies have made during the last 12 years is, likely to be eroded and the Taliban and other power brokers, will become increasingly influential, as the United States winds down its longest war in history. The post 2014 civil war will be localized and complex. With the military and political intervention of neighboring states, including Rus-sia, Pakistan, Iran and China, war will spread across the Durand Line and, war between new warlords and old warlords will also intensify.[1]

The increasing Taliban attacks and their collaboration with the officers of ANA, forced some NATO allies to think about the earlier withdrawal of their forces from Afghanistan. In 2011, in a White House meeting, President Obama once proposed earlier withdrawal from Afghanistan. The focus of US Secretary of Defense Robert Gates in a meeting with Afghan authorities was the same issue. Gates made no secret of his frustration in Afghanistan.[2]

In 2012, during his visit to Kabul, President Obama made it clear that the United States army will continue operation in Afghanistan beyond 2014. Paul D. Miller, an assistant Professor of International affairs at the National

---

1 *Daily Times*, 16 June, 2011.
2 *Daily Outlook Afghanistan*, 15 June, 2011.

Defense University in Washington DC, in his recent article (Survival-March 2013) revealed about the US withdrawal strategy:

> The United States is not scheduled to withdraw from Afghanistan in 2014. President Barak Obama made clear in his May 2012 speech in Kabul that the United States would continue to train Afghan security forces and undertake counter terrorism operations, which are likely to require thousands of US troops to operate in the country for years to come.[1]

The US-led international forces immediate withdrawal from Afghanistan was long awaited by other neighboring countries. President Zardari visited Russian and China and received Moscow's appreciation of the role his country played in Afghanistan. Russia fears that the US withdrawal will lead to civil war in the country or extremist fighters moving into the Central Asian region. In December 2013, suicide bomber killed dozens civilians in Volgograd Railway Station and local market.

An Islamic insurgency in the North Caucasus region has led to many attacks there in recent years. The quick or immediate withdrawal of US and NATO troops from Afghanistan has developed a new perception among Afghans that US again leave Afghans in a state of maroon. A recent study in the United Stats warned that faster withdrawal of troops from Afghanistan will cause economic collapse, as there is no proper revenue generation in the country. Afghans can suffer a severe economic depression unless proper planning begins.

Military experts understated that the main reason behind the US frustration might be the return of civil war after the NATO and US immediate withdrawal in the end of 2014. The war in Afghanistan, which is being conducted under NATO auspices, is a prime example of U.S. frustration at European inability to provide the required resources. In his various meeting with US officials in and outside the country, Afghan President Hamid Karzai also showed deep frustration. The reasons for his frustration are clear and understandable. In Karzai's view, the possibilities of ethnic cleansing or the return of civil war might push his country back into graveyard.

President Karzai also discussed the withdrawal of foreign forces from Afghanistan with Islamabad and Iran. The main focus of his visits to Islamabad was to seek Pakistan's cooperation in bringing the Taliban to negotiation table, which have been the basic objective of Afghan government and its allies for the future settlements of decades long civil war.[2]

Islamabad never designed a constructive policy towards Afghanistan after the fall of the Taliban regime in 2001. For President Karzai, the issue of security transition was more important, but Pakistan was not clear in its political and military cooperation with Afghanistan. Karzai told his Paki-

---

1　Paul D. Miller. *The US and Afghanistan after 2014, Survival, Global Politics and Strategy*, vole, 55, No, 1, February-March 2013.
2　*Daily Times*, 25 august 2011.

stani friends, that the recent terror attacks carried out by the Taliban in Northern Afghanistan are much irksome for him.

In Karzai's view, if his administration cannot maintain peace in northern parts of the country, how they would be able to control the troubled South? Pakistan promised to persuade the Taliban leader for talks with Afghanistan. There are three competing rogue armies in the country, Taliban militias, warlord militias and the Afghan National Army; therefore, after the withdrawal of US forces in 2014, the country will become the battle ground of these armies. Warlords do not accept the instruction and command of the ANA and do not help the state army in maintaining stability in the country. All these forces have been involved in violence since 1990s.[1]

Ethnic and sectarian violence on provincial level greatly disturbed the process of nation building. The present feature of governance structure in the country is nothing more than a mockery with the citizens of the country where political bargaining and corruption created an alarming situation.[2]

Each province has three governors; formal governor (appointed by Afghan Interior Ministry, informal governor (appointed by warlords and war criminals) and, invisible governor (appointed by the Taliban). The three run the country's administration on diverse directions, based on different politico-religious ideologies. Their source of revenue and their way of governance, prosecution and justice is quite different. They all collect taxes, shares poppy cultivation, protect containerized criminal trade and black market economy. They forcefully bring young people to the governor house, train and arm them for future civil war.[3]

As we read in history, governance is the manner in which communities regulate themselves and government is the consecutive exercise of state authority, but in Afghanistan, the case is different. Some analysts are of the view that Pakistan runs a shadow government and controls several provinces but majority term this perception exaggerated. Pakistan's religious and political influence cannot be ruled out, but in parts of Northern Afghanistan, Iran's political, religious and military influence is strongly felt.[4]

A part from international and regional influence, the way of intractable governance across the country has become a strong challenge to the sub national governance. Every governor has its own Inspector General Police, Maliks, Forces Commander, paid Community alders, Councils and Municipalities. Competition over political influence is another challenging prob-

---

1   *Breaking Point, Measuring Progress in Afghanistan.* Report of the Centre for Strategic and International studies, March 2007.

2   *Daily Times*, 25 august 2011.

3   *Ibid.*

4   *www.globalsecurity.org*, November 2011.

lem. Sometimes, the forces of these three governors attack each other, some-times negotiate for peace and sometimes entered into alliance with Taliban.[1] They operate separately and maintain their own militias and prisons. In the business of kidnapping, they do not rob or kidnap each other's member's houses. They are corrupt and unable to bring peace and stability in their managed provinces. They are involved in kidnapping, human trafficking and child abuse. Ordinary Afghans have become frustrated, alienated and dis-connected from all these policies. They are in disparity and dismal with the corruption, torture and administrative policies of these people.

All provincial governors have divided the total 166,000 mosques and 6,000 Imams across the country. In total 330 religious madrasas, more than 100,000 students are being taught with different syllabuses. They have failed and cannot exert control over the whole country. The issue of mapping con-flicts among communities has never been taken seriously. Community lead-ers have been humiliated, killed and their house were set to fire. Thus, tradi-tional administrative system came to an end gradually.[2]

Author Robert D. Lamb explains the disruption of social and traditional systems in Afghanistan:

> Informal governance includes not only patronage networks and corrupt practices, but traditional and customary structures as well, including tribal, religious, ethnic and kinship networks. The customary institutions, most people associated with Afghanistan—mainly Pashtun tribal codes, elders and community councils—have been greatly degraded over the past 40 years. The elders were attacked by communists in the 1970s, Soviets in the 1980s, the Taliban in the 1990s. Traditional authority was displaced by the elevation within Afghan society of Mujahedeen commander in the 1980s and religious leaders in the 1990s.[3]

Social systems of the country have been disrupted by the massive popu-lation displacement that took place during the thirty years of war. These socio-political fluctuations in Afghan society greatly impacted the tradi-tional way of governance. The present shadow governments have created more problems. Sectarian violence in Ghazni and Wardak provinces and ethnic violence in Northern parts of the country forced business and invest-ment communities to leave the country.

Kenneth Katzman highlighted the recent administrative reshuffle of the Afghan government in response to the corruption complaints of interna-tional community: "On September 20, 2012, acting subsequent to his July 2012 administrative decree, Karzai shuffled 10 out of 34 provincial governors,

---

1 Occasional Paper, No. 11, April 2012, *Formal and Informal Governance in Afghanistan,,* Reflections on a Survey of the Afghan People.

2 Kenneth Katzman *report, Specialist in Middle East and Eastern Affairs,* 2012.

3 Robert D. Lamb, *Report of the CSIS Program on Crisis Conflict and cooperation.* April 2012.

asserting that those taken out of their positions had fallen short on improving governance or combating corruption".[1]

Unfortunately, the Karzai government has failed to control corruption. The stark reality in today Afghanistan is that government doesn't know what to do and how to manage the affairs of the state. Power is in the hands of criminal and corrupt mafia groups, who control the whole economy of criminal market, poppy cultivation, human and arms trafficking.

International Crisis group in its recent report warned that Afghan police and army are unprepared for security responsibility. According to European diplomatic sources that the US backed Afghan government could be on course for what it calls a devastating political crisis after 2014. Foreign Policy Magazine suggests that international community should not abandon Afghanistan and should include Pakistan as the mediator.[2]

The recent report of the US Inspector General for Afghanistan is more alarming. According to his report, one-fourth recruits of the ANA are absent from duty in any given time. They do not inform their seniors. Their desertion is the biggest challenges faced by the ANA after the US and NATO withdrawal from the country.[3]

Many Afghans and Pakistani intellectuals often ask about the future of civil war in Afghanistan and an unending series of insurgencies in Pakistan. The partition of Afghan state is begun with the establishment of the Taliban office in Qatar, and the demand for federal system of government and independent provinces. Since the revelation of Britain MP plan for the future political structure of Afghanistan that appeared in newspapers, Afghans of different ethnic groups demonstrated and expressed concern about the dismemberment of their country on ethnic lines. The plan is supported in the North while rejected in the South.

As the country experienced a lot of torture, destruction and humiliation in the hands of Russia, Afghan communists, Mujahedeen and the Taliban, now NATO and US are treating its wounds with their own medicines; the recovery of the Afghan state seems to be impossible. The injection of the American and European tax payer's blood into the diseases infected body of the state gave no result.

The series of extra-judicial ethnic and sectarian killings from North to South and from South to North, and the hatred walls between the Pashtuns and other ethnic minorities, foreign intervention, poverty and national alienation, provided a ground to various ethnic groups to demand the partition of the country. The collapsed and deeply wounded, polarized and fragmented

---

1  Kenneth Katzman *report on Afghanistan*, 2012.
2  *BBC News*, "Foreign Forces in Afghanistan". 4 April, 2013
3  *Daily Times*. 13 March, 2011.

Afghan state caused a vortex of instability, corruption, regionalism and illegal militarization of society.[1]

The artificial Afghan state has no specific production or proper revenue generation, as there is no tax system, no electricity, gas and water bills system, no income tax, wealth tax, property tax, to support the day to day expenditure of the state and government. Interestingly, there is $11 billion worth of arms across the country, not under the government control. Based on these criteria, Afghanistan is considered to be a failed state.

If a country like Afghanistan is unable to extend its writ to the whole territory, unable to provide basic public services and cannot represent the whole country in the international community, it means the state has shrunken, withered and failed. Afghan army is still dependent on NATO for air support, ammunition and roadside bomb-clearing. Moreover, high rates of desertion and drug addiction, made it more vulnerable.

A recent report of the Center for Strategic and International Studies warned that militia commanders and warlords who took part in the disarmament drive have begun to rearm their cronies in Northern Afghanistan, and former warlords retain de facto control, blunting Karzai's influence in the region.[2]

The wave of partition has arrived and the horses of criminal militias are being prepared for the killing fields. One of the most destructive dimensions of this war is internal rivalries among factions divided along tribal, ethnic,' religious, and ideological lines. The ethno-civil war coupled with the Taliban-imposed Jihad on the country is considered, a protracted conflict, in which the focus of NATO and US forces has tended to fluctuate, depending upon their interests.[3]

Afghan returnees from Pakistan and Iran faced a threatening situation when ethnic commanders refused to leave houses they had occupied in 1990s. Some of these areas now have a different ethnic profile. There are no easy solutions to such problems. Kabul is not in full control of some Northern provinces, like Balkh, Mazar-e-Sharif and Bamyan, causing growing ethnic violence in the North. Governors of these provinces do not take any advice from Kabul. They are running their administration like independent states. They do not even share revenue with the Central Government.[4]

The state is on the verge of disappearance and dismemberment due to the recent power struggle. A combination of all these factors has led to unrest, ethnic and sectarian violence in the country. A new chapter of civil war is about to be opened after the withdrawal of US forces in the end of 2014.[5]

---

1   *Daily Times*, 26 March, 2011.
2   *Human Rights Watch*, 29 July, 2012.
3   *Afghanistan Justice Project*, 18 July 2005.
4   *Daily Outlook Afghanistan*, 19 May, 2011.
5   *The Bangladesh Today*, 11 February, 2011.

The recent debates about the partition of Afghanistan for peace in London and Washington received plenty of reactions from Afghanistan and Pakistan. Afghans understand that the old state machine of their country is no more working as it cannot accommodate all ethnic colors within its torn and bruised body. Technocrats believe that all parts of the machine have become outdated as it has not been able to address the issue of ethnicity, sectarianism and national reconstruction, since 1992. Conversely, there are different opinions in Pakistan. Some believe that Pakistan needs a strong and united Afghanistan, while some agree on the issue of partition for peace.[1]

The Federation of American Scientists (FAS) recently released a detailed report and identified important factors that gave rise to the threat of the jihadist Taliban inside the country. Military-grade weapons, the FAS say, are available to them in major towns and cities in all parts of FATA and Khyber Pakhtunkhwa. This means that the so-called Pakistani nuclear threat is only a pretext; Pakistan is the real target — owing to its role in the complex US-China geopolitical relations. Writing in the Cutting Edge Magazine, Shoshana Bryen revealed that the CIA has been using drones in Pakistan from bases in Afghanistan, because the US does not want to wage a war in Pakistan from Pakistan; the CIA wants to wage Pakistan's war from Afghanistan.[2]

The recent threatening statement of General Petraeus to undertake unilateral military operations inside Pakistan was followed by NATO violations of Pakistan's airspace in North Waziristan. All these challenges faced by Pakistan are linked with the availability of military-grade weapons to insurgents and terrorist groups.[3]

---

1  *Ibid.*
2  Shoshana Bryen *Cutting Edge,* June 22, 2011
3  *Daily Times,* 21, July 2011.

# Postscript

Since the fall of the Taliban regime in 2011, the issue of ethnic representation within the ANA and police ranks has not been addressed properly. Ethnic representation and discrimination in the Afghan National Army and the police, has been a major concern during the last 12 years. According to a US report, the division in the ANA, and ethnic hatred and factionalism within the ranks of the army is matter of great concern. Ethnic favoritism is on the rise. In July 2013, the US defense department published a detailed report, in which ethnic representation in the ranks of the ANA was focused upon with deep concern.

From 2005 to 2007, being an executive editor of *The Daily Outlook Afghanistan*, I still remember how Army Chief Mullah Bismillah Khan Muhammadi ordered officers and security guards from his Ministry to prevent Defense Minister Abdul Rahim Wardak from entering his office. He was adamant in saying that the Defense Minister was an ISI agent, because of his Pashtun identity. This irreconcilable policy of Mullah Khan further divided the Defense Ministry on ethnic lines. In Afghanistan, it is a common belief that Persian-speaking Afghans see all Pashtuns as agents of ISI or friends of al-Qaeda and Taliban.

Moreover, four months later, the Army Chief dismissed another Pashtun female general, Mrs. Khatool Ahmadzai, allegedly for her slight kissing moment with a NATO general. This decision created a formidable resentment of Pashtun officers against the Army Chief and his plan to build ethnic discord within the ANA.

This squabble and these ethnic rivalries forced ordinary ANA soldiers and officers to rethink their loyalties. Their wretchedness and misery, and the vulnerable future of their children, have raised serious questions. Their defection to insurgent forces is understandable from the fact that a corrupt and moribund Afghan army can no longer serve the interests of the state — they are serving the interests of the CIA and Pentagon generals. In 2013, Special Forces Commander Monsif Khan, defected to the Gulbeddin Hekmatyar group in Kunar province. The provinces of Herat, Farah, Badghis, Paktia and Kandahar are reporting the highest number of desertions.

The Afghan local police (ALP) have been running a chromate extraction operation in Kunar province for over a year. Not only the ALP but the ANA officers are also involved in robbing their country's mineral resources. Illegal extraction of mineral resources in several provinces of northern Afghanistan is a matter of great concern. Now, as this corrupt and ethnically divided army is unable to defend its country, President Karzai once again has started begging NATO, the US and UK for military cooperation after the end of 2014. Mr. Karzai wants a bilateral security agreement which will enslave his country for another 50 years. This agreement will further justify the illegal involvement of the Pentagon and CIA in Afghan security affairs after 2014.

Failure of the army to re-enlist 20% soldiers every year is a major problem for the military establishment. Generals cannot keep enough soldiers and officer in the field. The Afghan National army should number 250,000 men to effectively defeat al-Qaeda and Taliban forces, after the withdrawal of NATO and US forces in the end of 2014, but military experts in the United States note with regret that the number of ANA soldiers may never surpass 100,000, because 42% of soldiers are leaving their posts every year. Another problem is drug abuse; more than 50% of ANA soldiers are using drugs or have been involved in drug smuggling and fuel theft. Afghan government and its Army lack the domestic capacity to deploy forces across the country, or to provide security to the polling stations at election time.

Now, the ANA generals and officers have gotten weary in the endless battle against the Taliban. They want peace, but are divided on the peace process. The poor, illiterate and corrupt leadership, lack of accountability, and reported sexual assaults all fuel attrition. There are 1,700 to 1,800 women police officers in the ANP, but they face serious challenges including sexual abuse. In Mazar-e-Sharif, Balkh and Kunduz provinces, according to a US-based public radio report, senior policemen demand sexual favors in exchange for promotions. The same story is being repeated in the ANA as well. A negative attitude towards women officers, on top of sexual demands and verbal abuse, has forced hundreds of women officers to leave the armed forces. Women working in the army have no separate toilets — they are reported to have been raped and abused in shared toilets by ANA and police officers.

Warlords still control important posts in the Interior, Foreign, Intelligence and Defense Ministries and have also dragged intelligence agencies into this war. Military intelligence never investigated ethnic rivalries within the army headquarters, and other institutions, because its officers are also involved in corruption, land grabbing, arms and drug trafficking business. Mullah Bismillah Khan Muhammadi has failed to address ethnic and sectarian issues within his divided force.

War has become a profitable business in Afghanistan. When poor, alienated, homeless and jobless people enter this business and taste it, then the business of killing and destruction expands to all parts of the country. War criminals and warlords cannot live without war and destruction; they depend on it. Their way of life is war, rape, male prostitution, killing, looting and kidnapping.

Citizens of Afghanistan never experienced a single day in peace during the last three decades. Since 2001, every year the statistics on civilian and military causalities make record increases. Every year is bloodier than the preceding one. The lack of confidence in the Karzai government is growing, due to the gap between expectations and real political and economic achievement. Taliban have re-established their offices in several provinces of the country, while Pakistan's jihadists groups and TTP are also critical of US and NATO presence in Afghanistan, therefore; they may possibly join Afghan Taliban in disrupting the security network in the country.

During the last 12 years, Afghan army and the police has not been able to restore the confidence of the people. The state hardly exists, and its artificial institutions are so weak that they enable non-state actors to achieve political gain. The weak political party system is another challenging problem, which is characterized by clientelism. The judicial aspect of election infrastructure is weak and impartiality of Independent Electoral Commission (IEC) is doubtful. The integrity of some officers of election commission and their deficiencies in voter registration and identity card distribution raises many questions. During the last two elections, election security was maintained by ISAF, NATO, US and Afghan National army, while in 2014, election security will be entrusted to ANA and ANP, that face the challenge of corruption in their ranks.

Without any proper training of intelligence information collection, to prevent the Taliban infiltration into the ANA's rank and file, Afghan military intelligence is unable to process any kind of information. The leadership of the Afghan military intelligence has purchased expensive houses in major provinces of the country. Another secret agency, RAMA, which was established under the auspices of Indian intelligence agency RAW, in 2009, is working in an adverse direction. The National Directorate of Security (NDS) works for the CIA while Pakistani intelligence agency, ISI, runs its own business.

Iran has also increased its military and intelligence influence within the ranks of the Afghan intelligence agencies. Iranian intelligence has established several networks across Afghanistan, and fixed salaries for the NDS's double agents. In Northern Afghanistan, Iran's various intelligence activities, including Signal Intelligence, Human Intelligence and Counterintelligence, are operating under the auspices of the Ministry of Intelligence and security (MOIS), known as VEVAK.

Afghanistan is not a functioning modern nation state. The nation does not exist in any Western sense, so the Afghan 'National' Army was always going to be a problematic model. Even in Western countries, national armies are a relatively recent development. Humans have always fought other humans as part of groups. On November 24, 2013, the Loya Jirga (Grand Assembly of 3,000 elders) endorsed the Bilateral Security Agreement (BSA) between the US and Afghanistan, which allows U.S, forces to operate in the country beyond 2014. Members of the Loya Jirga were faced with a very awkward situation when President Karzai refused to sign the agreement. The gathering was arranged by the president himself but was humiliated and left rather speechless, when he said that he would not sign it until after the presidential elections in April 2014.

The agreement allows US forces to enter the houses of Afghan citizens day and night, and kill, injure and arrest their women, children and elders, on suspicion of their links with the Taliban and al-Qaeda terrorist groups. "From now on, the US troops searching houses, night raids, blocking roads and military operations are over and our people are free to go anywhere," Karzai said. He said, "if the US soldiers' raids on homes continue, then this agreement would not be signed". In fact, he insisted on the end of US night raids on Afghan homes, which have regularly been carried out since 2001.

The commonly called 'immunity' for US forces is a matter of great concern for all Afghans living in and outside the country. Experts say, immunity for US soldiers is directly related to the national sovereignty of the country. This means national sovereignty has been sold.

After the endorsement of the Loya Jirga, US Ambassador James B Cunningham issued a statement that said, "I am grateful that the Loya Jirga, which represents the Afghan people, overwhelmingly offered support for the Bilateral Security Agreement and asked President Karzai to sign it by the end of the next month." US National Security Advisor Susan Rice also told Mr. Karzai that the US was ready to sign, but Karzai acknowledged that there has been a trust deficit between his government and the US during the last five years. He also feared that the CIA and Pentagon might interfere in the coming elections. Mr. Karzai accused the US of meddling in the 2009 elections, saying it tried to change the voting process.

There was also a sharp reaction from Afghan forces when Mr. Karzai questioned the credibility of the Afghan security forces in fighting insurgency and terrorism. Afghan neighbors have shown reservations about the US military bases in the country and said\ these bases will endanger their security. The air bases that the US wants to establish in Bagram, Kabul, Kandahar, Herat, Mazar-e-Sharif, Helmand and Jalalabad, and land ports in Torkham, Spin Boldak, Tooghundi and the Sher Khan border in Kunduz province, are considered a greater threat to regional security.

In the general understanding, the US military base in Mazar-e-Sharif province will monitor Russia and China, while its military base in Herat might monitor Iran and the Gulf states. The Jalalabad and Kandahar bases would monitor Pakistan and its military activities and the Bagram base would monitor China.

# Appendix 1. Durand Line Agreement, November 12, 1893

## Agreement between Amir Abdur Rahman Khan, G. C. S. I., and Sir Henry Mortimer Durand, K. C. I. E., C. S. I.

Whereas certain questions have arisen regarding the frontier of Afghanistan on the side of India, and whereas both His Highness the Amir and the Government of India are desirous of settling these questions by friendly understanding, and of fixing the limit of their respective spheres of influence, so that for the future there may be no difference of opinion on the subject between the allied Governments, it is hereby agreed as follows:

1 The eastern and southern frontier of his Highness's dominions, from Wakhan to the Persian border, shall follow the line shown in the map attached to this agreement.

2 The Government of India will at no time exercise interference in the territories laying beyond this line on the side of Afghanistan, and His Highness the Amir will at no time exercise interference in the territories lying beyond this line on the side of India.

3 The British Government thus agrees to His Highness the Amir retaining Asmar and the valley above it, as far as Chanak. His Highness agrees, on the other hand, that he will at no time exercise interference in Swat, Bajaur, or Chitral, including the Arnawai or Bashgal valley. The British Government also agrees to leave to His Highness the Birmal tract

as shown in the detailed map already given to his Highness, who relinquishes his claim to the rest of the Waziri country and Dawar. His Highness also relinquishes his claim to Chageh.

4    The frontier line will hereafter be laid down in detail and demar-
cated, wherever this may be practicable and desirable, by joint British
and Afghan commissioners, whose object will be to arrive by mutual
understanding at a boundary which shall adhere with the greatest possible exactness to the line shown in the map attached to this agreement,
having due regard to the existing local rights of villages adjoining the
frontier.

5    With reference to the question of Chaman, the Amir withdraws
his objection to the new British cantonment and concedes to the British
Government the rights purchased by him in the Sirkai Tilerai water. At
this part of the frontier the line will be drawn as follows:

6    From the crest of the Khwaja Amran range near the Psha Kotal,
which remains in British territory, the line will run in such a direction as
to leave Murgha Chaman and the Sharobo spring to Afghanistan, and to
pass half-way between the New Chaman Fort and the Afghan outpost
known locally as Lashkar Dand.

7    The line will then pass half-way between the railway station
and the hill known as the Mian Baldak, and, turning south-wards, will
rejoin the Khwaja Amran range, leaving the Gwasha Post in British territory, and the road to Shorawak to the west and south of Gwasha in
Afghanistan. The British Government will not exercise any interference
within half a mile of the road.

8    The above articles of agreement are regarded by the Government of India and His Highness the Amir of Afghanistan as a full and
satisfactory settlement of all the principal differences of opinion which
have arisen between them in regard to the frontier; and both the Government of India and His Highness the Amir undertake that any differences
of detail, such as those which will have to be considered hereafter by the
officers appointed to demarcate the boundary line, shall be settled in a
friendly spirit, so as to remove for the future as far as possible all causes of
doubt and misunderstanding between the two Governments.

9    Being fully satisfied of His Highness's goodwill to the British
Government, and wishing to see Afghanistan independent and strong, the
Government of India will raise no objection to the purchase and import

by His Highness of munitions of war, and they will themselves grant him some help in this respect. Further, in order to mark their sense of the friendly spirit in which His Highness the Amir has entered into these negotiations, the Government of India undertake to increase by the sum of six hundred thousand rupees a year the subsidy of twelve lakhs now granted to His Highness.

H. M. Durand,
Amir Abdur Rahman Khan.
Kabul, November 12, 1893.

APPENDIX 2. DECREE OF THE PRESIDENT OF THE ISLAMIC
TRANSITIONAL STATE OF AFGHANISTAN
ON THE FORMATION OF AFGHAN NATIONAL ARMY [ANA]

1 December 2002.

In the name of Allah, the Compassionate and Merciful;

With the blessings of the Almighty, the Islamic Transitional State of Afghanistan (ITSA) hereby decrees that the Afghan National Army (ANA) shall be established.

1. The ANA will be subordinate to the command of legitimate civilian authorities. The President of the ITSA (or its successor government) will be commander-in chief of the ANA.

2. The ANA will not exceed 70,000 soldiers, officers and non-commissioned officers, to include all air and ground forces, air defense forces, civilian employees of the Ministry of Defense (MoD), student cadets of post-secondary institutions, and other specialized units.

3. The current organization of the army will gradually be transformed into four major commands. With the exception of the central command in Kabul, the location of the remaining commands will be determined on the basis of strategic and geographical factors. The ITSA is committed to promote the earliest restoration of security, the rule-of-law and the full exercise of human rights throughout the country.

4. The organization and staffing of the ANA and the MoD will take place on the basis of individual merit and in accordance with accepted prin-

ciples of balance among different ethnic groups and establishment of trust among all the citizens of this country.

5. The recruitment of soldiers for the ANA will be voluntary and inclusive of all social and ethnic groups. A Sub-commission on Recruitment of Young Soldiers will be established to recruit volunteers representing all the population of Afghanistan who meet the necessary conditions and are willing to abide by the regulations of the ANA. In order to qualify as soldiers of the ANA, recruits must successfully complete the training program of the ANA, as jointly designed by Afghanistan and the United States or other designated lead nations.

6. Another Sub-commission will be formed to propose criteria for and carry out the process of selection of officers for the ANA on the basis of merit, ethnic representation and national outlook. Officers selected will complete the aforementioned training program.

7. Concurrent with the recruitment and training of soldiers, a program of collection of arms and reintegration shall be carried out. The ITSA, with the assistance of the United Nations and the Government of Japan as lead nation, shall prepare a comprehensive program of collection of arms and reintegration based upon:

(a) The establishment of a Commission on Demobilization with its own chairman by the Defense Commission;

(b) Concentration on collection and integration into the ANA of heavy weapons (to include tanks, armored personnel carriers, artillery, field guns, multiple rocket launchers and towed air-defense weapons, etc.); and

(c) The development of a comprehensive disarmament, demobilization and reintegration plan for officers and soldiers who meet the necessary conditions with implementation timelines.

This process shall be subject to independent verification and shall be carried out as rapidly as possible with the assistance of the United Nations, Japan as lead nation and other interested countries.

8. The process of building of the ANA — including recruitment, training and equipping – will take several years to complete. Military formations, armed groups, and any other military or paramilitary units that are not a part of the ANA shall be prohibited.

9. Taking account of financial constraints, an essential element of the national security strategy for Afghanistan is the furthest consolidation of the ITSA's authority across all of its territory in the shortest period of time.

10. The Defense Commission, under the chairmanship of the Minister of Defense, will report on progress in development of the ANA, the reorganization of the Ministry of Defense, and the reorganization of the units and formations of the army, its relevant offices and appointments of responsible officials to the President of the Islamic Transitional State of Afghanistan. An Advisory Committee — comprised of members of the Defense Commission,

representatives of the United States and Coalition Governments, and United Nations officials — will periodically review the progress of the ANA recruitment and training process, promoting financial and technical support for the process within the international community.

11.  Financial contributions for the ANA and the process of disarmament, demobilization and reintegration shall be made in a transparent manner.

Contributions shall be made to the United Nations ANA Trust Fund, the Afghan Ministry of Finance or the United States as the designated lead nation for ANA restructuring. Disbursement of funds to the Ministry of Defense shall be through the Ministry of Finance and in accordance with all applicable budgetary, statutory and regulatory requirements of the ITSA. Military finances shall be subject to civilian oversight, auditing and control.

The nation has a special responsibility to recognize the historical legacy of the Afghan mujahedeen for the Afghan people's freedom and for Islam. The ITSA will give special consideration to Afghan mujahedeen who are qualified to make use of them in building the Afghan National Army. Those who do not join the ANA will be given special consideration in the reintegration process.

Hoping that our endeavor will be endowed with success by the Almighty God, we are embarking on the renewal and reconstruction of the ANA as an essential step for the realization of the ideals of the Afghan mujahedeen who were martyred during the Afghan jihad, of all the people of the Afghan nation, and for the securing of national unity, peace and stability in our country. Success is from God.

Hamid Karzai, President: Islamic Transitional State of Afghanistan.

*Sources: (Ministry of Foreign Affairs Afghanistan, Kabul).*

## Appendix 3. Afghan Security Forces Command and Control Structure

### Afghan National Army

1. Afghan National Security Forces Headquarters is based in Kabul
2. Commando Brigade headquarters, Kabul.
3. Division 111st is based in Kabul
4. Corps 211st is based in Kabul.
5. Corps 203rd is based in Gardez province.
6. Corps 205th is based in Kandahar province.
7. Corps 207th is based in Heart province.
8. Corps 209th is based in Mazar-e-Sharif province.
9. Corps 215th is based in Lashkargah.

### Afghan National Army Air Corps Command and Control System

1. Air Command headquarters is based in Kabul.
2. Kabul air wing.
3. Kandahar air wing
4. Shindand air wing.
5. Jalalabad detachment.
6. Mazar-e-Sharif detachment
7. Gardez detachment
8. Heart detachment.
9. NATO, US, UK, ISAF and Allies Command Operation.
10. US central command.

11. Combined joint task force.
12. Combined security transition command - Afghanistan.
13. Chief of mission.
14. US State department.
15. Islamic republic of Afghanistan.
16. ISAF joint command.
17. ISAF forces.
18. Interagency provincial affairs.
19. Joint force command.
20. NATO.
21. National command authority.
22. NATO and its training mission
23. PRT committee.
24. Regional command.
25. Regional platform.
26. Bureau of South and Central Asia.
27. Task force.

DEFENSE MINISTERS OF AFGHANISTAN

1. Lieutenant General Ghulam Haider Resuli: 1977 to 1978.
2. General Abdul Qadir Dagarwal: May 1978 to August 1978.
3. General Muhammad Aslam Watanjar: March 30, 1979 to July 1979.
4. Hafeezullah Amin: July 1979 to December 27 1979.
5. General Muhammad Rafi: December 1980 to 1982.
6. Brigadier General Abdul Kadir: 1982 to 1984.
7. Nazar Muhammad 1984 to 1986.
8. General Muhammad Rafi: 1986 to 1988.
9. General Shanawaz Tanai: 1988 to 1990.
10. General Muhammad Aslam Watanjar: 1990 to 1992.
11. Warlord Ahmad Shah Masood: 1992 to 2001.
12. Warlord Mullah Obidullah Akhund: 1996 to 2001.
13. Warlord Muhammad Fahim Qasim: 2001 to2004.
14. General Abdul Rahim Wardak: 2004 to 2012.
15. Warlord Bismillah Khan Muhammadi: August 2012 to Present.

GENERALS OF ANA MILITARY COMMAND

1. Defense Minister: Bismillah Khan Muhammadi.
2. Muhammad Zahir Azimi: Spokesman of Defense Ministry.
3. General Shir Muhammad Karimi: army Chief.
4. GeneralMuhammad Ikram: deputy Chief of General Staff.

5. General Ishaq Noori (without position).
6. Major General Abdul Abdullah: General Chief of Staff.
7. Chief of Military Intelligence: General Abdul Mana Farahi
8. Major General Abdul Khaliq Faryad: Intelligence Staff.
9. General Azizuddin Farahi: Logistics.
10. Major General Mehrab Ali Khan,: Communication.
11. Major General Jahandar Shah: Military Inspector General.
12. Surgeon General: Dr. Abdul Qayyum Tota Khel. Medical Corps.
13. Major General Muhammad dawran: Air Force.
14. Major General Muhammad Rahim Wardak, Corps commander.
15. Major General Abdul Khaleq: Corps Commander.
16. General Sher Muhammad Zazi: Corps Commander.
17. Major General Jahandar shah: Corps Commander.
18. Major General Murad Ali: Corps Commander.
19. Major General Aminullah: Commander ANA Military Academy.
20. Major General Razaq: Commander Military Staff College, Kabul.
21. Major General Muhammad Sharif: Military Academy.
22. Brigadier General Muhammad Amin Wardak: Military Academy Kabul.

*Sources: (Defense Ministry of Afghanistan).*

# Appendix 4. Size of the Afghan Security Forces 1978–2012

|      | Army, Soldiers and Officers | Air Force, Officers and Pilots |
|------|------------------------------|--------------------------------|
| 1978 | 80-90,000                    | 10,000                         |
| 1979 | 50-100,000                   | 5,000                          |
| 1980 | 20,000–25, 000               |                                |
| 1981 | 350,000                      |                                |
| 1982 | 40,000                       |                                |
| 1983 | 40,000                       | 5,000–7,000                    |
| 1984 | 40,000                       | 7,000                          |
| 1985 | 40,000 and Paramilitaries, 50,000 | 7, 000. (Total 87,000)   |
| 1986 | 40,000                       |                                |
| 1987 | 40,000                       |                                |
| 1988 | 300,000                      |                                |
| 1989 | 150,000 Paramilitaries, 100,000 | (Total 400,000)             |
| 1990 | 100,000                      |                                |
| 1991 | 160,000                      |                                |

## Afghan National Army plus Police

| 2003 | ANA 6,000   |                | |
|------|-------------|----------------|------------------|
| 2004 | ANA 24,000  | Police 33,000  | Total 57,000     |
| 2005 | ANA 26,000  | Police 40,000  | Total 66,000     |
| 2006 | ANA 36,000  | Police 49,700  | Total 86,000     |
| 2007 | ANA 50,000  | Police 75,000  | Total 125,000    |
| 2008 | ANA 57,800  | Police 79,910  | Total 137, 710   |
|      | ANA 68,000  | Police 79,910  | Total 147,910    |
| 2009 | ANA 82,780  | Police 79,910  | Total 162,690    |
| July | ANA 91,900  | Police 81,020  | Total 172,920    |

| | | 95,000 | Total 190,000 |
|---|---|---|---|
| | ANA 100,131 | Police 94,958 | Total 195,089 |

2010

| March | ANA 113,000 | Police 102,000 | Total 215,000 |
|---|---|---|---|
| April | ANA 119,388 | Police 104,459 | Total 223,847 |
| August | ANA 134,000 | Police 109,000 | Total 243,000 |
| Sept. | ANA 138,164 | Police 120,504 | Total 258,668 |
| Oct. | ANA 144,638 | Police 116,367 | Total 261,005 |
| Dec. | ANA 149,533 | Police 116,856 | Total 266,389 |

2011

| Jan. | ANA 152,000 | Police 118,800 | Total 270,800 |
|---|---|---|---|
| April | ANA 164,003 | Police 122,000 | Total 286,003 |
| May | ANA 168,037 | Police 128,622 | Total 296,659 |
| Aug. | ANA 169,076 | Police 134,865 | Total 303,941 |
| Sept. | ANA 170,781 | Police 136,122 | Total 306,903 |
| Oct. | ANA 173,150 | Police 139,070 | Total 312,220 |
| Dec. | ANA 179,610 | Police 143,800 | Total 323,410 |

2012

| Jan. | ANA 184,437 | Police 145,577 | Total 330,014 |
|---|---|---|---|
| Dec. | | | Total 344,108 |

Sources: Afghan Defense Ministry and the Police Department, Kabul

# Appendix 5. Foreign Forces Deployed in Afghanistan 2001–2012

2002

| February | 5,000 |
|-----------|-------|
| March | 5,000 |
| April | 5,000 |
| May | 4,500 |
| June | 5,000 |
| September | 4,700 |

2003

| April | 5,000 |
|-----------|-------|
| September | 5,000 |

2004

| April | 5,000 |
|-----------|--------|
| June | 6,000 |
| August | 6,500 |
| September | 8,000 |
| October | 10,000 |
| November | 9,400 |
| December | 8,500 |

2005

| | |
|---|---|
| February | 8,000 |
| June | 8,000 |
| August | 10,500 |
| December | 9,000 |

2006

| | |
|---|---|
| May | 9,000 |
| June | 9700 |
| August | 15,000 |
| September | 18,000 |
| October | 20,000 |
| November | 21,000 |
| December | 21,000 |

2007

| | |
|---|---|
| March | 21,750 |
| April | 21,750 |
| May | 24,000 |
| July | 24, 250 |
| September | 26043 |
| October | 30, 147 |
| December | 26,703 |

2008

| | |
|---|---|
| April | 28,000 |
| June | 29,350 |
| September | 29,810 |
| October | 30,100 |
| November | 31,150 |
| December | 31,400 |

2009

| | |
|---|---|
| January | 31880 |
| February | 31250 |
| March | 32140 |
| April | 32175 |
| June | 32280 |
| July | 34550 |
| October | 36230 |
| December | 38370 |

2010

| February | 38890 |
|----------|-------|
| April | 40139 |
| June | 41070 |
| July | 41315 |
| August | 40389 |
| October | 40432 |
| November | 40390 |
| December | 41730 |

2011

| February | 41893 |
|----------|-------|
| March | 42203 |
| May | 42400 |
| June | 42381 |
| August | 40697 |
| September | 40670 |
| October | 40638 |
| December | 40313 |

2012

| January | 40346 |
|---------|-------|
| April | 38961 |

Sources: (Defense Ministry and Interior Ministry of Afghanistan).

## TROOPS COMMITTED TO NATO's INTERNATIONAL SECURITY ASSISTANCE FORCE (ISAF) BY COUNTRY

Albania, 290, Armenia, 126, Australia, 1,550, Austria, 3, Azerbaijan, 94, Bahrain, 95, Belgium, 522, Bosnia & Herz., 59, Bulgaria, 605, Canada, 508, Croatia, 320, Czech Republic, 527, Denmark, 692, El Salvador, 25, Estonia, 153, Finland, 176, France, 3, 308, Georgia, 800, Germany, 4,900, Greece, 122, Hungary, 337, Iceland, 6, Ireland, 7, Italy, 3,816, Jordan, 0, Republic of Korea, 350, Latvia, 175, Lithuania, 245, Luxembourg, 10, Malaysia, 46, Mongolia, 113, Montenegro, 39, Netherlands, 274, New Zealand, 153, Norway, 525, Poland, 2,457, Portugal, 133, Romania, 1,843, Singapore, 39, Slovakia, 331, Slovenia, 89, Spain, 1,481, Sweden, 500, Macedonia, 177, Tonga, 55, Turkey, 1,327, Ukraine, 23, United Arab Emirates, 35, The United Kingdom, 9,500, The United States, 90,000.

Total: 128,961.

Sources: (Defense Ministry of Afghanistan).

## NATO Training Mission in Afghanistan

### Mission

NTM-A/CSTC-A, in coordination with NATO nations and partners, international organizations, donors and non-governmental organizations, supports the government of the Islamic Republic of Afghanistan in generating and sustaining the ANSF, develops leaders, and establishes enduring institutional capacity to enable accountable, Afghan-led security.

### Area of Responsibility

NTM-A/CSTC-A oversees training and equipping of Afghan forces throughout Afghanistan.

### Contributing Nations

NATO Countries: Albania, Belgium, Canada, Croatia, Czech Republic, Denmark, Estonia, France, Germany, Greece, Hungary, Italy, Netherlands, Norway, Poland, Portugal, Romania, Slovenia, Spain, Sweden, Turkey, U.K, U.S.

Non-NATO Countries: Australia, Finland, Jordan, Korea, Mongolia, Singapore.

Major Units Assigned:
1. 3-4 Infantry Battalions.
2. 1-17 Field Artillery Battalion.
3. 2-44 Defense Artillery Battalion.
4. 650th Regional support Group.

*Sources: ISAF Public Affairs Office, ISAF HQ, Kabul.*

# Appendix 6. Resolution against Drone Attacks

Submitted by
Dr. Shirin Mazari, on behalf of Tehreek-i-Insaf, 10 June 2013.

For nine years the US has rained drones over Pakistani territory killing innocent Pakistani citizens in far greater numbers than "militants". The people's elected representatives in the last NA passed unanimous resolutions condemning these attacks and demanding they be stopped. Today we, the newly elected representatives of the people of Pakistan in the National Assembly, express deep distress over the deaths of more than 3000 Pakistani civilians due to drone strikes since their initiation in 2004 and clearly recognize the following:

1. That drone attacks conducted earlier by the American Central Intelligence Agency (CIA) and now by the Pentagon, through direct missiles fired on Pakistani territory are in violation of Pakistan's sovereignty. The UN Charter, Article 2(4), states: "All Members shall refrain in their international relations from the threat or use of force against the territorial integrity or political independence of any state, or in any other manner inconsistent with the Purposes of the United Nations".

2. That US drone attacks violate the Geneva Conventions (1949). Drones do not even provide the chance for suspects to surrender and any person having characteristics of a militant are targeted by signature strikes, without confirming the identity of the suspect. Further, many drone strikes have targeted rescue workers that come to the site of a drone attack.

3. That drone strikes violate the International Covenant on Civil and Political Rights (ICCPR). Article 6 states that "Every human being has the inherent right to life. This right shall be protected by law. No one shall be arbitrarily deprived of his life."

4. That the Convention of 9th December 1948 with regard to punishment of the crime of Genocide, imposing prohibition against genocide, defined by Article 1 of the Convention includes the following acts: a) "Acts committed with intent to destroy, in whole or in part, a national, ethnical, racial or religious group; b) Killing members of the group; c) Causing serious bodily or mental harm to members of the group; d) Deliberately inflicting on the group conditions of life calculated to bring about its physical destruction in whole or in part; e) Imposing measures intended to prevent births within the group; f) Forcibly transferring children of the group to another group.

And calls on the Government of Pakistan, to immediately take steps to halt all drone attacks, including:

1. asking the US to end their drone strikes over Pakistani territory;

2. taking diplomatic and, if need be, military measures to respond firmly to any such attack immediately.

3. Furthermore, the National Assembly seeks to remind the Government of Pakistan of its obligations on the drones issue in view of the judgment of the Peshawar High Court of April 2013, on writ petition Writ Petition No. 1551-P/2012 in which the Court decided, inter alia:"Under the Constitution of Pakistan, 1973 particularly Article 199 thereof put this Court under tremendous obligation to safeguard & protect the life & property of the citizen of Pakistan and any person for the time being in Pakistan, being fundamental rights, hence, this Court is constrained to hold as follows:

i. That the drone strikes, carried out in the tribal areas (FATA) particularly North & South Waziristan by the CIA & US Authorities, are blatant violation of Basic Human Rights and are against the UN Charter, the UN General Assembly Resolution, adopted unanimously, the provision of Geneva Conventions thus, it is held to be a War Crime, cognizable by the International Court of Justice or Special Tribunal for War Crimes, constituted or to be constituted by the UNO for this purpose.

ii. That the drone strikes carried out against a handful of alleged militants, who are not engaged in combat with the US Authorities or Forces, amounts to breach of International law and Conventions on the subject matter, therefore, it is held that these are absolutely illegal & blatant violation of the Sovereignty of the State of Pakistan because frequent intrusion is made on its territory / airspace without its consent rather against its wishes as despite of the protests lodged by the Government of Pakistan with USA on the subject matter, these are being carried out with impunity.

iii. That the civilians casualties, as discussed above, including considerable damage to properties, livestock, wildlife & killing of infants/ suckling babies, women and preteen children, is an un-condonable crime on the part of US Authorities including the CIA and it is held so.

iv. That in view of the established facts & figures with regard to civilian's casualties & damage caused to the properties, livestock of the citizens of Pakistan; the US Government is bound to compensate all the victims' families at the assessed rate of compensation in kind of US dollars.

This Resolution demands the Government protect the sovereignty of Pakistan; the International Lawn cited above and enforces the judgment of the Peshawar High Court as soon as possible.

*[Reprinted with the permission of Pakistan Tereek-i-Insaf: www.insaf.pk].*

# Bibliography

Abbas, Hassan. 2004. *Pakistan Drift into Extremism. Allah, the Army and America's War on Terrorism.* M.E Sharp Inc.

Abbas, Hassan. 2010. Shi'ism and Sectarian Conflict in Pakistan: "Identity, Politics, Iranian Influence, and Tit for Tat Violence". *Occasional Paper.*

Abu Zahab, Mariam. March 19, 2009. "Sectarianism in Pakistan's Kurram Agency". *Terrorism Monitor.* Vol-7, Issue No-6.

*Afghanistan Election, Guns and Money*, August 2009. The International Council on Security and Development.

Afsar, Shahid, Chris Samples and Thomas Wood. 2008. "The Taliban: An Organizational Analysis." *Military Review, May June Issue.*

Ahmad, Ishtiaq. 2008. "Pakistan Inter Services Intelligence: *A Profile*," ISAS Insights, No. 35.

Ahmadzai Ashraf Ghani. April 2009, "Lecture at the Atlantic Council of the United States."

Ali Ahmad Jalali. 2002. *Rebuilding Afghanistan's National Army.* Strategic Studies Institute, USA.

Ali Banuazizi and Myron Weiner. 1986. *The State Religion and Ethnic Politics in Afghanistan, Iran and Pakistan.* Syracuse University Press.

Ahmad. Khalid. 2011. *Sectarian War: Pakistan's Sunni-Shia Violence and its Link to the Middle East.* Oxford University Press.

Anderson, Ben. 2012. *No Worse Enemy: The Inside Story of the Chaotic Struggle for Afghanistan.* One World Publications.

Avant, Deborah D. 2005, *The Market for Force: The consequences for Privatizing Security.* Cambridge University Press.

Azim Sharif. 2009. "The need for Security Sector Reforms in Afghanistan to curb corruption". *Peace and Conflict Monitor.*

Barfield, Thomas, 2010. *Afghanistan: A Cultural and Political History.* Princeton University.

Barry, Michael. 2006. *History of Modern Afghanistan.* Cambridge University Press.

Bashir Shahzad and Robert D. Crews. 2012. *under the Drones: Modern Live in the Afghanistan-Pakistan.* Harvard University Press.

Baxter, C. 2011. *The First Anglo Afghan War: A Country Study*, Baton Rouge.

Boera, Michael and Paul R. Birch. 2011. "Rebuilding Afghanistan's National Security Forces. Fighting Symmetry with Symmetry". *Military Review.*

Bowen, D. 2010. "Combatants in Afghanistan: What's in a Name"? *Canadian Army Journal. Volume 13, No 2.*

Bowen, Dominic. 2010. "Combatants in Afghanistan: What's in a Name"? *Australian Army Journal. Vol. VII, No 3.*

Brandt, Ben. 2011. "The Taliban Conduct of Intelligence and Counterintelligence". Combating Terrorism Centre. Vol. 4, No 6.

Cassidy, R. M., 2010–2011, *War, Will, and Warlords: Counterinsurgency in Afghanistan and Pakistan*, Marine Corps University Press.

Chandrasekaran, Rajiv. 2011. *Is NATO Counterinsurgency Strategy Working in Afghanistan? A Case Study*, Centre for International Policy Studies.

Chantelle, Taylor. 2011. *Bad Company, Face to Face with the Taliban.* DRA Publishing.

Chesser, Susan G. 2012. Afghanistan Casualties: Military Forces and Civilians. Congressional Research Service.

Choudhry Rudra and Theo Farrell. 2011. "Campaign Disconnect: Operational Progress and Strategic Obstacles in Afghanistan, 2009-2011". *International Affairs. Vol. 87. No-2.*

Clark, Kate. 2011. *The Takhar Attack: Targeted Killings and the Parallel Worlds of US Intelligence and Afghanistan.* Afghanistan Analysis Network.

Clukey, David. S 2010. "A District Approach in Afghanistan". *Small Wars Journal.*

Coffey, Luke. September 2009. "Detainee Operations in Counterinsurgency Operations, Lesson from Afghanistan 2005–2006." *Small War Journal.*

Cordesman, Anthony. H. 2008. *Winning in Afghanistan: Creating Effective Afghan Security Force*, Washington, DC, Centre for Strategic and International Studies.

Cordesman, Anthony H. 2002. *The Lesson of Afghanistan, War Fighting, Intelligence and Force Transformation.* Centre for Strategic and International Studies.

Cronin, Audrey Kurth. 2009. *How Terrorism Ends.* Princeton University Press.

Cronin, Stephanie. *Afghanistan's Armies Past and Present.* History and Policy, Institute of Contemporary British History. Kings College, London.

Crumpto, H. A., 2012, *The Art of Intelligence: Lessons from Life in the CIA's Clandestine Services*, Penguin Press.

Curtis, M., 2000, *Secret Affairs: Britain's Collusion with Radical Islam*, Serpent's Tail, London.

Dalrymple, William. 2010. "The Ghosts of Gandamak". New York Times.

Dimitrakis, P., 2013, *Secret War in Afghanistan: The Soviet Union, China and Anglo-American Intelligence in the Afghan War*. I. B Tauris. London.

Dimitrakis, Panagiotis. 2013. Secret War in Afghanistan. The Soviet Union, China, and Anglo American Intelligence in the Afghan War. I B Tauris. London.

Dodge, Billingsley, Greu Lester.W. 2011. *Operation Anaconda*. Kansas University Press.

Duncan, Alex. 24 May 2012. *Sweating the Metal: Flying under Fire: A Chinook Pilot's Blistering Accounts of Life, Death and Dust in Afghanistan*. Hodder.

Dunigan, Molly. 2011. Victory for hire: Private Security Companies, Impact on Military Effectiveness. Stanford Security Studies.

Edwards, David B. 2002. *Before the Taliban: Genealogies of the Afghan Jihad*. Berkeley University of California Press.

Edwards, David B. 1996. *Heroes of the Age: Moral Fault lines on the Afghan Frontier*. Berkeley University of California Press.

Emadi Hafizullah. 2010. *Dynamics of Political Development in Afghanistan*. The British, Russian and American Invasions. Macmillan.

Encyclopedia Britannica. "Muhammad Daud." 2010.

"Exploration of the Arbakai, (Tribal Police) in South Eastern Afghanistan". Contemporary Security Policy.

Ewans, Martin. 2005. *Conflict in Afghanistan: Studies in Asymmetric Warfare*. Routledge.

Fenzel, Michael. March–April. 2010. "The Maneuver Company in Afghanistan: Establishing Counterinsurgency Priorities at the District Level". *Military Review*.

Ferris, John. 2006. "Invading Afghanistan. 1838–2006: Politics and Pacification". *Journal of Military Strategic Studies. Vol 9, Issue 1.*

Finel, Bernard I. 2010. "Planning a Military Campaign to Support Negotiations in Afghanistan". *Small Wars Journal. Vol 6, No-10.*

Flynn, Michael T. 2010. *Fixing Intelligence: A Blueprint for Making Intelligence Relevant in Afghanistan*. Centre for a New American security.

Fountain, Richard and John Nagl. 2010. Contracting in Conflicts: the Path to Reform. Centre for New American Security, Washington DC.

Friesendorf, Cornelius. 2001. "Para Militarization of Security Sector Reform: Afghan National Police". *International Peace Keeping. Vol. 18, No. 1.*

Giustozzi, Antonio. 2008. *Koran, Kalashnikov and Laptop*. Columbia University Press.

Giustozzi, Antonio 2003. *Military Reforms in Afghanistan*. Crisis State Programme Development Research Centre, London School of Economic, London.

Gonaratna, Rohan, and Khuram Iqbal. 2011. Pakistan: *Terrorism Ground Zero*. Reaktion Books.

Goodson, P. 2001. Afghanistan's Endless War: State Failure, Regional Politics and the Rise of the Taliban. University of Washington Press. US.

Harden, Toby. 2011. Dead Men Risen. *The Welsh Guard and the Defining Story of Britain's War in Afghanistan*. Quercus Publishing Plc.

Jebnoun, Joseph. 2008. "The Denial of Failure in Afghanistan". *Small Wars Journal.*

Jockel, Joseph and Sokolsky Joel. 2008. "Canada and the War in Afghanistan: NATO's odd man out steps forward". *Journal of Transatlantic Studies. Vol 6, No-1.*

Kan, Paul Rexton. 2011. "Making a sandwich in Afghanistan: How to Assess a Strategic Withdrawal from a Protracted Irregular War". Small Wars Journal. Vol 7, No-2.

Katzman, Kenneth. 2012. *Afghanistan, Post Taliban Governance, Security and U.S Policy.* Congressional Research Service.

Katzman, Kenneth. 23 May 2013. "Afghanistan: Politics, Election and Government Performance." Congressional Research.

Krahmann, Elke. 2010, *States, Citizens and the Privatization of Security*, Cambridge University Press.

Ledwidge, Frank. 2011. Losing Small Wars: British Failure in Iraq and Afghanistan. Yale University Press.

Macroy, Patrick. 2002. Retreat from Kabul: The Catastrophic British Defeat in Afghanistan. The Lyons Press. USA.

Malevich, John J. and Deryl C. Youngman. May-June, 2011. "The Afghan Balance of Power and the Culture of Jihad". *Military Review.*

Maley, William. 2011. *PRT Activity in Afghanistan: The Australian Experience in State Building in Afghanistan.* Routledge.

Malleson, George Bruce, 1999. *History of Afghanistan: From the Earliest Period to the Outbreak of the War of 1878.* Adelgi Graphics LLC, London.

Mir Amir. 2009. *Talibanization in Pakistan.* Pentagon Security International. India.

Murphy, Eamon. 2012. *The Making of Terrorism in Pakistan. Historical and Social Roots of Extremism.* Routledge Critical Terrorism Studies.

Murshed, S. I., 2006, *Afghanistan: The Taliban Years.* Bennet & Bloom, London.

Nuzum, Henry. 2010. *Shades of CORDS in the Kush: The False Hope of "Unity of Effort" in American Counterinsurgency.* Strategic Studies Institute.

Oliker, Olga. 2004. *Aid during Conflicts: Interaction between Military and Civilian Assistance Providers in Afghanistan.* RAND Corporation, USA.

Omand, D., 2010, Securing the State. Hurts Company, London.

Oslon, L. 2007. "Challenges and Opportunities in Afghanistan and Beyond". *Journal of Military and strategic Studies. Vol 10, Issue 1.*

Panilonis, Brigid Myers. 2010. *Fighting the Irregular War in Afghanistan: Success in Combat—Struggle in Stabilization.* Routledge.

Pike, Tom and Eddie Brown. August 2011. "Population as Complex Adaptive System: A Case Study of Corruption in Afghanistan". *Small Wars Journals.*

Patterson, Malcolm Hugh. 2009. *Privatizing Peace: A corporate Adjunct to United Nation Peacekeeping and Humanitarian Operation.* Palgrave Macmillan.

Rana Amir. 2009. *A to Z Jihadi Organizations in Pakistan*, Mashal, Lahore, Pakistan.

Rashid Ahmed 2010. *Taliban: The Power of Militant Islam in Afghanistan and Beyond.* I B Tauris & Co Ltd, London

Samaranayake Nilanthi, Jerry Meyerle, Mark Markowitz, et al. 2011. *Conscription in the Afghan Army. Compulsory Service Versus an all Volunteer Force.* Academia.edu. CAN.

Schwartz, Moshe. March 29 2011. "Department of Defense Contractors in Afghanistan and Iraq: Background and Analysis." Report. Congressional Research Service. Washington.

Sedra, Mark. 19 April 2012. *The Army in Afghanistan: from Abdur Rehman to Karzai.* Middle East Institute.

Schmeidle, Susanne and Karookhel Massod. 2009. "The Role of Non-State Actors in Community Based Policing: An Exploration of the Arbakai (Tribal Police) in South Eastern Afghanistan.

Singh, Maj. General V. K. 2007. *India's External Intelligence.* Manas Publications.

Shaffer, A., 2011, *Operation Dark Heart: Spy-Craft and Special Ops on the Frontline of Afghanistan and the Path to Victory,* Thomas Dunne Books.

Steel, Jonathan, 2012, *Ghosts of Afghanistan,* Portobello Books Ltd.

Strick, Alex, Van Linchoten, Felix Kuehn. 2012. *The Enemy We Created, The Myth of Taliban-Al Qaeda Merger in Afghanistan,* Hurst & Co. London.

Steve and Schmeidle. 2008. "When Nobody Guards the Guards: The Quest to Regulate Private Security Companies in Afghanistan". *Security and Peace Journal,* Brookings, Vol-4.

Stoddard, Abby, Adele Harmer and Victoria Di Domenico. 2008. "The Use of Private Security Providers and Services in Humanitarian Operations". Humanitarian Policy Group, Institute HPG Report.

Taj, Farhat. 2011. *Taliban and Anti Taliban.* Cambridge Scholars Publishing.

Tanner. Stephen 2009. *Afghanistan: A Military History from Alexander the Great to the War against the Taliban.* Da Capo Press Inc.

Thomas, Jason. "Post 2014 Afghanistan: Another King upon an Ant Hill". *Small War Journal,* 5 July 2013.

# Index

## A

Abbottabad, 54, 71
ABC TV, 67
Abdul Abdullah, Major General, 171
Abdul Khaleq, Major General, 171
Abdul Khaliq Faryad, Major General, 171
Abdul Kadir, Brigadier General, 170
Abdul Mana Farahi, General, 171
Abdul Qadir Dagarwal, General, 170
Abdul Rahim Wardak, General, 18, 26, 38, 51-53, 66, 155, 170
Abkamari, 46
Academi, 57
Addis Ababa University, 74
Aegis Defense Service, 58, 59
Afghan Air Force, 28, 39, 54
Afghan Border Police, 31, 44, 80, 81, 83, 84
Afghan Civil National Order Police, 80, 81
Afghan Conference (January 28, 2009), 100
Afghan Defense Commission, 166
Afghan Defense Ministry, 21, 25, 27, 31, 73, 105, 174
Afghan Independent Human Rights Commission, 52
Afghan Intelligence, 24, 25, 28, 31, 47, 49, 50, 73, 82, 93, 94, 111, 113-120, 125, 126, 157
Afghan Intelligence Transition Directorate, 120
Afghan Local Police (ALP), 62, 65, 80-83, 156
Afghan Military Intelligence, 38, 157

Afghan Military Law, 27
Afghan Governmental Ministries, see Government
Afghan National Army Air Corps Command, 169
Afghan National Auxiliary Police, 79
Afghan National Civil Order Police, 80, 81
Afghan National Police, 41, 74, 79-84
Afghan National Security Forces, 15, 22, 53, 54, 135, 169
Afghan Parliament, 53, 67
Afghan Peace Council, 18, 90
Afghan Public Protection Program, 79, 81
Afghan Security Council, 63
Afghan Strategic Partnership, 133
Afghan Territorial Police Force, 81
Afghan TV, 92, 121, 142
Afghan Uniformed Police, 81
Afghanistan Justice Project, 152
Af-Pak (Afghan-Pak), 69
Ahmad Gul Khan, 54
Ahmad Shah Durrani, 6, 12
Ahmad Shah Massoud, 18, 105
Ahmed Al-Khalifa, 60
Aimal Faizi, 15
Aina Television of Afghanistan, 93
AITD, 120
Akbar Khan, Prince, 12
Al Quds Brigade, 117
Al Shabab, 93
Albania, 177, 178
Algeria, 93
Ali Ahmad Jalali, 13, 35
All Volunteer Force, 14

Allen, John, US General, 11, 22, 30
Allied Command Operations, 82
Al-Qaeda, 3, 22, 23, 26, 54, 64, 65, 68-70, 74, 75, 93, 95, 96, 98, 107, 112, 124, 133, 147, 155, 156, 158
Amanullah Khan Jabbar Khel, 13, 50
American Enterprise Institute, 99
Aminullah, Major General, 171
Amir Abdur Rahman Khan, 13, 161, 163
Amnesty International, 50-52, 75
Amrullah Saleh, former Chief, National Directorate of Security (NDS), 39
Anglo-Afghan War, 12
Ansarul Muslimeen, 25, 117, 122
Anthony, A. K., 53
Anti Crime Police Force, 80, 81
Arab Spring, 134
Arghandab, 82
Arghandi, 46
Argu of Badakhshan, 46
Ariana Network Service, 130
Arnawai, 161
Arnold, Terrell E., 93
Arsala Rehmani, 40
Asad Durrani, 9, 21, 43
Asadullah Khaled, 49
Ashfaq Kayani, Army Chief, 108, 144
Ashfaq Yousufzai, 88
Asia Consultancy Group, 130
Asian Human Rights Commission, 145
Asian Tribune, The, 57
Asif Ali Zardari, President of Pakistan, 71, 148
Asif Haroon Raja, Brigadier, 57, 134
Assadullah Khalid, 48, 49, 116
Atta Muhammad Noor, 65, 68
Australian Intelligence Secret Service, 117
Australian Special Forces, 65
Azeem Ibrahim, 87
Azizuddin Farahi, General, 171

**B**

Babrak Karmal, 14
Bagram Air Base, 53, 73, 159
Bahrain, 60, 61, 177
Baitullah Mehsud, 19, 90
Balkh, 46, 65, 152, 156
Baluchistan, 43, 99, 142-145
Bamyan, 28, 45, 83, 106, 152
Bangladesh, 86, 141, 152

Behsud, District of, 46
Bhadrakumar, M. K., 106
Bilateral Security Agreement, 156, 158
Bismillah Khan Muhammadi, General, Interior Minister, 26, 38, 48, 51, 155, 157, 170
Blackwater (See Academi or Xe)
Blue Attacks, 21, 29
Boko Haram, 93
Bonn Agreement, 14, 15, 35, 52, 79
Bonn Conference, 79
Border Police, 31, 44, 80, 81, 83, 84
British Army, 13
British India, 12
British Parliament, 62
Burhanuddin Rabbani, former Afghan President, 18, 40, 66, 68, 90
Bush, George W., former US President, 58, 71, 107

**C**

Cambridge, 104
Cameron, David, British Prime Minister, 26
Camp Integrity, 57
Canada, 49, 65, 112, 117, 177, 178
Canadian Forces Intelligence Branch, 117
Canadian Major-General David Fraser, 49
Carnegie Endowment, 35
Central Intelligence Agency, 25, 39, 64, 67-73, 75, 94, 111, 112, 116-121, 126, 128, 134, 137-139, 153, 156-158, 179-181
Chageh, 162
Chagh Charan, 46
Chaman, 162
Chanak, 161
Chatham House, 16, 17
Chechens/Chechnya, 145
Checkering, A. Lawrence, 38
Cheney, Dick, Former US Vice-President, 8
Chicago Conference, 17, 22
Chicago Summit, 3, 17, 22, 44, 45
China, 41, 95, 100, 107, 120, 127-129, 133-135, 137-140, 145, 147, 148, 159
China Daily, 128, 135
China-Phobia Policy, 133, 134
Chinese Muslims, 41, 137, 140
Chinese Turkistan, 145

Chisht, 46
Chitral, 161
Christian Science Monitor, The, 119
Churchill, Winston, 11
CNN News, 39, 40, 80, 82
COIN, 101
Cold War, 57-59, 100, 111, 112
Combating Terrorism Center (at West Point), 125
Combined Security Transition Command-Afghanistan, 43, 79, 170
Conscription, 13-16
Constitution of Pakistan, 180
Constitutional Commission, 14
Contractor Identification Cards, 62
Contractors, see Private Contractors
Control Risk Group, 59
Cordesman, Anthony H., 25, 116, 117
Corruption Perceptions Index, 68
Critical Threat Project, 99
Croatia, 177, 178
CRS Reports (see US Congressional)
CSIS, 2, 25, 150
CSTC-A, 178
CSTM-A, 79
Cunningham, James B., US Ambassador, 158
Cyber Reconnaissance Infrastructure, 126
Cyber Terrorism, 123, 126-129
Cyberspace, 123, 127-130
Czech Republic, 177, 178

**D**

Daily Frontier Post, 70
Daily Independent, 27, 44
Daily Mail, 108, 128
Daily Nation, 51, 68, 75
Daily Outlook Afghanistan, 27, 29, 38, 39, 41, 44, 50, 53, 62-68, 82, 83, 101, 108, 115, 135, 137-140, 147, 152, 155
Daily Tech News, 127
Daily Telegraph, 115
Dande Darpkhel, 75
Daud Khan, former President of Afghanistan, 13, 14, 106
Dawar, 162
Daykundi, 46
Defense Clandestine Service, 137-139
Defense Commission, Advisory Committee, 166
Defense Signal Directorate, 112
Demobilization, 22, 166, 167
Democratic Party of Afghanistan, 14
Demonstrations, 24
Denmark, 177, 178
Deobandi, 86
Department of Defense Report No DODIG-2013-058, 120
Der Spiegel, 1
Dera Ghazi Khan District, 91
Desertion, 1, 4, 7, 14, 15, 22, 26-28, 36, 38, 44, 97, 135, 151, 152, 156
Detainees, treatment of, 48-50, 53, 126
Digital Journal, 87
Din Muhammad Jabar Khel, 50, 66, 68
Disarmament, 22, 152, 166, 167
Doha, 19
Dost Muhammad Khan, 12
Dostum, Abdul Rashid, General, 7, 41, 51, 52, 66, 68
Drones, 32, 57, 63, 69, 71, 73-77, 91, 101, 127, 128, 142, 153, 179, 180
Drugs, 2, 30, 37-41, 43, 62, 63, 65, 69, 83, 90, 96, 98, 105, 136, 149, 151, 152, 156, 157
Dubai, 92, 113
Durand Line Agreement, 12, 13, 94, 106, 147, 161
Durand, Sir Henry Mortimer, 12, 13, 94, 106, 147, 161, 163
Durrani dynasty, 106
Durrani, Asad, General, 9, 21, 43
DynCorp, 40, 62

**E**

Economist, The, 23
Education Committee, 43
El Salvador, 177
Elections, 15, 104, 106, 142, 156-158
Elite Security Company, 66
Ervin International, 59
Espionage, 113, 124, 129
Estonia, 177, 178
Euro Police Mission, 80
European Union, 35, 80
Europol, 80
Euros, 80
Ex-Servicemen Society, 60
External Intelligence, 113, 114
Ezzat, Abdul Hamid, 49

F

Facebook, 93, 116, 124
Faiz Ali Chishti, 60
Faizabad, 46
Farah, 29, 156
FAS, 153
FATA Research Center, 95
Fauji Foudation of Pakistan, 60
Federal Bureau of Investigation, 73
Federation of American Scientists, 153
Financial Times, The, 74
Finland, 177, 178
First Anglo Afghan War, 11
Florida, 24
Flynn, Michael T., Major General, 114, 118
Foreign Affairs, 54, 74, 127, 167
Foreign Policy Magazine, 39, 151
Fort McNairy, 74
Forward Operation Base of International
    Security Assistance Force, 88
Fox News, 42
France/French
    French Directorate of Military Intel-
        ligence, 117
    French President Sarkozy, 25
Frontier Corps, 121
Frontiers Post, 76

G

G. C. S. I., 161
G4S, 61
G8, 22
Gandamak, 12
Gandamak Treaty, 12
Gardez, 83, 169
Gardi Jangle of Baluchistan, 43
Gates, Robert, US Secretary of Defense,
    54, 147
Geneva Convention, 76
Genghis Khan, 11
Genocide, 180
Georgia, 12, 177
Germany
    German Army, 65
    German Intelligence, 117, 118, 120
Ghazi Abad, 52
Ghazni, 46, 49, 150
Ghosts of Gandamak, 12

GHQ, 144
Ghulam Farooq, 88
Ghulam Haider Resuli, Lieutenant Gen-
    eral, 170
Ghurkha, 59
Giga Noor, 131
Gilgit, 138
Gilgit Baltistan, 138
GIP, 117
Giustozzi, Antonio, 96, 104
Global Policy Forum, 58
Global Politics, 148
Global Risk International, 59
Google, 124
Government Ministries of Afghanistan
    Ministry of Communication, 123, 131
    Ministry of Defense, 18, 28, 33, 44, 129,
        139, 142, 165-167, 170, 171, 177
    Ministry of Education, 84
    Ministry of Finance, 167
    Ministry of Foreign Affairs, 74, 167
    Minister of Frontiers Affairs, 50
    Ministry of Interior, 24, 28, 40, 72, 79-
        81, 83, 84, 86, 88, 121, 125, 149, 177
    Ministry of Intelligence, 116, 123, 125,
        158
Grand Assembly, 14, 15, 158
Great Britain (see also UK), 6, 11-14, 17, 18,
    23, 26, 27, 32, 33, 38, 48, 50, 58, 59, 61-
    64, 93, 94, 100, 106, 112, 113, 120, 128-130,
    136, 137, 151, 161, 162
Great Game, 35, 47, 48
Greece, 11, 177, 178
Green Book, 144
Guangxi Zhuang Autonomous Region,
    140
Gul Muhammad, 64
Gul, Imtiaz (Centre for Research and Se-
    curity Studies, Pakistan), 74
Gulabuddin Hezb-e-Islami, 105
Gulbuddin Hekmatyar, 99
Guradian, 144
Gurgin, 12
Gwasha, 162

H

Habibullah Khan, 12
Hackers, 127, 128, 130
Hafeezullah Amin, 170

Hague, William, 46, 106
Haji Din Muhammad, 50, 66, 68
Haji Toor Jan, 65
Hakimullah Mehsud, 69, 75
Hamid Gul, General, 119
Hamid Jan Wardak, 66
Hammond, Philip, UK Defense Secretary, 33
Haqqani, 6, 19, 23, 35, 99, 121
Hari Singh Nalwa, 12
Hashish, 39, 40, 43
Hasht Nafari, 13
Hazara, 13, 39, 52, 93, 141
Heart Province, 45, 46, 169
Hellfire, 73
Helmand, 45, 63, 64, 82, 125, 159
Herat, 28, 83, 156, 159
Hezb-e-Islami, 91, 105
Hindus, 12, 138, 143
Hindustan, 12, 138
Holy Quran, 1, 3, 24, 68
Holy Warriors, 100
Hotaki Dynasty, 12
HRCP, 144
HRW, 29
Hujattullah Mujaddidi, 126
Human Intelligence, 81, 91, 116, 125, 127, 158
Human Rights Watch, 28, 51-53, 64, 92, 93, 152
Hungary, 177, 178

I

ICCPR, 76, 180
Iceland, 177
ICT Solution, 130
ID cards, 119
IDG Security Ltd, 58
IDIL, 131
Imam Hasan, 15
Imams, 150
Independent Electoral Commission (IEC), 157
Independent Human Rights Commission of Afghanistan, 92
India
  Indian Consulate, 88
  Indian Defense Minister, 53
  Indian Intelligence Service, 112, 114, 116, 119, 157

Indian Defense Review, 91
Indian Ocean, 137
Indrani Baghchi, 106
Inner Mongolia Autonomous Region, 139
Inter Services Intelligence (ISI), 9, 21, 25, 43, 71, 73, 94, 95, 116, 117, 119, 121, 141, 142, 145, 155, 157
Interior Ministry of Afghanistan, 121, 177
Interior Ministry of Pakistan, 72, 86
International Court of Justice, 180
International Crisis Group, 36, 44, 51, 74, 98, 151
International Intelligence Limited, 59
International Security Assistance Forces, 27, 32, 45, 53, 73, 87, 88, 114, 127, 177
Internet, 116, 120, 123, 127, 130
Iran, 3, 12, 25, 28, 41, 42, 63, 68, 73, 91, 98, 114-117, 119-122, 129, 136-138, 141, 145, 147-149, 152, 157-159
Iranian Ansarul Muslimeen Secret Service, 25, 117, 122
Iranian Intelligence, 63, 68, 116, 121, 122, 157
Ireland, 177
IRIN, 92
ISAF, 1, 3, 4, 15, 17, 21-27, 29, 30, 32, 38, 44, 45, 49, 52, 54, 63, 66, 73, 94, 96, 114, 118, 120, 126, 127, 135, 157, 169, 170, 177, 178
Ishaq Noori, General, 171
Isfahan, 12
Islamic Emirate of Afghanistan, 42
Islamic Movement of Uzbekistan, 145
Islamic Republic of Afghanistan, 44, 170, 178
Islamic Transitional State of Afghanistan, 165-167
Ismail Khan, 1, 68
Israel, 58
Italy, 22, 117, 177, 178
ITSA, 165-167
IWPR, 49

J

Jahandar Shah, Major General, 171
Jalalabad-Torkham Highway, 88
Jamia Masjid Zakriya Kondali, 90
Jamrud, 12
Japan, 22, 41, 166
Javed Nasir, General, 145
Jayant Singh, 35

JCMB, 16
Jeddah, 85
Jelriz of Wardak Province, 46
Jirga
    Constitutional Jirga, 15
    Emergency Loya Jirga, 14
    Loya Jirga, 14, 108, 158
Jordan, 177, 178
JRIN, 92
Judicial Reforms, 22
Judicial Security Unit, 81
Juma Khan Humdard, 105

**K**

K. C. I. E., 161
Kabul Airport, 7
Kabul Bank, 68
Kabul Conference, 54
Kabul Province, 45, 46
Kabul Reconciliation Plan, 108
Kabul University, 49
Kadimkhel, 49
Kalashnikovs, 86
Kaleed Research Report, 66
Kandahar Jalalabad, 119
Kandahar Security Group, 66
Kandak, 22
Kandak-e-Amniat-e-Uruzgan, 65
Karachi, 70-73, 89, 90, 143
Karakoram Highway, 138
Karzai, Hamid, Afghan President, 11, 13, 15-17, 21, 22, 24, 26, 36, 37, 39, 40, 42, 44-46, 48, 50, 53, 54, 58, 63, 64, 66-68, 70, 80, 96, 99, 100, 104, 106-108, 117, 126, 133, 137, 148-152, 156-158, 167
Karzai, Hashmat, 66
Karzai, Wali, 40, 66, 68
Kashmir, 145
Kayani, General, 108
Kaynat Technologies, 131
Kerry, John, US Secretary of State, 74
KGB, 111
Khalid Iqbal, 77
Khalq, 14
Khost, 6, 48, 106, 115, 118, 119, 142
Khyber Pakhtunkhwa, 85, 142, 144, 153
Kohat, 91
Konduz, 83
Korea, 129, 137, 139, 177, 178
Kosovo, 145

Koz Kunar, 46
Kuchi, 39
Kunduz, 28, 29, 64, 106, 156, 159

**L**

Lahore, 71-73, 145
Lal Bibi, 29
Lashkar Dand, 162
Lashkar Gah, 45
Lashkargah, 169
Latif Mehsud, 75
Latvia, 177
Libya, 97
LinkedIn, 124
Lisbon Summit, 3, 44
Lithuania, 177
Liwal, 130
London Conference, 100, 101
Luxembourg, 177

**M**

Macedonia, 177
Maidan Shehr, 46
Maidan Wardak Province, 24
Mehrab Ali Khan, Major General, 171
Makran, 145
Malacca, 137
Malalai Joya, 2
Malaysia, 177
Malik Palawan, 51
Maliks, 144, 149
MANAMA Conference, 105
Maratha Empire (Hindu), 12
Marketing Terrorism, 85, 92-94
Massod Ashraf Raja, 91
Matiullah Khan, 64, 65
Mazar-e Sharif, 51
Mazare-e-Sharif, 45
McChrystal, Stanley, General, 3, 38, 70, 73, 99, 106, 108, 117, 124
MCIT, 123
McKiernan, David, General, 79
McRaven, William H., Admiral, 73, 80, 82
Mehtar Lam, 45
Mengal, 14
Mercenaries, 57-60, 66, 72
Mexico, 69
MI5, 117, 120

MI6, 117, 119, 120
Mian Baldak, 162
Middle East Institute, 13
Military Law of Afghanistan, 25
Militias, 1-4, 21, 22, 26-31, 36, 37, 39, 41, 47, 49, 57, 59-61, 63-67, 70, 79, 83, 87, 97, 98, 112, 149, 150, 152
Mills, Richard P., US Marine Lt. Gen., 127
Mir Ali District of North Waziristan, 91
Miranshah, 43
Mirwais Khan Hotak, 12
Mirza Aslam Baig, General, 100
Mohmand, 142, 144
MOIS, 116, 158
Mokoor, 49
Mongolia, 11, 139, 177, 178
Monitoring Board, 16
Monsif Khan, 156
Montenegro, 177
Moscow, 136, 148
MOSSAD, 117
Muhammad, Major General, 171
Muhammad Rahim Wardak, Major General, 171
Muhammad Sharif, Major General, 171
Muhammad Aslam Watanjar, General, 170
Muhammad Atta Noor, 65, 68
Muhammad Daud, 13, 14
Muhammad Fahim, 68, 170
Muhammad Hassan Kakar, 125
Muhammad Ikram, General, 170
Muhammad Rafi, General, 170
Muhammad Zahir Azimi, 170
Muhammad Zahir Shah, 13
Muhammad Zai Salehi, 63
Muhammad Zaman, General, 30
Mujaddidi, 66, 68, 126
Mujahedeen, 1, 6, 7, 14, 22, 36, 37, 47, 70, 87, 100, 105, 112, 141, 145, 150, 151, 167
Mullah Bismillah Khan, Army Chief, 26, 38, 48, 51, 155, 157, 170
Mullah Khan, 155
Mullah Omar, 42, 43, 99, 143, 145
Mullen, Mike, Admiral, 108
Munich, 19
Murad Ali, Major General, 171
Murder, 31, 32, 49, 70, 87, 136
Murgha Chaman, 162
Musahibeen, 14
Musharaf Zaidi, 71

Musharraf, Pervez, Former Pakistani President, 71, 73, 119, 141
Muslim Hui people, 140

**N**

Nahr-e-Saraj, 46
Najeeb, 7
Najjam Sethi, 3
Narai, 43
Nashita, 130
Nasim Ahmed, 76
National Assembly, 71, 76, 179, 180
National Civil Order Police, 44, 80, 81
National Clandestine Service, 137
National Crisis Management Cell, 86
National Defense Research Institute, 21
National Directorate of Security, 39, 49, 50, 115-117, 157
National ID Card, 107
National Security Agency, 112
National Security Council of Afghanistan, 95
Nawah, 46
Nawaz Sharif, 142, 144
Nazar Muhammad, 170
NCL Security Company, 66
Nek Muhammad, 69
Netherlands, 177, 178
New Chaman Fort, 162
New Delhi, 53
New Dunya, 123, 130
New Silk Road, 8
New Zealand, 28, 112, 177
Niamatullah Ibrahimi, 96, 104
Nigeria, 93
Nilanthi Samaranayake, 14
Ningxia Hui Autonomous Region, 140
Noor Muhammad, 68, 87
Nooristan, 113, 115
North Atlantic Council, 17
North Caucasus, 148
North Korea, 129, 137, 139
North Waziristan, 23, 30, 75, 89-91, 99, 153
Northern Alliance, 7, 26, 41, 65, 68, 97, 104, 105, 119
Northern Provinces, 39, 115, 152
Norway, 128, 177, 178
NTM-A, 178
Nuristan, 142

NWFP, 99

**O**

Oath of Afghan National Police, 84
Obama Administration, 19, 23, 24, 55, 75, 76, 96, 134, 135, 138, 139
Obama, Barack Hussein, US President, 8, 17, 19, 23-25, 30, 36, 55, 58, 74-76, 96, 99, 107, 118, 128, 133-135, 138, 139, 147, 148
Omand, Sir David, 112, 113, 124
Operation Enduring Freedom, 15, 22
Opium, 2, 40, 43, 70, 96
Opposition, 72, 73, 94, 135
Osama Bin Laden, 54, 55, 71
OSCIA, 130

**P**

Pactec, 130
Pajhwok Afghan News, 141
Pakistan
    Pakistan Army, 7, 30, 60, 72, 99, 141-144
    Pakistan Security Forces, 144
    Pakistan Tehreek-e-Insaf (PTI) political party *****
    Pakistani Blackwater, 60
    Pakistani Defense, 30, 57
    Pakistani Mullas, 85
    Pakistani Taliban, 43, 75, 85, 95
Paktia, 13, 66, 115, 119, 156
Paktika, 13, 105, 119
Panetta, Leon, US Defense Secretary, 134, 145
Panipat, 12
Panjgur, 145
Panjshir Province, 9, 45, 89, 119
Panjshiri Tajik, 114
Panjwai, 3, 31, 32
Paramilitaries, 57, 63, 80, 97, 166, 173
Paris, 100, 101
Parwan, 46
Pasha, General, 108
Pashto/Pashtun, 7, 13, 18, 25, 37, 38, 48, 51, 52, 65, 86, 100, 108, 112, 115, 121, 137, 142, 144, 145, 150, 155
Pashtun Taliban, 86
Pashtunistan, 13, 35, 141
Pavan Duggal, 128

PDPA, 6, 7
Pentagon China-phobia, 134
Persian Gulf, 61, 97
Persians, 12
Persian-speaking Afghans, 155
Peshawar, 12, 43, 48, 71, 72, 90, 143, 144, 180, 181
Peshawar High Court, 180, 181
Petraeus, David, US General, 39, 72, 82, 99, 106, 153
Philippines, 145
Political Rights, 76, 180
Port Qasim, 73
Portugal, 177, 178
Poverty, 2, 86, 92, 98, 100, 151
Prince, Erik, 72
Prisoners, 43, 50-52
Private Contractors, 3, 37, 57, 62, 67, 72
Private Militias, 2-4, 27, 29, 37, 39, 41, 57, 59-61, 63-67, 98
Private Security Companies, 57, 58, 62, 66
Privatization of Security, 58, 60-62
Propaganda, 96, 107, 128
PSCs, 61
Psha Kotal, 162
Pul-e-Charkhi, 52
Punjab, 12, 86, 89
Punjabi Taliban, 91
Pure Theory of Law, 6
Putin, Russian President Vladimir, 128, 136

**Q**

Qala Jangi, 51
Qarghai of Laghman, 46
Qari Hussain, 88
Qasim Fahim, General, 66, 68
Quetta Council, 43
Quetta Shura, 19, 43, 99
Qulbars, 28

**R**

Radicalization, 86, 87
Radicalization of Pakistan, 86
Radio Free Europe, 88
Rahman, Abdur, 13, 137, 161, 163
Rahmatullah Nabil, Former Afghan Intelligence Chief, 48

RAMA, 17, 111, 116, 119, 157
RAND Corporation, 81
Rasmussen, Anders Fogh, 54
Rasul Seyyaf, 68
Rawalpindi, 12
Razaq, Major General, 171
Reagan, Ronald, former US President, 58
Recruitment Committee, 43
Recruitment of Young Soldiers, 166
Red Cross, 89
Refugees Committee, 43
Regional Command of Gardez, 83
Regional Command of Kandahar, 83
Regional Command of Mazar-e-Sharif, 83
Regional Command Structure, 83
Regional Training Centers, 83
Rehman Malik, 72
Repatriation Committee, 43
Revolutionary Association of Women, 105
Rice, Susan, US National Security Advisor, 158
Romania, 177, 178
Roshan, 123
Rudd, Kevin, former prime minister and foreign minister of Australia, 64
Russia, 1, 3, 11, 12, 41, 58, 68, 86, 98, 100, 115, 117, 119, 120, 127-129, 134, 136, 138, 139, 145, 147, 148, 151, 159
Russian FSB, 128

S

Sabghatullah Mujaddidi, 66
Safavids, 12
Salafi, 86
Salehi, 63
Samangan, 46
Sararogha Peace Agreement, 19
Saudi Arabia, 60, 61, 73, 85, 92, 117, 141
Saudi Intelligence, 117
Save The Children, 70, 71
Sayyaf, Abdul Rasul, 66
Sayyed, 46
Scotland, 87, 94
Scotland Yard, 94
Serbs, 145
Shah Waliullah Dehlavi, 12
Shakai Agreement, 19
Shalimar Bagh, 106
Shanawaz Tanai, General, 170

Shanghai Cooperation Organization, 100
Sharobo, 162
Sheberghan, 46
Sheikh Hamad, 42
Sheikh Khaled, 60
Sher Khan, 159
Sher Muhammad Zazi, General, 171
Sherzai, 68
Shia/Shias, 52, 60, 61, 88, 97
Shindand, 46, 169
Shir Khan Farnood, 68
Shir Muhammad Karimi, General, 31, 170
Shiwari, 46
Shorawak, 162
Shoshana Bryen, 153
Shuja Nawaz, 143
Shuras, 43, 118
Siahghered, 46
Signal Intelligence, 112, 116, 121, 125, 126, 129, 158
Sikhs, 12
Singapore, 177, 178
Singh, VK, General, 112-114
Sirkai Tilerai, 162
Slovakia, 177
Slovenia, 177, 178
Smuggling, 22, 30, 31, 39, 50, 80, 156
Social Media, 116, 123, 124, 126
Socialist Unity, 32
Somalia/Somalis, 73, 92, 93, 145
Sorkhrud, 46
South China Sea, 137
South East Asia, 138
South Waziristan, 19, 69, 99, 180
South-eastern Afghanistan, 67
Southern Afghanistan, 23, 48, 65, 70, 86, 100
Sovereignty, 9, 71, 72, 75-77, 133, 158, 179-181
Soviet Invasion, 6, 125, 141
Soviet Union, 1, 6, 7, 14, 105, 125, 141, 150
Spain, 177, 178
Spin Boldak (town), 91, 159
State-Owned Criminal Militias, 79
Strategic Partnership Agreement, 3, 133
Strategic Solution International, 66
Sudan, 93, 145
Sufis, 19, 91
Suicide Bombers, 77, 85-93
Sunnis, 60, 61, 65, 97
Sunni Awakening, 65

Super Highway, 90
Surveillance Unit, 81
Swat, 19, 93, 142, 144, 161
Sweden, 177, 178
Syed Iftikhar, 95
Syria, 85, 86, 94, 97

## T

Taiwan, 139
Tajikistan/Tajiks, 2, 18, 30, 41, 65, 114, 141
Takfiri Jihadists, 93
Takhar, 46
Talat Farooq, 76
Taliban Office, 19, 29, 41, 42, 45, 151
Taliban Peace Talks, 19
Taliban-imposed Jihad, 152
Taluqan (village), 28
Tamil, 145
Tarin Kot, 64
Tatars, 11
TechNet Land Forces, 127
Tehreek-e-Taliban Pakistan (TTP), 75, 90, 144, 157
Tehreek-i-Insaf, 179
Tibet, 139, 140
Tirah Valley, 144
Tokyo Conference, 45
Tokyo Mutual Accountability Conference, 44
Tonga, 177
Tooghundi, 159
Torture, 24, 48-50, 52, 82, 105, 114, 115, 119, 126, 145, 150, 151
Transparency International, 68
Tribal Areas, 49, 180
Tribal Force, 40
TTP, 75, 90, 144, 157
Turkey/Turkish, 13, 98, 131, 177, 178
Turkmenistan, 41
Twitter, 93, 116, 124

## U

Uighur Islamic Movement, 139
Uighur Muslims, 139
UK Ambassador, 32
UK Foreign Office, 28
UK Ministry of Defense, 28, 33, 44
Ukraine, 177

Ulema Council, 43
United Arab Emirates (UAE), 72, 130, 177
United Nations
    United Nations ANA Trust Fund, 167
    United Nations Assistance Mission in Afghanistan (UNAMA), 51, 52
    United Nations Development Program (UNDP), 82
    United Nations Secretary General, 45
    UN Charter, 179, 180
    UN General Assembly, 58, 180
    UN High Commission, 75
    UN Security Council Resolution, 14
United Press International (UPI), 45, 60
Urdu, 38
Uruzgan, 27, 28, 64, 65
United States
    USAID, 59
    US Armed Services Committee, 29
    US Congress
        Congressional Executive Commission, 140
        Congressional Research Service (CRS), 15-17, 23, 24, 58, 140
    US Department of Defense, 28, 30, 41, 59, 62, 81, 120, 134, 145, 155
    US Joint Special Operations Command, 69, 71
    US Special Operations Force Joint Afghan-US Special Operations, 16, 82
    US State Department, 40, 170
Uyghur Muslims, 137-140
Uzbekistan/Uzbeks, 2, 41, 51, 65, 98, 138, 145

## V

Village Stability Operation, 79, 82, 83
Volgograd, 86, 148

## W

Wakefield, Alison, 61
Wakhan, 161
Wali-ur-Rehman death of, 28, 32, 40, 54, 55, 66, 75, 76, 88, 92
War Crimes, 2, 21, 31, 40, 41, 47-51, 66-68, 70, 105, 107, 112, 115, 149, 157, 180
War of Perceptions, 19
Wardak, Afghan Defense Minister Abdul

Rahim, 18, 26, 38, 51-53, 66, 155, 170, 171
Warlords
  Ahmad Shah Masood, 170
  Bismillah Khan Muhammadi, 26, 48, 51, 155, 157, 170
  Gulalai, 65
  Matiullah Khan, 64, 65
  Muhammad Fahim Qasim, 170
  Mullah Obidullah Akhund, 170
  Nazari Muhammad, 65
Waziri, 162
West Point, 96
White House, 30, 96, 147
Wiki Leaks, 40, 62
World Security Network, 62, 106, 120
World Socialist Website, 39
World War II, 69

**X**

Xe Services LLC (Xe, or Blackwater, now Academi), 1, 57-60, 62, 63, 69-73
Xinhua News Agency, 87, 88, 92, 103
Xinjiang Uyghur Autonomous Region, 137-140
Xu Feihong, 139

**Y**

Yahoo, 124
Yellow Sea, 134
Yemen, 60, 61
YouTube, 93, 116, 124
Yunus Qanooni, 68

**Z**

Zabihullah Mujahid, 89
Zahid Hamid, 30
Zahir Azimi, General, 27
Zahir, Muhammad, Shah (last king of Afghanistan), 13
Zakaullah Khan, 89
Zhang Xin, 128
Zia-ul Haq, 106
Zulfiqar Ali Bhutto, 60